PENGUIN BOOKS

Tribe

Bruce Parry began his adult life as an officer and physical training instructor in the Royal Marines. He left to become an expedition leader, and then worked in the film industry. He now combines his love of exploration and filming in his award-winning documentaries. When he is not travelling the world, he spends his free time at his home in Ibiza.

Tribe

Adventures in a Changing World

BRUCE PARRY

WITH MARK McCRUM

PENGUIN BOOKS

PENGUIN BOOKS

Published by the Penguin Group
Penguin Books Ltd, 80 Strand, London WC2R ORL, England
Penguin Group (USA) Inc., 375 Hudson Street, New York, New York 10014, USA
Penguin Group (Canada), 90 Eglinton Avenue East, Suite 700, Toronto, Ontario, Canada M4P 2Y3
(a division of Pearson Penguin Canada Inc.)
Penguin Ireland, 25 St Stephen's Green, Dublin 2, Ireland (a division of Penguin Books Ltd)
Penguin Group (Australia), 250 Camberwell Road, Camberwell, Victoria 3124, Australia
(a division of Pearson Australia Group Pty Ltd)
Penguin Books India Pvt Ltd, 11 Community Centre, Panchsheel Park, New Delhi – 110 017, India
Penguin Group (NZ), 67 Apollo Drive, Rosedale, North Shore 0632, New Zealand
(a division of Pearson New Zealand Ltd)
Penguin Books (South Africa) (Pty) Ltd, 24 Sturdee Avenue, Rosebank, Johannesburg 2196,
South Africa

Penguin Books Ltd, Registered Offices: 80 Strand, London WC2R ORL, England

www.penguin.com

First published by Michael Joseph 2007
Published in Penguin Books 2008

2

Copyright © Endeavour Productions Ltd, 2007
All rights reserved

Maps courtesy of David Atkinson, handmademaps.com
Photography supplied by the BBC and taken by
members of the production team on location

The moral right of the author has been asserted

Set in Bembo
Typeset by Palimpsest Book Production Limited, Grangemouth, Stirlingshire

Printed in England by Clays Ltd, St Ives plc

ISBN 978-0-141-02683-1

www.greenpenguin.co.uk

Penguin Books is committed to a sustainable future
for our business, our readers and our planet.
The book in your hands is made from paper
certified by the Forest Stewardship Council.

To all those in faraway places who have ever called me brother, cousin, uncle or son. You have taught and given me more than I can ever repay.

Contents

TIC OCEAN
BERING SEA
NENET
Siberia
DARHAD
Mongolia
ASIA
PACIFIC OCEAN
ADI
LAYAPS
Himalayas
Bhutan
PENAN
Malaysia
KOMBAI
West Papua
ANUTANS
Polynesia
INDIAN OCEAN
AUSTRALIA
EAN

Introduction

One of the Tribe

The idea behind *Tribe* was simple: to make a series of compelling programmes about indigenous peoples living traditional lives in some of the world's most remote places. This was never intended to be a scholarly anthropological ethnography, more a hands-on look at a group of people, in a particular place, at a particular time in their lives. What is it like to eat only what you can hunt and gather from the land? How do the husbands, wives and families interact in these societies? What do they feel threatened by? What do they believe?

The BBC production team felt that the best way to answer these questions would be for its presenter, Bruce Parry, to actually live with each community for a dedicated period of time. Not to stay in the nearby tented crew camp, but to actually live with the people, day and night, in their huts, *gers* or tree houses; to hunt and eat the food they were eating, be bitten by the insects that were biting them, undergo their rituals and join in their family life.

Bruce would become, for a month or so, as the title sequence of the programme puts it, 'one of the tribe' . . .

1. Initiation

The Babongo of the Congo Basin, Gabon

On the overnight flight from Paris to Libreville, I was learning about *iboga* and wishing I'd had the time to check my research notes more thoroughly before leaving the UK. 'In high doses', I read, '*iboga* produces a hallucinatory inebriation with motor incoordination and sometimes a state of lethargy lasting four to five days. In massive doses, the drug may cause death as a result of paralysis of the respiratory muscles.' The two Europeans who were known to have died from an overdose of *iboga*, the notes went on, had both had 'pathological Q waves' on their heartbeats, an otherwise minor cardiac abnormality easily revealed by an electrocardiograph reading. Libreville, Gabon, I was thinking, was maybe not the best place in the world to get your Q wave checked out.

Not that my producer or anybody else was going to force me to take this powerful hallucinogenic drug, which is ingested by chewing the root-bark of the shrub *Tabernanthe iboga*. But my central philosophy in this new TV-presenting career I'd embarked on was that I wanted to live as much as possible like the tribespeople we were filming – not just alongside them, but actually with them, in their huts, eating their food, drinking their water, experiencing their lives for real. With the jungle-dwelling Babongo people of Gabon, with whom we were hoping to spend a month for our very first *Tribe* programme, *iboga* is a crucial part of their culture. Their religion, called Bwiti, involves an initiation ceremony where a large amount of the drug is taken and the initiate goes off into a trance, seeing visions of God and confronting, so it is said, his entire past in vivid detail – in particular what he's done wrong in his life. There was a big part of me that wanted to do this.

Down on the ground in Libreville I met up with a man who I hoped might help me. M. Hugues Poitevin had been recommended to us as a possible fixer. I say 'possible' because all the information we had on this long-term-expat Frenchman made him sound eccentric, to say the least. 'English not very good', read my research notes. 'Difficult to get information from him without a commitment to work with him.' Having used the services of a wide range of fixers over the years, I'd been keeping an open mind.

But once I set eyes on Hugues, I was sure he had to be on the team, if indeed not in the programme. With his tousled dark hair and baggy, well-lived-in face, Hugues – or 'Oouge' as his name is pronounced – looked as if he'd walked straight out of a Graham Greene novel. The laughter creases ran from his eyes in furrows across his cheekbones to his chin. His forehead was a Gallic question mark of wrinkles. As we sat out on the terrace bar of the downtown Tropicana Hotel, he told me in the thickest of French accents that he had originally come to Libreville for two weeks thirty-three *yee-ears* ago. He had fallen in love with the place and the people and had stayed. He was an expert on both Bwiti and *iboga* – an initiate, and one of the first Europeans ever to have taken the drug. He was happy to act as driver and local contact while I sorted out the final bits and pieces for our expedition.

In the morning producer Steve Robinson and cameraman Jon Clay flew in and we got straight on the road south out of town. The well-laid tarmac of Libreville gave out within a few kilometres and we were soon rattling along dreadful roads. We travelled in two vehicles. M. Hugues drove a battered white Toyota Land Cruiser, awash with feathers and charms, which the crew immediately nicknamed the Fetish-mobile. It was equipped with a heavy winch, without which we'd never have got to our chosen village at all, as our other hire car kept getting stuck in the mud.

As he drove, eyes fixed on the road under his round straw hat, M. Hugues reassured me that my time in the jungle was definitely going to go well. An archetypal hippy, he saw meaning in everything. *Parry* in a local language meant 'jungle' and *en bruse* (sounding like Bruce) in French meant 'going rough' or 'into the bush'. When I told him that my birth certificate had no mention of any hospital for my place of birth but simply read 'The New Forest', he was ecstatic.

'It's like you were born to be here, Mister Bruse, this day, going into the bush, *en bruse*, ha ha, with me. I can feel it in my bones, it's very exciting, everything that is good is coming together.'

We reached the village of Mimongo in the early evening of our second day on the road. This is a Babongo village, until a couple of years ago deep in the forest. Then a logging concession pushed a road through and overnight the villagers stopped being forest people and became roadside people. Now they live where the track runs out, some in dwellings made of timber, others in more modern mud-brick shacks with corrugated-iron roofs.

Our assistant producer Alison Quinn and anthropologist Judy Knight had been here some days before, so we were expected. Having slung up our hammocks by the vehicles and set up our makeshift overnight camp, we sat down with the chief and elders and negotiated with them for porters for the next stage of our journey, the half-day trek into the jungle. Pretty much everyone was keen to get involved – remunerated work isn't common in such an out-of-the-way place. Steve and I decided the easiest thing would be to employ the whole village for the morning's journey. That sorted, we lit a fire and got supper: the crew staple of pasta and tuna washed down with a powdered fruit drink.

Steve Robinson was not just producer/director of this first programme, but series producer and the hub of the *Tribe* team. We'd spent the last seven months side by side in the BBC offices in Cardiff developing *Tribe* from newly commissioned pitch up to this point, so we knew each other pretty well. Steve's a true Welshman: poetic, proud, always brutally honest with his opinions, passionate about the project and, more importantly, deeply caring about doing the right thing for the people we were filming. Jon Clay, the cameraman, I knew less well. Good looking and very bright, he knows almost as much about environmental issues as he does about ornithology – his understanding of the local birdlife had already proved impressive.

We sat up late around the fire that evening, talking everything through. We were all enjoying the company of larger-than-life M. Hugues, who was full of opinions and stories about this place and these people. The sky had cleared and the stars shone bright overhead. As the noise from the village died down we could hear the sounds of the jungle beyond; over the insistent croak of the frogs, the squawks and cries of unknown birds and animals: owls, monkeys, gorillas – who knew? Tomorrow we would be walking right in to join them.

In the morning we left the vehicles behind and set off on foot, down a wide, overgrown logging track. It was quite a sight, a cavalcade of villagers in a long line, each transporting an item or two in their traditional wicker carriers, which strap on their shoulders like a knapsack without the covering. Despite the help, I carried my own gear: I like to be self-sufficient and I enjoy the exercise, once I actually get going. Annoyingly, I was tremendously out of shape. I cursed myself repeatedly.

When we finally got to Mikoko, our destination, it had a welcoming feel to it, looking down from its hillside to a valley where mist floated through the tall green treetops. Alison and Judy were already in situ, camping on the edge of the village, so once more there was no need for explanations. And the people, at first meeting, seemed lovely: warm, gentle and genuinely pleased to see us. I was surprised to hear French being spoken throughout the village. We sat down with the men in the central communal hut, which has a thatched roof so low you have to bow to enter – a deliberate feature, as the far end is a sacred space, for initiated males only. With Judy acting as our interpreter, we explained what we wanted to do; if they agreed, I would try to live with them in their village while the rest of the team camped just outside, coming in by day to film. In what was to become the norm for every shoot, I suggested that I stay with the crew for the first few days so that the villagers could get to know me properly before I moved in, then they could decide in their own time where I should live and what exactly they wanted to do with me. There were big smiles all round and no objections in principle.

Later that day they staged a wonderful series of songs and dances for us. One man was almost invisible at the centre of a whirling, gyrating mass of green foliage; another had his face whited out with kaolin, in a costume that made him look like the spookiest of ghosts. They represented forest spirits; indeed, their dancing, we were told, would call real spirits from the forest.

We spent the next two days pitching camp and sorting out our equipment. On a site at the top of the village, we set up toilet and kitchen areas, hung our hammocks and sorted out the solar panels and camera gear. On our second night, after a crew evening chatting around the fire, we were woken in the pitch darkness by an awful screaming and wailing from the village. The eerie sound was deeply troubling and we all knew something terrible had happened. We stayed put, but in the morning our worst fears were confirmed: a baby girl had died. We did our best to express our sympathy in halting French, then backed off and left the villagers to it, not wanting to get in their way.

We were also worried they might take this tragedy as a bad omen – or even blame us. But it wasn't so. Not only were they keen that we should stick around, they wanted me to visit another woman who was very ill. She was lying in the corner of her hut in the darkness, just wasting away. She was only twenty-five, but so thin and weak and haggard that she looked twice that age. Nobody said it was AIDS, but I felt sure that it was. Such cases were known where the loggers had been. Her eyes were still bright, but you could see she knew she was dying. Hugues explained that the villagers were hoping we'd have some medicine that could cure her, but even if I'd been a trained doctor with the best drugs in the world, I wasn't sure if there was anything I could have done. I held her hand and talked to her, but she was beyond help. That night we woke to more howling; I knew instinctively that she had died.

The next morning it was raining: real, hard, tropical rain that drummed on the tent walls and splashed up off the orange-brown dirt. When it had stopped, we went over to the village. I was right; the poor woman had passed away. With such high infant-mortality rates, this second, adult death was a much bigger deal for these people. The funeral rites that followed in the afternoon involved pretty much everyone in the village. While the men drummed and chanted, the women smeared their bodies all over with thick, chalky-white kaolin and danced up and down like human ghosts, ululating a very public grief. The dead woman's children were even more expressive, moaning and howling as they rolled in the dirt outside their hut.

For us visitors, this was complicated. On one level we hardly knew where to put ourselves; we certainly didn't want to intrude on their grief. On another, we had come all this way to see how these people lived and here we were witnessing big and all-too-real events. We had decided not to film, but they were insistent about us doing so. Then: 'Is everything OK?' they kept asking us in French, which was not an easy one to answer. Obviously we were sad for them, but if we said, *'Non, nous sommes tristes,'* they might take that the wrong way, feel they hadn't made us welcome. We ended up gesturing a lot as we tried to explain that we were perfectly OK in ourselves, but obviously sad about what had happened. Luckily, we still had M. Hugues with us, and he was a brilliant link, both as interpreter and someone who better understood the culture we were dealing with.

Though the funeral was an expression of grief, it somehow seemed more than that: a ritual cleansing of the village, almost; at some level, a celebration. As the dancing, drumming and chanting continued, the women of the village washed the body and wrapped it tight in a white cloth, then it was tied to a bier and carried at a near-sprint by two of the men to its final resting place in the forest, with the other men forming a loose cortège around them. Steve was struck by the contrast between this village's open, vocal, shared grief and the more private and prolonged mourning of our own culture.

After three days and nights, the ceremony was over. M. Hugues drove off in the Fetish-mobile back to Libreville, and I judged that the time had finally come to leave spaghetti bolognese dinners and other camp comforts behind and move into the village. Until this moment I had hidden behind the undeniable force of Hugues's character; now it was time for me to take a more prominent role, if I was to learn more about these people and make any worthwhile friendships. I was both petrified and excited now, our experiment finally about to begin. I'd worked as an expedition leader before, taking young people on science and conservation trips through the jungles of Indonesia and elsewhere, and had often spent time with indigenous peoples, staying with them and *seeing* how they lived. But I'd always had my Western stuff with me – sleeping bag, mosquito net, dried food, iodine and nail scissors – which had created a small but undeniable barrier between us. Now I was going to leave all that behind and really try to live like the locals. What insights would that throw up? Maybe I would realize that I'd been viewing these communities through rose-tinted specs, going back to the UK and rhapsodizing about how great their lives were. Perhaps I was going to discover a life of boredom and misery. I was extremely apprehensive.

All of us on the project felt that this look at indigenous peoples was important. We knew it was a hell of a subject: anthropologists cannot agree what course of action is best for the future of indigenous peoples around the world, while the United Nations hadn't at the time even decided what an indigenous person was. There were so many issues involved: the environment, sustainability, human rights and land ownership, quite apart from sex, drugs, religion, family values, stress-free living – you name it. No doubt about it – our plan was controversial. We'd been told by academics in the anthropological world that if they could think of one type of programme they would hate the most, this would be it! That didn't exactly help my confidence much.

None the less, we were all convinced that if we got our series right it could put all these important subjects back into the living room in a brand new way. It was television, so it had to be entertaining. It couldn't preach or people would switch off in droves. We wanted to reach an audience who wouldn't normally watch this kind of programme, but we also had to do justice to the pace and style of the culture in question. How the hell were we going to do it? There was so much riding on how I got on in the coming weeks and it was all about to start. The long months of preparation were over and I was bricking it.

*

The men in the village had decided to mark my integration into the village by building me a *tudi*, or traditional house. This looks like a jungle igloo, with a substructure of saplings, curved to join at the top, layered over with broad green leaves to keep out both the sun and the rain. It's the traditional dwelling that the Babongo would have built when they were more nomadic, on the move every three months or so. Now they live in more permanent oblong dwellings, with walls made from a stick lattice, plastered in mud and covered with a thatched roof of palm fronds.

On this morning half the men of the village, it seemed, had turned out to help and demonstrate their traditional skills. We walked in a big group into the jungle, found a grove of palms, and hacked off leaf after leaf with our machetes – shiny, green, each leaf at least thirty centimetres long by fifteen. These were then bundled up into neat packs that we hoisted on to our backs and carried to the village, where another bunch of guys was already hard at work on the sapling framework, which looked, when finished, exactly like a makeshift wooden igloo. With deft, practised hands, the leaves were layered on, section by section, and by early afternoon my *tudi* was finished. I pulled a few weeds from the dirt that comprised my floor and got to work sweeping out my new home.

A young guy called Jean-Jacques appeared, carrying a board on which he'd painted THIS NEW HOUSE OF MISTER BROSE. Jean-Jacques was only a teenager, but he was clearly one of the brightest people in the village, as well as being a bit of a show-off – in this case English was his third language, after Babongo and French. He would end up being either one of the programme's stars or a real problem.

My initial euphoria at being alone in my brand new jungle dwelling didn't last long. The sky darkened, thunder rumbled and lightning flashed among the treetops down in the valley. A few heavy drops of rain on the roof were followed by a tropical downpour designed to test the efficacy of tradition against modernity. Unfortunately here, at least, tradition lost out –

streams of water were soon pouring in through the roof. I knelt on the dirt, cursing quietly as I tried to rearrange the leaves to block them out.

The men's communal hut was completely empty that evening. It looked as if there was going to be no more welcome for me, so I thought I might as well get an early night in my new pad. I was sleeping on an old flour sack on the uneven ground. Ants crawled over me, announcing their presence with a sharp nip. Just as I finally dozed off there was the loud rhythmic *thump* of a drum, three metres from my head. It was a bunch of kids right outside my door, eyes gleaming and teeth white in the darkness. They wanted to celebrate my moving in, they indicated with expressive gestures, with a dance. I hauled myself to my feet, went out and joined them. It was fun, out under the stars, and I felt as if I was finally where I was meant to be: in the village, doing my best to be part of the scene.

Sometime later, back on my flour sack in the dark, the ants stepped up their welcome. I lay on the dirt, without a sleeping bag or mosquito net, wide awake and listening to the unfamiliar village sounds all around me: over the incessant chirruping of crickets, the odd dog barking; and beyond, the ever-present jungle noises. Then, at first light, just as I'd finally nodded off, cocks started to crow, dogs woke up with a vengeance, and human chatter followed soon after. The crew didn't pitch up for ages, and when they did, they already looked different: well rested from a comfortable night in sleeping bags under mosquito nets, with breakfast in their bellies. I can't deny that I was jealous.

My legs were itching badly, not only from the ant-nips, but from the bites of the evil little insect the locals call the *feroux*. This is more like a midge than a mosquito and it moves in silently at dusk or dawn, with no warning whine to alert you. One layer of insect repellent will keep them away, but I was adamant about my plan to live exactly the same as the people with whom I was staying: with the result that my uncovered arms and legs were already a mass of vivid crimson bites.

That first week wasn't easy in lots of ways. I had imagined the crew would be around a lot more than they were. And though the guys in the village were friendly, I felt decidedly awkward sitting in the men's hut in the evenings, not speaking their language, not really able to join in except with clumsy remarks in my terrible French. Then I'd go back to my *tudi*, and there was nothing to do there either, except stare out of the door. I could hear life going on in the mud houses all around, but I didn't feel I could just march in without being invited. I didn't want to commit some terrible cultural faux pas.

Every evening one of the village women would bring me supper – a small bowl of boiled potatoes. Later I realized they thought I still had access to the crew's food in camp. For them it was a no-brainer. Why would I voluntarily be eating nothing but potatoes when I could be having *tinned food* with my colleagues? So they gave me something very simple, without the meat and vegetables which at the time I didn't realize they had regularly in their diet. Some of them were even hanging around the crew camp when the crew were cooking, and getting the odd impromptu takeaway as a result. So ironically – and unwittingly – I ended up living a harder life than not just the crew, but the locals too. I was hungry all day and, as a result, irritable and lethargic. Steve was worried about me.

'You're starving, mate,' he said after a few days. 'Please come and eat with us up in camp.'

The temptation was so strong. 'No, I can't, Steve.' I knew that if I succumbed once, it would all be over. 'If I have a meal with you because you're feeling sorry for me, it's a slippery slope . . .'

I was determined to do what I'd told myself I'd do – live like the locals for as long as I could. At the very least, I had to last a week.

In the meantime, we were spending part of each day filming the ordinary life of the Babongo. One morning I went out with the women collecting crabs in the nearby freshwater streams; on another we went off to see the little clearings in the forest where they cultivate maize, manioc (cassava) and taro. But I was still finding it hard to bond. Even when I mucked in with their tasks I felt a bit of an outsider.

Then one evening, just as we arrived back at camp, one of the women invited me into the communal cooking hut to join them as they made supper. The room had a roof, but no mud between the sticks that made up the walls, so it was nice and cool. They cooked round an open fire. There was no crew around, just me, and as we conversed in sign language and snippets of French, and they teased me and laughed loudly at my halting replies, I started to feel that at last I was getting to know them.

Feeling altogether better about things, I left the big kitchen and wandered up to the top of the village on my own. I was quietly sitting watching the stars above – so intense and bright you could have read a book by them – when I felt a hand on my arm. It was one of the guys, Jean-Claude, gesturing sideways with his head. I followed him past a bush to where four or five other men sat round a big wooden tub of mud, splashing it over themselves. They gestured for me to join them. I dipped my hands in up to the wrists, then made a couple of prints on my T-shirt and smeared my face in mud, which made everyone laugh. Then we went down to the central compound and had a wild dance round the fire, drums beating, the guys chanting, some of the women coming over from their hut to watch and join in. This was my first breakthrough with the adults, my first real sign of acceptance coming pure and unsolicited from them. It felt fantastic.

A couple of days later I went out with a group of villagers on a search for honey. It took more than one trip. The first time we saw a bees' nest at the top of a tree, which they climbed, using natural ropes and cutting little steps in the trunk with an axe. But after all this effort, when they finally reached the top there was no honey. On our next excursion they went for a more radical approach. When after a couple of hours spent scouring the jungle they found another bees' nest, they started to make steps in the trunk for climbing as before. Then one of the steps became larger and larger ... until it dawned on me that they were going to chop the whole tree down.

Steve was thinking the same as I was.

'Bruce, what's going on?' he questioned from behind the camera.

'Well, erm, shit, I didn't think they'd be chopping the whole thing down.'

'And ... ?'

Now I was flummoxed. From an environmental point of view, chopping down a hardwood tree in the middle of the rainforest isn't great. Especially as one of the guys had said that it probably didn't contain any honey anyway – they were just doing it to have a look.

I was on the spot. I found myself stumbling and waffling in front of the camera like the sappy apologetic Englishman that I am. It wasn't as if I didn't understand the arguments. It is the Babongo's land to do with as they wish. Selective felling isn't such a bad thing. Issues of protecting the environment surely have more to do with our potential in the developed world to do massive harm than a little local event like this. I have opinions on all these things, that I could defend with gusto down the pub, but now I was talking to an international audience which would doubtless include anthropologists, naturalists, agroforesters and others who had spent their entire lives studying these matters. It was a truly seminal moment, for Steve as well as for me.

That day I realized something important – I had to take a stance. This may sound terribly obvious to an outsider, but I realized then that I couldn't answer to everybody. Some elements of my TV audience were always going to disagree with me. I was lucky to have Steve as my director. He let me experiment endlessly on camera, but always made me feel safe. I knew that he would look after me as I learnt my new craft and not stitch me up to make me look like an idiot when it came to the edit, which allowed me to relax and slowly start being myself.

Back in camp, Jon had fallen ill with a fever, so Steve and I decided we'd take a couple of the men up on their invitation to accompany them on a three-day hunting trip, deep into the jungle. Two in particular, Jean-Claude and Jean-Philippe, were very easy-going and friendly and, importantly, quite natural on camera. Unlike teenaged tearaway Jean-Jacques – the guy who'd painted the board for my *tudi* – who bounded into shot at every opportunity, singing, dancing and showing off his undeniably strong personality, but in an artificial way. He might have done all right on a Gabonese version of *Pop Idol*, but he was totally wrong for the programme we were trying to make. Steve had decided the best way to stop him hijacking the film was to employ him behind the scenes as a camera assistant. He was delighted and so were we.

Before we left, Jean-Philippe showed me how to make a bow and a quiver full of poisoned arrows. The bow was fashioned out of a curved ground vine which we found down by the river. Quite the most dainty, childlike bow I'd ever seen; even Cupid would have scoffed at it. The power of the hunter came in the arrows. To make them, we went out to a nearby grove and cut off sections of a tough, thick reed-like grass. Back at the village these were sliced down into thin, rounded shafts, about sixty centimetres long. The ends were sharpened and then coated with a special poison made from ground seeds, crushed into a paste and smeared on a leaf. The poison was very strong, Jean-Philippe told me. If a man was shot with one of the arrows he would die pretty much instantly.

We set off early, moving quickly down a narrow track through the jungle. The guys were up ahead, superbly fit, chattering like starlings as they paced along on bare feet, legs protruding from tatty sports shorts. Jean-Claude, who always wore the same ripped T-shirt, was the more relaxed and easy-going of the two; Jean-Philippe, whose daily uniform was a once-smart, red and white Hawaiian shirt, was quieter but no less friendly. Steve and I did our best to keep up, but were not as used to the dense foliage as they were. After two or three hours we came to their special hunting camp, in a lovely spot by a bend in the river. Ironically, after all our earlier efforts to find honey, it was swarming with wasps and bees. Great for me too – I'm allergic to their venom.

It was impossible to keep out of the insects' way, so, trying not to disturb them too much, Steve and I sat down, grateful for the rest. Before we knew it, the guys were off down the river, fishing for lunch. They returned with a basket full of their slippery catch, which we gutted on the spot and cooked wrapped in leaves over a fire. After my days and days of bland boiled potatoes, this fresh and succulent white flesh, picked with fingers off the bone, tasted as good as anything I could remember. I was suddenly fired up with energy again, but now all the guys wanted to do after their impromptu feast was sleep. Steve and I watched them flat out on their backs in the shade, snoring fitfully as the bees buzzed around. No, there would be no filming of any hunting that afternoon. In the evening we sat around the fire doing our best to make conversation, in French and the few words of Babongo I'd learnt. The flip-out screen of the camera provided our only other amusement; seeing their own faces grinning, laughing and jostling into the frame was a novelty which the guys never seemed to tire of.

After three days in the jungle we had to go back to the village empty-handed. But even with nothing to show for our hunting trip, I got a terrific reception. All kinds of people appeared from their huts to say hello to me, to shake my hand and welcome me home. I think they had been worried that something terrible would happen to me in the jungle. It was a great moment, and it showed me that I had a true relationship with the villagers of Mikoko after all. There was talk of my initiation, and alone in my *tudi* that evening I decided that I trusted them fully and would go ahead with the Bwiti ceremony.

How could I hope to gain even the smallest understanding of their culture if I wasn't even willing to undergo this ritual? I would have felt as though I'd let myself down if I'd gone back to Libreville without having done it. Which is not to understate my fears. I had no real idea what *iboga* was, what it might do to me – even what state my Q waves were in. But I knew it was not just any old hallucinogen. M. Hugues had explained that if you take LSD it's like watching a cartoon version of the world: you might see kaleidoscopes or trees breathing or people's faces twisted into caricature. But with *iboga*, you actually *enter into* that cartoon world, become a cast member and participate. This is no happy-go-lucky three-hour mushroom trip on a sunny English country afternoon. It is all or bust and the dose has to be taken in one huge ingestion. There is no 'Let's see how you get on and we can ramp it up later if you're feeling OK.'

But the element that scared me the most was one I'd read about on the flight out and that M. Hugues had elaborated on further: that when you take the drug in this massive dose you are somehow forced to confront exactly who you are; specifically any remorse you feel about bad things you've done in your life. Not that I had any huge sins or veteran's horrors that I feared coming face to face with. Yes, I'd been in the Marines, to Iraq even, but only to do humanitarian work. I've never fired a shot in anger. The worst things I've done were probably in my private life, in relationships. If they were going to come back and haunt me now, perhaps I deserved it; perhaps, at thirty-four, it was time for me to take a really searching look inside myself.

Steve and I sat down with Chimika, the young chief of the village, and a few of the elders in the men's hut and talked about how exactly they were going to manage my initiation. I needed to be well and strong, they said, before we went ahead with it. But the elders were also concerned about the correct dose. Being this far into the jungle, the Babongo had never known of a European doing this before. They had all the traditional antidotes ready for things that had gone wrong in the past, but it was a question of how much I should be given. We had just about decided to start the very next day, when Steve suggested that maybe we should ask M. Hugues back. He had overseen many Bwiti initiations, of both Africans and Europeans. He, surely, would know the right dosage. He could also act as intermediary and translator. It was a great idea, so Steve got on the satellite phone and called the charismatic Frenchman in Libreville.

I was glad of this delay, because I wasn't on top form. I'd been feeling a bit shivery and had diarrhoea. Steve was keen that I should be as fit as possible for my upcoming ordeal, so we agreed that I should bring a few Western elements back into my lifestyle, primarily a cotton sleeping sheet and insect repellent. That night, protected at last from mosquitoes, ants and evil *feroux*, I slept soundly for the first time since I'd come to Mikoko.

M. Hugues arrived and immediately took charge of the preparations for my initiation in his own inimitable style. In the urban versions of the Bwiti faith anyone can invent their own form of the religion, start their own sect and become their own high priest – the only common denominator being that you have to undergo the *iboga* overdose as the initiation. M. Hugues had done this, establishing his own rituals and form of service, more Gaian than Christian.

One of Hugues's additions was that I should have a whole day of contemplation, during which I must work out my lifetime's wrongdoings and write them down – everything bad I'd ever done. So I sat in my *tudi* with my diary and thought it all out, stretching back to childhood. The list lasted some pages and the process was highly cathartic. Most of the nastier entries were one-offs and, I would argue, circumstantial, but this of course was where the drug was going to do its work. Were they really circumstantial, or was that my ego forcing me into denial and trying to make me feel better? What was I really going to discover about myself when I took a deep look inside? I had read that many people after taking the drug had changed their lives completely. They saw who they were so vividly that they couldn't go back to doing what they'd done for a living before. Lawyers and politicians beware! People make similar claims for ayahuasca, DMT, San Pedro and mescaline, but their chemical compositions are entirely different. And those, like M. Hugues, who have done many or all of these drugs will tell you there really is nothing out there like *iboga* for going deep inside.

All of a sudden there was a problem. The chief of a neighbouring village, who was more in touch with the Gabonese authorities than our community, had got cold feet about negative repercussions that might come his way if things went badly. He was seriously worried that because I was a white man I might have a bad reaction to *iboga* and die. There was also a concern that I might be some kind of sorcerer; in which case the drug would surely finish me off. If that happened, the Babongo would be in deep trouble.

M. Hugues tried to reassure him. White people are the same as black people, he said. He had done this with European people before; it was all going to be fine. In the end Chimika and the other chief asked me to sign a document, absolving them of all responsibility for anything that happened during the initiation. It was a surreal moment, putting a pen to this formal piece of paper in the middle of the jungle.

Finally we could begin. The following morning I was taken to the men's hut and sat on the floor in my shorts. My tongue was pricked with a pin to stimulate speech; then I was fed a mixture of honey and shredded *iboga* leaves. Meanwhile I was surrounded with chanting Babongo. Drums beat in the background. Then everyone in the hut gathered round and breathed on me, warm and close, three times, followed by a group shout. This was the traditional blessing.

I was led off to a smaller mud hut. Now I just had Jean-Claude – my outgoing friend from the hunting trip – M. Hugues and a couple of the village elders. Jean-Claude took a knife to a long hard *iboga* root and cut off a thick, creamy-white slice and held it out for me to eat. It was at this moment that I realized he was to be my Bwiti Father. Hugues had made much of the importance of this relationship, and I couldn't think of a better choice.

However, even Jean-Claude's benevolent presence didn't take away from the fact that the *iboga* tasted foul, acrid and indigestible, like chipboard soaked in battery acid. Even when I had chewed it thoroughly it didn't go into a mash, just woody chunks. Somehow I crunched it up and swallowed it down. My lips and mouth were burning painfully, then went into a very unpleasant numbness. I was handed another piece, then another. Looking back I can honestly say that this *iboga* root was by far the nastiest thing I ate during all the *Tribe* programmes. Give me rats' intestines, live bugs, grubs, tepid stringy cow's blood – anything rather than that again. Hugues took a mouthful and had to agree that, compared to his smaller, newer, urban plants, it was an exceptionally bitter specimen.

Jean-Claude started humming, a repetitive, soothing mantra to calm me as I kept on chewing and swallowing. Opposite me M. Hugues was nodding and smiling, encouraging me to keep eating. The force-feeding went on for hours. I started to become very cold. I was told that I couldn't cover up, or cross my legs, or get comfortable in any way. I just had to sit in the same position munching down this toxic wood. I was the *banzi*, the initiate, and I had to do as they said. I had been desperately thirsty since the first morsel, but I hadn't once been allowed even a glassful of water. I was told that once I drank I would start to vomit, and I needed to ingest enough poison first. Finally, towards dusk, they brought me a drink. I was a little spaced by now, but I could see that the drink was more slices of bark mixed in with leaves and water – a concentrated infusion of *iboga*. They told me to gulp it down in one. Pure poison. I instantly felt my stomach churning violently. Then I vomited. They were ready for me – there was a girl beside me with a big leaf. It was the right and expected thing to be sick at this stage, Hugues told me. As I knelt, moaning, retching my guts out, my blood felt like hot pepper sauce pumping round my veins.

Suddenly it hit me. The sceptical chief had been right – I was going to die. Panic welled up inside me as I reached for my pulse, finger and thumb clutching at my burning throat. My veins were pounding like I'd just sprinted an Olympic hundred metres. I tried to rationalize it as the paranoia which usually accompanies such trips, but that didn't help me. I truly thought I'd gone one step too far and would expire there and then in the remote jungle of Gabon. My happy-go-lucky approach to life, which had always served me so well in the face of danger, had finally run out. Idiot! At least it would be recorded on camera for posterity.

Now Jean-Claude and Hugues were asking the crew to leave. The next part of the ceremony, when I was to tell the elders what I saw in my hallucinations, was secret and sacred. Even if there were no cameras, the uninitiated couldn't stay. I didn't even wave goodbye as Steve and Jon backed out through the door into the darkness. Jean-Claude was still feeding me the *iboga*, but it was harder now to get it down my throat. My gag reflex had kicked in. No sooner had I forced a piece down than I would be on my knees again, retching violently on to the hard mud. There was nothing left in my stomach but bile. I'd been eating this poison for ten hours.

Then I was gone, off into a trance. Different visions came and went. Adulthood first, then younger and younger. I was a young Marine in Scotland, driving to Edinburgh. Then I was in my bedroom at home in Hampshire, lying on the bed, a small boy looking up at a photograph of an English cathedral on the wall. Now I was in Germany with my parents, aged three, feeding some ducks with my mother. I could see the ducks in front of me, the knee-length brown skirt my mother was wearing, the bright green car behind us on the road. Wow, I thought, surfacing for a moment, that's exactly how it was.

Beside me Jean-Claude kept up his soft humming. His dark face was side-lit in the yellow firelight, the whites of his eyes shining. Every now and then he or one of the others would lean forward to ask me what I was seeing. When this was translated by Hugues I'd try and explain, but they weren't in the slightest bit interested in my childhood memories.

'What else?' they kept asking. 'What do you really see?' But whatever I was supposed to be seeing, it clearly wasn't right. They grunted and nodded at each other, and still Jean-Claude fed me the foul woody slices.

I was spinning off again but this time it felt different: I was entering the remorse phase of the trip. I was travelling down a wormhole, a swirling vortex, like that sequence at the start of *Doctor Who*. I saw a huge finger, like Kenny Everett's comedy preacher's hands. This was no laughing moment though: the giant finger pointed back up at me and a voice of God cried, 'Look at yourself, Bruce, you're like this as well, aren't you? Forgot to mention *that*, didn't you?' And then I remembered a couple of other bad points to my life which somehow I'd omitted to put on my list of sins.

Then I was in a bedroom in Maida Vale with an old girlfriend, Madeleine, the love of my life. We met when she'd come on one of my expeditions in Indonesia, and we'd got it together three years later, one wonderful night in Jakarta. We'd had a wild time together back in England and I was crazy about her. She'd then become desperately ill and our relationship had fallen apart.

Now I was in the bedroom of the flat we'd shared in London. Madeleine was standing over on the other side of the bed, by the window. I could clearly see the books on the shelves, the names of the books, even the pattern of the blue duvet cover, the time on the clock on the wall. Madeleine was looking at me.

'I love you, babe,' she said. Somehow I was out of my body and floating up by the ceiling, looking down on both of us. Then I was inside *her*, looking across at me *through her eyes*.

'I love you too,' I saw myself saying. But I could see all too clearly that I didn't mean it any more. Instantly I felt her heart break in two as if it were mine. I felt her pain there and then, looking at myself through her eyes. I saw myself not care and that made it so much worse. How could I ever have done that to someone, anyone? But especially her, in her time of need. Somehow, I suppose, all that time ago, I'd known this had been the time I'd hurt her the most, and I had obviously subconsciously stored the moment in all its vitality somewhere in my head.

I was back in Gabon, in a little hut with torchlight flickering on dried mud walls; with Jean-Claude and M. Hugues and a silently watching row of Bwiti papas.

'What did you see?' they asked earnestly. I told them about Madeleine. They shook their heads; they weren't interested in that. 'What else?' they asked.

'Nothing. Well, there were, like, some shapes too.'

They sat forward eagerly. 'Shapes? What? Describe them.'

Because I don't speak Babongo and have terrible French, this was all being translated by M. Hugues. I was using a lot of gestures and struggling to find the right words.

'Well, there were, like, these two glowing balls . . .'

'Bawls?' Hugues repeated.

'Balls. *Boules*? *Ballons*?'

'Ah, *balles* . . .'

Now they were interested. They wanted to know everything about them. No leading questions though. They just repeated 'What else?' to my every additional description. As M. Hugues and I stumbled out an image, they sat there nodding and staring at me until, suddenly, they cried, '*Oui!*' and broke into a gentle cheer. Because they knew I had seen one of the shapes that they knew was a key. After describing the balls, I realized I had seen other things too – I just hadn't known these were what they wanted to hear about. The papas didn't give a toss about my awful guilt trip; they just wanted details of these shapes.

It reached the point where they didn't even need M. Hugues to translate. My gestures, grunts and hand shapes were enough. They had names for all these things. Over the hundreds, perhaps thousands of years these people have been taking *iboga* they had categorized these visions. A few images I depicted got little reaction at all while most, once described in full, were given a murmur of approval and another name.

What were they? Symbols of some sort, who knows, but they certainly had potent meaning to the Babongo. To me they were the key to my Bwiti acceptance, proof of the depth of my trip, justification of all the agony I'd been through. I was sworn to secrecy as to these images' dimensions, movements, colours and so on. The Bwiti elders had taken clippings of my toe- and fingernails, mixed them up with soot and gum and stuck them on the roof of the sacred section of their men's hut. If they ever needed to cast a spell on me, they said, just that residue would be enough. They needn't have bothered, their secret was safe with me.

On his various *iboga* trips, M. Hugues had talked to trees, flown through the air like a bird, and met and had a conversation with someone he called God. I didn't go as deep as that, unfortunately, but I did, somewhere in my trance, see and meet a Being. He wore what looked to me like a big white puffa jacket and he was sitting on a cloud that went up and down. The Bwiti elders were very impressed with this character and wanted precise details. Again they nodded in recognition, as I talked of the conversations we'd had.

As my trip progressed the mood got lighter. The remorseful

agonies had passed. Now I looked round the little room and shivered as the blue-grey morning light started filtering in from outside. I saw a swathe of green mist passing between us. It left my chest and passed to M. Hugues's chest and then on to Jean-Claude and all round the circle of Bwiti papas. Then it stretched outside to where the sun was now starting to light up the treetops, a golden yellow. This mist joined us to the forest and all the animals and plants within it. We were all connected. Every action had a reaction. We were all just tiny parts of our huge breathing organism of a planet and we should always be aware of that, whatever we do or take from it. This was a philosophy I'd been coming closer to in any case and I found this visualization of it profoundly moving.

When the sun was fully up, I was taken out into the village. It was now twenty hours since I'd started eating the root. There was drumming and chanting and everyone gathered around me as I was carried down to the river, then anointed with water infused with *iboga* leaves. To ritual chants, I was made to climb through an oval of sticks that symbolized a vulva: I was being reborn. They made me lie in the river while they washed me, many hands touching and rubbing me. Then I was carried back to the village and people danced all round me. There were so many different songs and musical drumming sessions. It was non-stop, and all clearly deeply symbolic. Where did they get their energy from? They had each taken a tiny sliver of *iboga*. This provided enough stimulant to keep them all going for the allotted two days, so God alone knew how high I was.

I wish I knew what all the songs and dances meant. I was still relatively off my nut, everything melted into a mad blur. The main thing was that I was looked after and never left alone. I rarely even touched the ground. I would sit in the crook of someone's feet with his toes turned up and his shins as my backrest and his hands gently swaying my shoulders from side to side; or be carried aloft on another's shoulders. Someone always made sure I had human contact, so that I didn't spin off into a bad trip. Once I was left alone for a brief minute and an elder pointed at me and shouted. Instantly five men came over, picked me up and hugged me back into the group. They knew exactly what they were doing.

As the sun went down on the second day, they all donned magical colourful costumes which in the gilded light to me now seemed fluorescent. They then started to run at me, some drumming and some holding leafy branches dripping with water. Back and forth they came. As they crowded round me and sprinkled me with water, I went from hot to cold, loud to quiet, bright to dark – my senses were pulsating. I've been to some very well-organized parties where fireworks and laser shows are put on to elicit some form of audiovisual response, but these guys were masters of sensory overload. They were partying like pros.

Then it was dark and they were dancing round with fire sticks, making great swirling patterns of light against the bright stars. Was that a dragon or just a trail of sparks? More creatures appeared, running forward and vanishing back into the night. I was still tripping, so although part of me knew these were humans decorated in leaves and branches, part of me saw them as forest spirits.

After three full days the end came. They brought me meat and rice which I swallowed gratefully. The Bwiti papas gathered round and gave me a name: Minanga, after the first vision I'd seen when I'd left the hut: a blue star. I was a new person; I hadn't died and I'd become one of them. I was permitted to sit with the elders in the sacred initiated part of the communal hut.

In just that one month, I'd learnt so much about myself and the world around me. I'd had many of my views confirmed and a number of other ones challenged. I'd been reborn back into my own world with new insights. I'd been truly initiated. Furthermore, I had experienced life in another culture and now realized that that carried with it a wonderful and important responsibility. By being paid public money to be here in the first place, I felt I had a duty to report back home on what our own world looked like from their perspective. I'd just had the most extraordinary experience of my life, terrifying but profound, humbling but ultimately very positive. How was I going to explain all that to anyone?

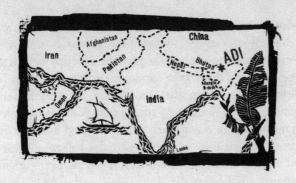

2. Spring Festival

The Adi of Arunachal Pradesh, India

The Adi people live way up in the far north-eastern corner of
India, in an area known by the British until 1986 as the North-
East Frontier Agency. To the west is the mountain kingdom of
Bhutan. To the north, over the peaks of the Himalayas, Tibet and
China. To the east, beyond the state of Nagaland, lies Myanmar,
formerly known as Burma. This remote region of Arunachal
Pradesh – as it's now called – has, since Partition in 1947, enjoyed
a unique autonomous status. China never recognized it as a part
of India, so Nehru pragmatically opted to leave the area to be
governed independently by tribal law. Until 1995 Indians from
other states weren't even allowed to enter without special permission. Now they may visit or work there, but are forbidden from
owning land or running businesses. Outsiders from other countries
may also go in, but permits are restricted, expensive and hard to
obtain. As a result, the contrast with neighbouring Assam is all
too visible – one state deforested and overpopulated, the other a
tribal homeland with huge areas of wilderness left intact.

In Victorian times the Adi were known as the Abor, which means 'unruly' or 'savage' in Assamese. Certainly they were a highly independent people who gave the colonial British a run for their money. There were sporadic confrontations with the administration of Assam throughout the nineteenth century, culminating in the murder of an assistant political officer who was touring the region in 1911. This provoked a savage retaliation from the British, who returned the following year and asserted their dominance in no uncertain terms, burning villages and hanging ringleaders.

Whether long Adi memories might influence the welcome for us present-day Brits remained to be seen. For the moment we had our work cut out just getting there. A flight from Delhi brought us to the plains of Assam and the sacred Brahmaputra River at Dibrugarh. In the wet season, the river runs next to the town and airstrip; now in the dry autumn, the depleted waterway was some kilometres away. Driving through the silty flood plain in the dark to where our boats were waiting involved over an hour of muddy vehicle rescues. At first light we set off in a colourful little vessel for a day's journey up that huge, wide, magical expanse of water – at one point passing a pod of playful river dolphins. As our boats moored that evening at a pre-arranged spot, long gangplanks were lowered and the figure of Ozing Dai, our fixer, was pointed out, waiting for us on the high banks with mugs of tea on a silver tray. What a great welcome! As soon as I saw him, I started to feel better about the month ahead. He was a stocky-looking guy with a lovely smile under a droopy moustache that made him look like Fu Manchu.

We were now in the hands of Ozing's team of drivers and cooks, who would be with us for the rest of the trip. Ozing had also arranged for two local Adi-language speakers, Bitton and Tajir, to act as translators. They seemed equally easy-going, with a gentleness of manner that I was starting to recognize as typical of the Adi. It was Tajir who had found our proposed destination village, Jorsing. Not only was it suitably remote, but he had relatives there too.

After more travelling, we stopped off at Pasighat, the capital of the East Siang area. That evening Ozing took us all off to his uncle Jarrah's house on the edge of town, a traditional dwelling on stilts with a thatched roof. Jarrah worked for the government and earned a good salary, and in his house he had all the accoutrements of modern-day living: television, telephone, electric light and heat. His extended family joined us for a meal. There were friendly cousins and pretty daughters and, before we knew it, the traditional fermented local beer – *apong* – came out. It was much tastier than other local brews I've encountered on my travels – and this was a particularly strong one, saved for special guests, Jarrah told us. I asked Jarrah about hunting methods, and he produced a bow and arrow, and a paper target was pinned up in a corner of the room. The party collapsed in hysterics as the crew and I took shots at it. One arrow went so wide of the mark it plunged into a nearby chest of drawers; it was buried at least an inch in and it took three of us to pull it out. Jarrah was loving all of this, and I wondered how my family at home would react if drunk strangers had fired arrows into their finest furniture.

I had a different producer/director for this trip – James Smith, a solid-looking guy with a ready smile and a great sense of humour. James was confident and good fun, and we got on instantly. His approach to directing was different from Steve's – standing back less and taking charge more. As well as recording video diaries as I'd done before, he wanted me to be more of a traditional presenter and do pieces to camera. Nor was he slow to ask me to do retakes if I hadn't done it to his satisfaction first time. The cameraman was tousle-haired Irishman Sam Gracey. The third member of the crew was Hannah Griffiths, our assistant producer, a bubbly Scottish redhead who had – usefully for us – a Master's degree in anthropology. She was laughing her head off that evening, although her tuneless singing didn't help our cause much. Not that she could care less; she was another highly outgoing character.

We left Pasighat the next morning and for another long day we drove north. Now we were way up in the mountains. There were thick woods above and below the road, and many scary hairpin bends to negotiate. Late in the afternoon we came to our camping ground by the edge of the river, the same mighty sacred waterway as the Brahmaputra, though up here it is called the Siang. In Tibet it's known as the Tsangpo.

We set up camp at dusk on a sandy beach where the roar of the deity over the rocks was thunderous. This second *Tribe* expedition already felt very different from our Gabon trip. Ozing's crew were extraordinary: they wouldn't let you touch or do a thing. For the first time in my life my tent was put up by someone else. Tea was brewed for us. Supper was an elaborate meal of rice and nan bread with several curry sauces and *dhals*, and we sat on chairs round a table – a far cry from my early days as an expedition leader, when we carried all our own gear. It was all very nice, but more like a five-star Kenyan safari, and, to be honest, I felt a little uncomfortable with it. Even though we'd been together all day, the cooks and porters wouldn't eat while we were still up and talking. Eventually I decided to go to bed just so that they could have their meal.

It rained throughout the night, drumming on the tent roof as I sank into sleep. In the morning, after an arm poked into my tent and served me tea in bed, I looked out to find a magical view: the steep valley on both sides silhouetted dark against a backdrop from a Chinese scroll painting; layer upon layer of receding grey, the gleaming silver river below.

While breakfast was being cooked, Tajir and Bitton leapt around the rocks, turning over stones and collecting beetles – an Adi delicacy, apparently. Naturally James wanted me to try one on camera. It was a bit odd munching down a live wriggling crustacean, and the first one didn't taste too bad: crunchy on the outside, soft inside (though I could have done without having to keep it on my tongue while Sam got a good shot). But the *second* one still had its poison sac intact: this exploded in my mouth like chilli sauce. My tongue and lips went numb, and stayed that way all day. Ozing's son Nino asked if I'd like to try another Adi delicacy: the intestine and lower bowel of a newly killed rat. Although it was all but burnt and tasted like charcoal, I could still make out its arsehole. Nice. Well, I had a job to do: I chewed it down.

'Why's it so overcooked?' I asked. Nino laughed. It had been writhing with worms, he said, so they'd given it rather longer in the fire than they would normally. They had done this just for me – they actually *liked* the taste of the live worms.

After breakfast we headed off on foot, first crossing a magnificent wire bridge over the river. A good day's walk brought us to a village where they had electricity and had encountered Europeans before, so we were only relatively unusual. After another long morning's hike, around lunchtime on our second day we reached Jorsing. It had been a delightful trek, I thought, looking across the valley at the thatched houses climbing on terraces up the steep wooded hillside. It felt wonderfully remote; Ozing explained that few Europeans had visited the village in the last fifty years.

As we walked down into the centre you could see we were a curiosity. People watched quietly from doorways. When we got to the *moshup* – the village or communal hall – the atmosphere was noticeably subdued. Looking round the silent crowd, if you met someone's eye, they would immediately glance down and away. I tried to break the ice by shaking the hands of a couple of kids, but they ran off.

This was considerably more awkward than my first meeting with the locals in Gabon, and it didn't exactly make me confident. There was wariness on their side of this strange white man with his camera-laden crew; and on mine, too, because I genuinely had no idea how things were going to shake down here. Who knew what folk memories might lurk in the minds of these people? They knew where we were from.

The headman – or *gam* – of Jorsing was out of the village on business, so we decided to keep a low profile until he got back: we all knew that his approval would be important. We didn't unpack our main gear and did minimal filming. Ozing found a place at the top of the village for the crew to set up their tents, behind a house belonging to Tajir's maternal uncle – a traditionally respected figure among the Adi, so he was being clever politically. Meanwhile, I had decided to settle down in the *moshup* as this is the usual place for visitors to stay. It had been a cold night, and I had now developed a chest cold – the last thing I needed at this crucial early stage.

The next morning I was woken by laughter: a group of little kids peered at me through my mosquito net. Curiosity had overcome their initial shyness. They were fascinated by my gear: penknife, torch, radio; they turned them over in their hands, eyes wide.

Later I walked up the stony track out of the village and looked back at the huddle of thatched roofs nestling in the valley. I felt very privileged to be here, especially in the run-up to the important spring festival, called Aran, which we hoped would make a colourful conclusion to our film. But, as in Gabon, I was aware that our very presence was problematic. In a romantic way, I loved it that these people lived here without electricity; yet we were bringing the latest, smallest hi-tech cameras, solar-powered, with night vision. I wanted to breathe the clear mountain air and hunt with a bow and arrow; they probably wanted tobacco and shotgun cartridges. Again a typical dilemma of this series we were making was brought home to me: how could we observe and record a way of life without in some way impacting on it? And maybe impacting in a negative way. The issue was to be central to the whole series.

The next afternoon the *gam* was back. He looked like a real wise village elder, a skinny, elegant man with a thin moustache and a suitably inscrutable expression. Ozing arranged a formal meeting with him in the *moshup* to explain what we wanted to do. Then the *gam* had his own meeting with the village council. It went long into the night. In the morning he informed Ozing of their collective decision: they had embraced our proposal and he wanted me to move not just into the village, but right next door to him. The men of Jorsing would build me a hut alongside his house. This was way beyond what we'd asked for, and showed genuine acceptance of us as a team. We were delighted.

Early the following morning it seemed most of the able-bodied men in the place had turned out to help build my new home. We started by walking up to some bamboo groves on the hillside to cut poles for the basic structure. The bamboo is five to seven centimetres across, sturdy yet flexible. I was keen to join in with the work, but I'm not sure I was that helpful. As a welcome gift, Ozing had given me a local *parang*, a sharp, broad-bladed knife, which I'd managed to chip while cutting some wood. I was of more service carrying the bamboo back into the village, but even this wasn't easy, the great length of the poles making it hard to hold them straight. Resting them on my shoulder, the rear end jolted down each step and terrace so much I thought my teeth would fall out.

As in Gabon, the men were experts at all stages of the building work. The basic structure was soon up, a criss-cross of bamboo tied together with thick natural twine. After lunch there was a second expedition, to collect the broad, brilliant-green palm leaves they use to cover the roof struts. This meant shinning up skinny tree trunks carrying a *parang*. Both the crew and the locals discouraged me. It wasn't safe, they said. This was starting to become a theme in *Tribe*. Compared to the locals, I was so crap at most of the physical stuff which they did with ease, and so they naturally thought that I'd be bad at everything; whereas for me climbing a tree was really not a problem. Just occasionally it was good to show I could hold my own.

Not that I was particularly steady with this one. You have to find purchase for your feet on the bases of previously sliced-off fronds, which can give way alarmingly as you climb. But I managed to get high enough to chop off a few palms for them. Then there was the laborious job of gathering the big leaves into bundles and carrying them back to base. On your head, as ever – very uncomfortable if you haven't balanced them well. But it all made for good bonding – during the day there had been much slapping of backs and laughter. I was starting to break the ice and make friends.

By dusk the house was three-quarters built, just the last of the wall-covering and thatched roof to go. The next morning the job was quickly finished. Special trees were planted round about and little latticed arrangements of bamboo, like mobiles, were hung outside – to give me good dreams. After lunch it was time to celebrate my moving in. A domestic pig was caught and strangled in the V made by two vertical sticks, its death-squeals ringing out horribly through the village. Then the *gam* and his family appeared with big brass and copper plates: moving-in gifts and, it transpired, heirlooms, because the *gam* now announced that he was adopting me as his son. When a bachelor sets up home away from his parents, he explained, they are duty-bound to give him basic crockery and implements.

'These are all for my son,' he said and then, eyes twinkling and playing up to the camera like a natural actor, added to the guys on one side, 'Don't worry: we'll get them all back later.' He did, too; most of the bits and pieces were back in his house again the next day. He left me with one big brass pot and a plate. 'After all,' he said, 'you'll be dining with me every day now anyway.'

That evening the *apong* was brought out, my house was blessed by the *gam*, and in the company of half the village I was given a new name: Opang Moyong. There was much hilarity as we tried to get an accurate translation of what this means:

Moyong is the *gam*'s family name, while *opang* means 'sudden arrival' or, as Tajir initially put it, 'one who comes quickly'. (Hannah and Sam weren't going to let this pass, and the joke persisted for ages among the crew.)

The party continued in the *gam*'s house. As the drink went down and people helped themselves to freshly roasted pork, my new position in the Moyong family was rehearsed and rere-hearsed. Beking Moyong, over in the corner, was my older brother; Lulu Moyong was my younger brother; the *gam* was my father; his wife, with a wonderfully wizened, smiling face, was my mother. The phrases 'This is your older brother', 'This is your younger brother', 'This is your mother' and so on kept us going for hours. After that a whole lot of the younger women of the village turned up, dressed in colourful long skirts and tops, and there was dancing in a line, which I joined in with, even though I wasn't sure which hand to wave and when.

The pig we'd slaughtered wasn't just any old pig; it was one of the animals the Adi prize most for its rich flesh – a toilet pig. This happy animal spends its entire life eating shit. Literally. It lives in the closet under the household toilet and when you go there for your daily business you dump on its head. That and a few scrapings off the odd plate is its regular diet. So it was rather warily that I tried the meat that evening; but it lived up to its reputation; if you didn't think too hard about what had gone into it, it was delicious. *you are what you eat*

Every morning in my little house I woke to a gathering cacophony. First off, at about a quarter to five, was a cock who roosted right outside my door. The noise was more like a strangled goat than traditional crowing, and he would soon be joined by seven or eight others; they didn't stop all morning. Next up were the pigs, squealing as they fought. Then the village dogs joined in; then the squawking chickens. If I was still trying to sleep at this point a *mithun* (their traditional animal – a heavy, clumsy-looking cross between a cow and a water buffalo) would often start rubbing against the wall of my hut, shaking it. Then the ants appeared. I was usually up by five-thirty.

Once settled in, I started to meet some of the village characters. The next day a guy in a bearskin hat turned up at the crew tents; rising from the black fur on each side were twin boar tusks and mounted on the top was a hornbill's skull and beak. Under this amazing headgear he was wearing full Adi battle dress and had a large sword. It turned out that he was renowned for being the best archer in the village, one of the few left who didn't have a shotgun, and the perfect person to show me how to make a bow and arrow. We went out to the fields to collect the right kind of wood; then I came back and watched as he fashioned the bow with his *parang*, strung it with twine, then cut thin arrows from the thick stems. I tried to help, but he did 90 per cent of the work. My attempt at an arrow must have been one of the least straight ever to have been made. He then showed me how to fire it, starting by aiming at the ground.

While we were out practising our archery, we met another wonderful old fellow, who explained that he was more of a gatherer than a hunter. He was coming up from the bottom of the valley, with a tub full of frogs and toads and little fishes that he'd just collected from his fish traps in the river. His name was Taman Tamak, and he possessed an amazing smile that drew you in; I could instantly tell he had a very warm, thoughtful personality. As the days went by I got used to seeing him appearing in the afternoon from the woods with a basketful of nuts and berries and assorted fungi. Even though we didn't share much language, we soon became friends. I would go and sit on his veranda in the evening and drink *apong* with him. If I could persuade Tajir or Bitton to go with me, all the better: I could understand his stories. If not we just smiled and nodded at each other, while his wife occasionally brought us food titbits. Sometimes she would come out and sit with us, but she rarely said much. They were a great couple, with a delightfully easy

'This new house
of Mister Brose'

Cupid at work

Non-stop banter in the men's hut

The most talented tribal dancers and musicians I would ever come across anywhere in the making of *Tribe*

Crossing the Brahmaputra

Curiosity overcomes shyness

The Adi of Arunachal Pradesh, India

Mummy's little helper

My farewell song

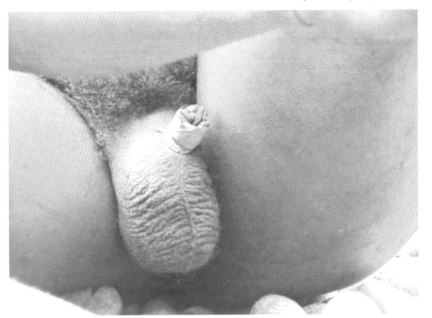

The vestige of the penis and foreskin is wrapped tightly in a leaf and bound closed with a tiny piece of bark thread to avoid its re-emergence

Late afternoon sunlight and breeze – bliss after a day in the humid forest

A rather large wild boar

An unusual headdress – later he turned it round to show his face and as a mark of his change of mood to one of happiness

Suri land

Proper hard stuff

The Suri of the Omo Valley, Ethiopa

Bargulu with
his cattle

Suri kids
made my stay

manner with each other. Their children had grown up and left the village long ago.

Taman Tamak told me that his traditional leaf roof would need changing again this year and he was considering using corrugated iron instead. Down the valley it was all the rage, he explained. When, with Bitton translating, I told him I thought this was a terrible shame, he said that the traditional style might be better to live under, but it had to be frequently renewed. To do that he needed five or six neighbours to help him, which then put him under an obligation to help them when they needed their houses renovating. However nice-looking the thatched roofs might seem to an outsider like me, the fact was that he spent half his time helping to build houses for other people, whereas he could do the corrugated iron himself and it would last three times as long.

I often use this as a good example of the changes coming to traditional life when discussing these issues with people back home. As in so many places, modernity here represented a perceived easier life. Taman Tamak was fed up with spending all his time helping his neighbours, and although he happily agreed that a tin roof was noisier in the rain, hotter in the sun, and less picturesque generally, he'd rather have the easier new version because it gave him more free time. However, by joining our modern world in this way, he would inevitably interact less with his neighbours. It was just a step on the ladder to where we are in the industrialized world; where in cities one can live in total ignorance of who our neighbours even are. I could have pointed that out to him from the perspective of someone who'd seen the benefit of community living and the greater human interactions that it brings, but for me to advise him not to change, or even to try to find ways to keep him ignorant of what could help him, would have been deeply patronizing – a bit like telling a friend not to buy a fast car because it might kill him. Any mate of mine would tell me to just get lost with that advice – and Taman Tamak likewise. What right did I have to stop another human being from wanting exactly what I want – an easier life?

I was now eating all my meals at the *gam*'s house, with the *gam*, his wife, his younger son Lulu and his wife and children (his other son, Beking, had his own house). This was a sea change from my experience in Gabon. I could escape if I needed to, to my own space, but always had a reason to call in on my welcoming next-door neighbours. The food was delicious too, served up on a leaf or a plate: rice and cooked vegetables as staples, with meat or fish every now and then. Not that I could ever see it – they had no windows in the hut, for fear of letting in the spirits. Sometimes they would produce a leaf full of ground chilli, and peering through the gloom to pick it up – as I soon discovered – I had to be very careful not to put too much on my rice.

I encouraged Bitton to come and hang out with me at the *gam*'s so I could communicate properly and ask the *gam* and Lulu questions about their life: how they farmed, how they hunted, the transition from boy to man in the community and so on. Other times the *gam* would tell me traditional Adi tales. 'Today,' he'd say, 'I'll tell you a story about how the moon was made.' He told it as if I were a six-year-old. 'Once upon a time, years ago, there used to be two suns. But the frog got annoyed in the morning and fired his arrow into one of the suns; it bled and died and became the moon.' I love these kinds of stories and would have been happy to listen to him all evening. Sadly Bitton didn't always stay as long as I'd have liked him to; the temptations of crew camp were too much for him – up there they still had the retinue of cooks and bottle-washers, not to mention European food and alcohol. Tajir wasn't much help either. Although he'd been recruited as a translator, he spent most of his time either chatting up the girls around the village or out in the woods hunting.

So on many long evenings I was on my own, doing my best with sign language when it wasn't too dark, and then just sitting quietly in the gloom while the family got on with things. It could often be boring, sitting for hours watching them do their stuff; but then every now and then I'd be rewarded with a golden moment or insight into the difference of their lives which would make all the waiting worthwhile. I found watching the children perhaps most illuminating: they didn't get told off as much as kids do in our culture. They were just allowed to get on with it day and night, enjoying their games, picking up whatever they liked – I'd even see them playing with knives without a hint of concern from their parents. And I could see how they copied their parents much more clearly, because their parents' work was never far from the house, rather than being miles away in an office.

The *gam* and his family saw my interest in these children and asked how ours differed back home. 'Of course,' I said, 'kids are kids everywhere.' But I added that in our society, with its advertising and consumerism, there is a danger that even children are being weaned on materialism. It is not uncommon for kids to get upset at not having the newest thing they've seen on TV, and they can be bored even when surrounded by the most expensive toys. Here, by contrast, you'd see a child running gleefully past the doorway with a home-made fishing rod in hand. But things were changing fast here too and the *gam* knew it. Ironically for me, TV would be in the first wave of the modern world's assault that the village would have to deal with. Electricity was due in the next year or so, and they were excited about that already.

The crew and I spent our evenings apart, but during the days we went out and joined in typical activities with individual villagers. I had one great day gathering fungi and looking at traps with my friend Taman Tamak. The season was changing, and now that spring was coming the fish were starting to swim upstream. Taman showed me how he was turning round his lobster-pot-style basket traps to catch them. Then I had a day in the fields with the women, gathering wood. They were amazed that I wanted to help carry it back to the village; in Adi society this is very much a woman's role. Another couple of days I spent with Lulu making and laying traps to catch rats and squirrels for the upcoming festival. They are made from a big bow of bamboo, with a noose hanging within, and a trigger mechanism on the bow itself. The trap is stand-alone and can be put anywhere that a rodent is likely to use the bow as a pathway to cross a gap in the forest. It then walks across the bow, touches the trigger and springs the trap. We spent all of one day in a production line making over 200 of these devices, which were then set and placed the next day.

Then the *gam* himself took me out to show me some bigger traps he had laid for boar and deer. On our way home he told me, in his usual teasing way, that I couldn't be his proper son unless I got to know their *mithuns*. With long horns each side of a large head and longer front than hind legs, these *mithuns* look pretty comical. They are left to roam free around the village and act as a kind of living currency. When an owner wants to bring his *mithun* into the village, he takes a handful of salt out to it, for the *mithuns* will go anywhere for a lick of salt. If they go for long enough without it they will eventually wander into the village, and will even know which is the house of their owner. The *gam* had a new *mithun* calf; he wanted to track it down, he told me, mark its ear and give it a name in honour of our arrival. I got quite excited about the idea of naming a *mithun*, but when he and Lulu and I went out into the woods around the village we had no luck at all; it seemed that every other Jorsing *mithun* was there except his new calf.

Another character I soon became aware of was the *miri* – the village's traditional healer and shaman. Unusually, in Jorsing she was a woman. She was small, skinny and old with a great face, as wrinkled as a walnut, around wise and kind-looking brown eyes. My chest cold was still clinging on, so Hannah suggested this would be a good reason to visit her; we could ask her to examine me.

The *miri* lived on her own at the top of the village. Her hut was small and dark and full of all kinds of odd stuff: as well as the usual pots and cauldrons, there were feathers and snakes' heads and odd little animal skulls – some were rats, she explained. The drying rack above her fire was thick with soot. The roof was hung with cobwebs and each was outlined with tiny soot particles. The *miri* sat me down by the fire to discover what was wrong with me. Was it an illness that came from the spirits or just an ordinary human one? She laid hands on me and if I'd thought I was going to get a gentle woman's touch I was mistaken. Years of hard manual labour had left their mark: the *miri* had the roughest hands I'd ever felt in my life. But I was OK, she said: my sore throat and chest weren't a malevolent gift from the spirits – it was just a cold.

After my diagnosis we stayed with her for quite a while and talked about her life. She had been married twice; first to 'the most handsome man in the village', whom she had loved very much, but who had died young. Her bright eyes shone with tears when she talked of him. Then, later, someone else had asked for her hand and she'd accepted. He had died too. So that was it – she wouldn't get married again. She had always, she said, been someone who had vivid dreams and a sense of something beyond, so she had decided she would become a *miri*.

We were planning in a day or so's time to join some of the men on a hunt in the forest to get meat for the festival. So now we decided to ask the *miri* to apply her powers to predicting how well it would go. Her method of divination was to rip a leaf, twice, then follow the way the rip tore down the leaf.

'You will get monkeys, squirrels and rats,' she told us. We would also take a shot at something big and miss. I personally would have no luck at all. I might get a shot or two at a deer, but I wouldn't hit anything. She met my eyes with a smile. If she turned out to be wrong, then she wanted to be able to eat whatever it was I'd caught. 'I have no teeth, so I will eat the head,' Bitton translated, as we laughed. She was definitely keeping her options open.

But she was endearingly humble about her abilities. There were other *miri*, in other villages, she said, who were better at contacting the spirits than her. She shrugged. She knew her power was waning: the young people no longer danced the traditional Adi dances, they copied what they had seen on television, in other villages that had electricity, or in Pasighat. And among a sizeable group of them a new religion had taken hold – Christianity. The converts met each week in a makeshift church at the top of the village, supervised by a young man who had been repeatedly ill as a child, until some Christians had treated him with massage oils and he had been cured. So he had come to believe in the power of Jesus Christ.

This was not a side of the village I saw much of, to be honest. Hannah had been finding storylines for the film which could be intercut with the experiences I was having. Under James's direction, this second film was definitely becoming less about me and more a portrait of the actual people themselves. With its *iboga* initiation, the Gabon shoot had turned out to be quite a personal trip and Steve had commented that there was a danger that the series could become a bit of a 'Can Bruce Parry hack living with the locals?' extravaganza, and none of us wanted that. But we were still feeling our way a bit, so I continued to comment on issues here, there and everywhere, to use if required. James was making sure he had covered all bases; we could deal with the fine-tuning when we got home.

On the day after my session with the *miri* the rain finally stopped. The sun shone from a brilliant blue sky and the air was crystal clear. At last we could see the mountain peaks, towering white above us in the distance. For the first time I had a proper sense of where we were, in the foothills of the Himalayas.

Everyone came out of their houses and I spent the day

wandering round the village in the sunshine, meeting characters I hadn't come across before. Two old men were sharpening stones and sorting out their traps for the upcoming hunt. They reminded me of Statler and Waldorf from *The Muppets*, laughing and teasing each other continually. Then I sat for a while with one of the young girls, who was weaving. Traditionally, she explained through Tajir, they had got their yarn from a local cotton plant in the forest, spun it, dyed it with vegetable or plant extracts, then woven it. Now they bought yarn from town, so their clothes had much more vibrant colours. It was good to sit and talk to her. The other Adi women I'd spoken to so far had been very shy; when I'd given them the traditional greeting, they had just giggled and run away.

The sun set in a glorious blaze of crimson and the stars were brilliant that night. It was easy to understand why these people had traditionally worshipped the sun, which they called Donyi, and the moon, Polo. Not literally, but as the visible manifestations of the Supreme Power of the universe, which they call Donyipolo. Beneath that central power is a host of other spirits, both benevolent and malign, who must be appeased and satisfied. To me, from the standpoint of being brought up strictly Christian, I found myself admiring Donyipolo. There's a great and undeniable wisdom in the idea of the sun and the moon representing the central spirit of our fragile planet, whatever name you want to give to it. And, as the *gam* explained, Donyipolo came with a clear code of conduct to define relations not only between human and human but, equally importantly – as we are only now beginning to understand in our frenzy of overdevelopment – between human and nature, our sustaining force.

Early the following morning, Ozing, Tajir, Bitton, I and several other village men set off for our day's hunting. Before we left, offerings were laid out in the woods to appease the watching spirits: eggs, rice, and *apong* in containers made from slices of bamboo – the traditional belief is that the spirits love to taste earthly pleasures.

The hunt itself was a slow process. We spent a large part of the day just sitting up in a tree waiting for the game to show itself. And when it did, the Adi had no problem making full use of their shotguns, on everything they saw: monkeys, squirrels, rats, flying foxes, tiny coloured little songbirds that you'd have been hard-pressed to get a mouthful out of. The only reason we didn't bag any deer or wild boar was because we didn't see any. The *miri* was right on all counts: with my bow and arrow I got nothing. And Tajir did see and miss a big animal, or so he claimed: a bear. I found it a little hard to believe, given that earlier in the day he'd been perfectly able to shoot down the tiniest birds.

Despite Donyipolo, our day had certainly dispelled any romantic notions I'd held about indigenous peoples treading lightly on the ground. Maybe the Adi had done so by accident when they only had bows and arrows; but now, equipped with guns, they were as voracious at destroying the local game as any other human community. Part of me lamented their over-hunting and found it sad, but who was I, with my nation's track record, to criticize?

This was also a special and particular time of year. A key part of the Aran festival is that there is plenty of meat for people to give each other and enjoy. Without any booty of my own, I was given a dead squirrel, beautifully wrapped in a lattice of dried rattan, to present to my 'father', the *gam*.

The Aran festival reminded me very strongly of Christmas. There was the same sense of a community stopping work completely and kicking up its heels, and the same emphasis on family. On the eve of the main feast day there was a real feeling of anticipation in the air, as is traditional in Britain. People were coming back into the village with the spoils of their traps and hunts. 'Opang Moyong!' they called to me cheerfully as I wandered round. There were relatives and friends arriving from other villages.

Everyone – myself included – was going from house to house, drinking *apong* and eating traditional delicacies.

The chief one of these, of course, incorporates dead rat. I called it rat-cake. It still wasn't as disgusting as the *iboga* drug, but it was far from delicious. The pudding-like mixture is made of rat and frog and fish all roughly chopped up in a dough of water and rice powder, wrapped in a leaf and then boiled until it's gooey and congealed. When a rat has been roasted over the fire, you can crunch through it and it's not too bad; but boiled it has a very different texture, so I really wasn't looking forward to my first mouthful. But when I pulled out a bit of meat and tried it, I was pleasantly surprised: it was like liver or fish stomach, and tasted fine. I was just starting to think it was all going to be OK ... when the smell hit me. It was grim – an acrid, dead-animal stink. On screen I said it was like a mixture of 'death and toilets' – and it really did conjure up an image of a rotting corpse on the floor of a sweaty public toilet.

This was the first of many occasions when I had to tread a fine line between saying what I really thought to my home audience, while at the same time not upsetting my hosts. The fact that my companions couldn't understand me was irrelevant; often they could tell by my face that I was saying something negative. Also, soon enough, some people of that culture will learn English or have our film translated to them. (How rude would it be to have an Indian film crew describe roast beef as being like something fished out of a sewer?)

As if to test me further, the next morning was the first day of the festival proper, when a *mithun* is slaughtered. The animal is calmly led with salt-lick to the village, where its head is put in a noose; later, with most of the village watching or helping, it's strung up on a big A-frame, writhing and kicking as it dies of strangulation. Get out of this one, I thought to myself. How was I supposed to react on camera to something that would undoubtedly shock some of my British viewers? I couldn't be seen to be enjoying myself too much; and yet I didn't want to offend my hosts by not joining in. Had I been trekking alone, with no camera in sight, I would probably have put aside my personal views and abandoned myself to the prevailing mood to avoid upsetting the villagers.

Like many communities around the world – rightly or wrongly – the Adi don't see animal cruelty as the same as cruelty to humans. Of course they all could see that the *mithun* was having a pretty nasty death, but they didn't take any special delight in the animal's pain. When we discussed it later, they simply stated, 'This is how our ancestors taught us to do it. Maybe we'll change one day, but we enjoy the ceremony.' Similarities with the UK fox-hunting debate coursed through my head. Their obvious joy was not at all in the pain, but the occasion.

And so, with the crew recording my every reaction, I stood to one side and gave the camera my honest feelings about the sacrifice, which were in truth that I found it hard to watch the *mithun* expire in this way, over several long, painful minutes, its big eyes wide with the knowledge that it was suffocating to death. Even doing this wasn't easy, because several of the villagers could see my obvious negative vibe to camera. When I'd done the piece, I went back over to the group by the rope, tapped somebody on the shoulder and joined in the ceremony. Maybe it was hypocritical, but it seemed the only thing to do; and I found it interesting, because it was an entirely modern dilemma. Travel writers of yore could react as they pleased; television had precluded that for me.

Having said that, if given the choice between being an English cow or an Adi *mithun*, I'd be a *mithun* every time. They get to roam around freely for their entire lives; they're not fed hormones, or kept in confined spaces, or driven miles in cramped conditions to an abattoir, smelling and hearing death on arrival. For the *mithun*, sacrificial ones at least, it's only their last ten minutes that are grim. And it's not as if they die for nothing. As soon as the sacrifice was over, this one was butchered and divided around the village: ears, bones, blood, hooves – the lot. There was nothing left over. One reason for the strangling, after all, is to preserve the blood within the body so that it can be shared out among the villagers in bamboo containers, carried off to individual households.

That afternoon and evening the Aran festival kicked off properly. After feasting in their own and their neighbours' houses, loads of people headed down to the *moshup* to drink *apong* and play games and dance. During my weeks in Jorsing I had met a lot of these people individually, but it was great to see them all together. In a group, they had a wonderful sense of humour, which was cheeky, bordering on rude. All the women, for example, would get up together and pull a man to his feet and sing an explicit song about him: 'We know you've got the smallest dick in the world' or 'We saw you screwing round the back of the bushes.' Everyone was in hysterics. 'What are they saying?' I kept asking Tajir and Bitton – I could hardly believe the translations.

Then the men fought back: 'It may be small but I know how to use it' or 'At least my wife's fanny isn't full of cobwebs.' The ruder it got, the more they all loved it. I had to pinch myself, and asked myself why I was surprised. Did I really think indigenous peoples were somehow more puritanical than us? Just because they were generally shy and respectful with an outsider, why wouldn't they have a sense of humour every bit as blue as ours? Even the oldest grannies were getting really stuck in, and tiny kids were giggling with puzzled looks on their faces.

We were, after all, in the *moshup*, which I've described as a communal hall, but until very recently was used as a house where adolescent boys would stay for periods of time away from their parents (living as a group and a potential defensive force). The girls had a similar homestead. Boys and girls would visit each other and were quite free to have sex, experimenting with each other until the time came to behave like an Adi adult, settle down with one person and have children. So they presumably all knew each other very well; and maybe some of these jokes harked back to knowledge acquired during their freer youthful days.

As the evening went on there was more dancing and even, at one point, a conga. Well lubricated with *apong*, we all joined in. James, Sam, Hannah and me all traipsing around with the old fellows. Eventually the party broke up and there was a sort of Scottish-style first footing, where people called at each other's homes, for more *apong* and special Aran delicacies. I drank my fill, but discreetly avoided the rat-cake.

With the end of Aran, it was time for us to go. We had come to witness the build-up to the spring festival and now it was over. On my penultimate day I found out the answer to a question that had been puzzling me. Why, when there were loads of chickens running around everywhere, did I never see an egg? I was woken by these chickens every morning, and last thing at night I helped put them into baskets to protect them from marauding predators. I collected eggs from them and gave them to the *gam*'s wife, but they never appeared on the menu. Now I realized why. The *gam* had been selling them to the crew. Ozing's team of cooks had been using them to prepare elaborate breakfasts for James, Sam and Hannah. Bastards.

Then, suddenly, the night before our departure, I heard some terrible news: Taman Tamak's wife had died. The poor man had come back home to find her lying flat out on the floor of his house. I had no idea how to express how sorry I felt. With no children in the village, he had no one to look after him. He looked devastated. 'I'm going to be lonely now for the rest of my life,' he told me. I had no idea what to say to comfort him.

The villagers thought evil spirits had taken her, because she had died so suddenly and was bleeding from the eyes. That night, a group of men gathered in the *moshup*, lit torches of split bamboo and ran through the village, screaming and whooping, to chase the spirits away. Though my rational mind told me otherwise, it all felt pretty real in this village without electricity, shrouded in mist, with the huge dark forests all around.

It was hard leaving the *gam* and his family; they had been so good to me. With and without translation, we'd had wonderful rambling conversations about many things. Now he made a heartfelt speech, saying how he would always be my father, even though I had another father elsewhere. I was profoundly moved. I'd learnt a lot from him, and I'd been very happy living with the people of Jorsing.

Later Ozing told me that the *gam* had used a special word to describe me: it meant 'love from our village' and carried with it a great honour. It wouldn't have been used, for example, about an outsider like Ozing, even though he had relatives in Jorsing. I was very touched by this. It confirmed what I'd already felt – that I had found real acceptance in Jorsing. In the short amount of time we'd spent with them, our presence had made a big impact on their lives, and equally they'd had a huge effect on us. It was a sad day when we left, and we all had tears in our eyes.

3. The Real Thing

The Kombai of West Papua, Indonesia

Right at the start of the whole series, when we were still in the planning stage in Cardiff, I had been pestering my producer Steve Robinson to let us visit a tribal group in the Indonesian province of West Papua. Formerly known as Irian Jaya, this huge stretch of jungle wilderness makes up the western half of New Guinea Island, mirroring Papua New Guinea in the east. It was renamed in 2002, in an attempt to curb support for the local separatist movement, the Organisasi Papua Merdeka (OPM or Free Papua Movement), whose stated aim is to break away from Indonesia completely.

It was here that I'd made my first ever film, in 1999–2000, with my friend and fellow expeditioner Mark Anstice (also now a TV presenter). It was called *Cannibals and Crampons* and it followed the pair of us as we trekked through near-impenetrable jungles, forded treacherous rivers and climbed the extremely remote Mount Mandala, the third highest peak geographically between the Himalayas and the Andes. During this expedition,

Mark and I had a 'first contact' with a clan of the Korowai tribal group – we were the first people from the outside world, let alone white people, they had ever seen (traders included). This is quite a claim – it is generally considered that not even the 'un-contacted' tribes of the deep Amazon can be found in this traditional state of being: without traded metals, T-shirts, fish hooks or knife blades of any kind. The experience of meeting this band of naked men, who cowered when they first saw us, then followed us later to warn us off, had impressed us both powerfully; Mark and I still talk often about the encounter and our possible effect on those people.

This subject is deservedly controversial – and when discussing making our first *Tribe* episode in West Papua, Steve and I had agreed it wouldn't be ethical to deliberately attempt a first contact of this kind. None the less, I'd been very keen to get back to New Guinea: for me it's still the most exciting place on earth. I was very disappointed when our formal application for permits was denied. 'For your own protection,' was the official line; we might be kidnap targets for the OPM. Unofficially, it was clear that the Indonesian government didn't want an organization like the BBC going into and sniffing around an area where there have been accusations of harsh military intervention – to say the least. So we'd let the idea go.

But now, back from Arunachal Pradesh in April 2004, when I met up with Steve in Cardiff he had a familiar glint in his eye.

'We're going to New Guinea,' he said.

I could hardly allow myself to believe it.

'Really?'

'Really.'

'That's fantastic, mate. How on earth did you get the permit?'

'We didn't get the permit.' He grinned.

Steve knew how much I wanted to go back. With two films in the can and another three in advanced stages of preparation, he had decided to take a risk. BBC guidelines allow you to film in areas without permits if there's an overriding public interest. If we'd applied for permits again, the best we could have hoped for from the Indonesian authorities was a military guard escort 'for our own protection' during the shoot – disastrous to any kind of relations with our prospective hosts.

Three of us would go, taking small cameras and nothing that could identify us as BBC. We had thirty-day tourist visas. As far as anyone at Customs was concerned, we were just a trio of backpackers with some amateur video kit. Directing and producing was Jon Clay, who had been the cameraman on the Gabon trip. Cameraman this time was Tim Butt, who'd worked alongside Steve on the BBC series *Extreme Lives*. A tall, fit, extreme-sports enthusiast, Tim's the sort who can snowboard backwards while simultaneously filming with a big digi-beta camera under his arm – definitely the right man for this sort of adventure.

To handle things on the ground in Papua, Steve and Jon had signed up a fixer called Kelly Woolford, an American tour operator based in Bali. He had long experience of Indonesia, we'd been told, and excellent contacts across New Guinea. I hadn't originally wanted a fixer. I knew Indonesia well already, and if we were going to have help at all, I wanted to use a couple of the Indonesian guys I'd worked with on previous expeditions.

Steve, as always, tactfully put me back in my box. 'Stop being such a control freak, Bruce. There's no way you can organize and lead each trip as well as present it. Who's going to look after the crew when you're living with the tribe?'

So Kelly was on board. He'd identified an area for us to go to, near a defunct missionary airstrip called Wangemalo, where, he said, there were remote groups of the Korowai people we wanted to spend time with. I wasn't so sure about this: I'd done some research on the Net and Wangemalo seemed to be in Kombai territory. Not that we had anything against the Kombai per se – they're very similar to the Korowai – but the production company Keo Films had recently made a programme about the Kombai with Nick Middleton for *Living at the Extremes*. Steve didn't want to risk in any way replicating that. But Kelly stuck to his story: Wangemalo was a Korowai area. We bowed to his greater knowledge.

We flew to Bali and drove out to meet our fixer. Kelly lived up in the hills, in the famous cultural centre of Ubud. He had a tiny house there – more of a hut, really, made of plaster and full of antique West Papuan carving and sculpture. He was a forty-something American with shoulder-length strawberry-blond hair, usually tied back in a ponytail, and thick brows over hazel eyes. My earlier reservations melted away; we all took to him instantly.

Sitting in a bar that evening, I repeated my concerns about Wangemalo. 'Don't worry, man,' Kelly said. 'It's an incredible place. You've only got to go a day or two into the jungle and there are stone axes everywhere.' He knew Papua well and had found Wangemalo by accident a year earlier, when he couldn't land at the better-known airstrip at Yaniruma. It wasn't a place he normally took people. And yes, he reiterated, it was definitely Korowai.

After a couple of days spent acclimatizing, we flew down to West Papua's scruffy, coastal capital city, Jayapura. I couldn't sleep in our hotel that night. I could hardly believe it: tomorrow I would be finally heading back into Korowai territory, four years after Mark and I had left. OK, so the airstrip we were flying into might not be as remote as Kelly made it out to be – until ten years ago they'd had missionaries there. But as we moved away into the jungle, who knew what we'd find? The Korowai mostly live in family homesteads in relative isolation from each other, and they are all fearful of other tribal groups. The further we went, the more likely we were to come across a group who would be more suitable for the programme. As long as it wasn't a first contact and we weren't upsetting their world view, and provided that they actively wanted us to be there, then the more traditional the better.

The next morning we took off in a tiny chartered plane and flew high over the deep green hills. Looking down under the wing, I could see nothing but trees. There were no pylons, mines, towns or visible settlements of any kind. Yet there are people there, living their own life in the valleys and swamps as they have done for generations.

We bumped down on a grassy airstrip which hardly seemed long enough for the plane to land. We were immediately surrounded by people in scruffy, ripped T-shirts and shorts, curious to see what this aeroplane might be bringing them.

Kelly introduced us to the chief, Britop – a skinny guy with wide, humorous eyes, a choker of red beads around his neck and a cassowary bone through his septum – who showed us round the scattered wooden houses of the village. He was a bit of a local hero, apparently, having once killed an Indonesian soldier by firing an arrow through his eye. After this incident, the military had returned to take revenge, and the area had been wasted. Britop had been hauled off to jail for ten years, and it was during that time that missionaries arrived. The Christians had enticed the locals out of the forest and encouraged them to settle, showing them how to grow bananas and potatoes and corn, converted them, then departed. They had left behind a church and a local preacher, Naftali, a tall man with a half-beard and a fierce expression. He was an intelligent guy, but had a scornful attitude to his 'unsaved' cousins who remained in the forest. 'They live like wild pigs,' he told us. 'They still kill and eat people. If they see you wearing clothes they will run and hide.' I wondered where such negative sentiments had originated from. Not his parents, I guessed.

Even if some of the people wore T-shirts and shorts, Wange-malo was hardly stocked up with imported goods. The one shop had a few tins and a couple of bars of soap for sale, and that was it. There had been no supply plane for a long time.

One thing was immediately apparent to me: these people were not Korowai. The Korowai decorate themselves with parallel welts on their skin that they make with smouldering tree bark – these start at the shoulder, come down towards the nipple, and go straight on to the navel, with a gap of perhaps two centimetres between each one. This lot had none of these markings, and the thorns in their noses were different too. I decided to tackle Kelly about this straightaway; not aggressively, but I was puzzled.

'I don't want to cause a problem here,' I said, 'but this doesn't seem to be Korowai territory.'

'What d'you mean?'

'I've been with Korowai people before; these people are Kombai. They've got different ornaments. And markings.'

I explained in detail and I could see Kelly's face fall. 'I never said they were *all* Korowai, man. It's on the border of the different territories. It's half Kombai and half Korowai.'

I was sure he'd told us in Ubud that this was an exclusively Korowai area. I decided to stay cool, but I would listen very carefully from now on to whatever he told us.

That evening we sat in the missionaries' house with Britop and another guy called Yambu and listened to them talk about a controversial topic – cannibalism. They had some gruesome tales to tell. Yambu had once – he told us with the camera rolling – cut the top off a man's head, scooped out the brains, mixed them with sago and cooked them. It sounded like something out of a Victorian traveller's tale and although I nodded along, I didn't know what to believe. I'd heard stories of this sort of pantomime occurring at Yaniruma for the small, specialized tour groups who go in there. But surely Kelly would be above that with us. He understood that our bottom line with *Tribe* was telling the truth. If the people we came across didn't use stone axes then that's how we'd tell it. Even if we found a satellite TV dish, we'd be honest about that. The world was changing fast and we'd always intended that any change would be part of our programme anyway.

We started to prepare for our journey, checking our food and kit and cameras, weighing up our bags. With Britop's help, we set about recruiting a team of porters to help carry our stuff into the jungle. Once again, as in Gabon, there were more volunteers than we needed. We were faced with the same dilemma: how do you discriminate when this is the only source of income on offer all year?

The problem was exacerbated because many of the locals didn't fully trust us to give them what they wanted in return for their work: pots, pans, knives and so on – the informal currency we carried with us as well as cash. The last outsiders who had been through Wangemalo had been *gaharu* traders, who operate by swapping Western goods for *gaharu*, an incredibly valuable resinous heart wood extracted from the aquilaria tree in South-East Asia and used in the preparation of incense and perfumes; in Java it costs more per ounce than gold. A team of them had been through Wangemalo a couple of years before, had persuaded the villagers to find this wood, then had not fulfilled their side of the bargain, so tensions were running high. During Britop's negotiations, our potential helpers came to blows over the deal, and one man was left with a gashed head. So we decided to employ them all: every male over a certain age and half the women as well. There were smiles all round.

In addition to the porters, we also recruited a couple of translators. The one who had the best Indonesian turned out to be Naftali, the preacher. Somewhat reluctantly on my part, we employed him and another guy. I liked Naftali tremendously as a character, but remained wary of his translations and second agendas. He was, after all, an evangelist preacher, with a deeply prejudiced attitude to those still living a traditional life. I was always alert to the fact that he might adapt what he heard in some way.

The next morning we set off into the rainforest. I shouldered my own pack as always, but we now had so many porters that they each carried next to nothing – a camera case, pot or pan apiece. So Jon, Tim and I were by far the most heavily laden of all. The New Guinean lowland forest was just as I'd remembered it: dense, green, luxuriant and sodden. The track was muddy and we were often splashing through little streams and swampy expanses.

Kelly's porters knew exactly where they were taking us. After only about four hours of trekking, we came to a settlement built around a festival longhouse. These people were not like the semi-Westernized folk of Wangemalo. They all wore completely traditional dress, the women in short grass skirts and the men naked apart from genital adornment: their testicles were out and visible, but the penis itself was in either a dried and hollowed-out vegetable (gourd) or a hornbill's beak; this was then tied with a fine bark thread around the waist to keep the appendage vertical. Some of the men had no gourds at all, and a cursory look seemed to reveal a missing penis, something I'd first noticed on my original trip with Mark. In fact, they had worked out a way of pushing the soft flesh of the penis back inside the body, leaving a wrinkly rolled parcel of skin smaller than a thimble. This was then tied up and left, or wrapped in a leaf, or covered in a walnut-like shell. Both men and women also wore dog- or pig-tooth necklaces and earrings of cassowary feathers, with lizard-skin straps across their foreheads, and whittled bones piercing their septums. The tips of their noses were also perforated – with toothpick-like sticks poking straight forward, or else holding a tiny cowry shell stapled in place.

Their welcome too was traditional – a seemingly aggressive stand-off with stern-looking guys training bows and arrows on us as they waited for us to explain who we were. But then I noticed some of our porters from Wangemalo sniggering; and I heard one of Kelly's team talk to the locals in Indonesian rather than the local language. When we were then told we couldn't go into the village until I took all my clothes off, alarm bells really began to ring. This had never happened with my previous encounters in this part of the world and I thought I could smell a very large rat.

I decided to go through with it. With my penis wrapped in a leaf, I walked naked up to their headman and very gently and respectfully offered a pouch of tobacco – a locally grown crop, it is the longstanding local currency. Without meeting my eyes, he reached out and took it. After more words from Kelly and Naftali, we shook hands. All was suddenly OK. We were accepted. We went into their longhouse and sat down for a smoke. There were two of them, an old man and a young one. Naftali translated from the local language into Indonesian, then Kelly from Indonesian to English. This all seemed genuine enough. There was the usual greeting stuff, how they were happy to make us welcome and so on. But then came the line: 'You are the first white men we have ever seen.'

No way. I looked at Kelly, who had just translated this from Indonesian. 'Are you serious? They're saying they've never seen a white man ever before?'

He nodded. 'Yeah, man.' Then: 'I told you this was an amazing area.'

Ten minutes later I went round the back of the longhouse with my private Bruce-cam and recorded two video diaries. One in case my instincts were up the spout and I'd got it completely wrong, saying how incredible this all was, here were these people who'd never seen white men before, and so on. And a second, where I said what I really thought: that it was all a bit far-fetched.

I was right. When we got back to the UK and I looked through the rushes with Steve, he saw this bit and said, 'I'm sure I've seen that bloke before.' He went and got Nick Middleton's film – when we played it back it was exactly the same village. There were these same people saying they'd never seen white people before, and there they were on British television. Imagine if Steve hadn't noticed it and we'd included the comment in our film! It didn't bear thinking about.

At the time I still wasn't 100 per cent sure. What was frustrating was that this area was magical enough *without* any fakery. Most of what we were seeing was real. I hated putting so much emphasis on such token issues – like some colonialist explorer – that we were being forced into debating. What to do? I didn't want to piss Kelly off, and, in any case, I was still partly thinking – indeed hoping – that I was wrong and that he might genuinely believe that this was all authentic. So I took him to one side.

'I really want to have a chat with you,' I said, 'because I just get this very strong gut feeling there's a couple of things wrong here.'

'Yeah?'

'I just don't think these guys are genuine. Put it this way: I don't think we're the first white men they've ever seen. And all that stuff with me having to get naked just struck me as phoney. I think they're pulling the wool over our eyes.'

Kelly was deadpan. 'I don't think so, man. I know what you're talking about, but these guys are for real. Nobody's been to Wangemalo for years. It's about as remote as you can get in Papua.'

I didn't expect him to confess to the whole thing being a fake; I just wanted him to know that I was on to them. We had to work together and I wanted to stay friends, but I needed him to know I wasn't a mug.

'Just tell them,' I went on, 'that we don't want them to fake anything. If they've got a satellite dish round the back of the longhouse, or they normally wear T-shirts, that's fine. As far as we're concerned, this is all cool enough anyway. We just want it to be authentic.'

'OK.' Kelly nodded. 'I'll tell them.'

We left it at that and went back into the longhouse and smoked some more of our tobacco and ate sago grubs, which is a real delicacy and a sign of welcome. We slept that night camped by the longhouse, then in the morning we were off again, deeper into the jungle, this time with a smaller entourage. The Wangemalo guys returned home, and we kept just Kelly, Naftali, Yambu, and a few new people from this longhouse settlement. We'd already sent a guy ahead to warn the next place along the track that we were coming. This was Kelly's suggestion, to make sure all was well and avoid dangerous surprises.

After four or five hours of trekking we came to the next place; and once again we went through the same ritual with the bows and arrows. Nobody told me to get my kit off this time, though. Kelly told us we'd reached an area that was definitely free of outside influences, but I noticed a felled tree which had cuts much too clean to have been made by a stone axe.

'That's a steel cut there, definitely,' I said.

He couldn't disagree. This was all made worse by the fact that I really liked Kelly.

We spent the night there and then pushed on. Kelly was going along more with what I wanted now, to go deeper and deeper into the jungle until we found a more isolated group. Now that he understood what I was after, I found him easier to work with.

Jon and Tim, meanwhile, had become totally paranoid about everything. I'd shared my doubts with them in private. Without the language or experience I had they started doubting everything. I was having to calm them down and explain that, yes, this was truly an incredible place, and nearly everything we were seeing was real enough.

We reached another homestead that afternoon, and another ritual stand-off. When that was concluded and we were let into the homestead, we saw that these people were using bamboo knives and stone axes and everything seemed much more genuine. Quite apart from the cut to the wood, you can tell when someone has used a steel axe before because the technique is quite different to a stone one.

I was happier now, but decided to push it one stage further. So we sent off three or four of our guys into the depths of the forest to see what other homesteads were around. They came back, one by one, with tales of this or that treehouse, but nothing that really inspired us. Then, after dark, just as we were having our supper in camp, Yambu returned with a dead piglet slung over his shoulder. It was a gift from a homestead whose people wanted us to come and stay. Fantastic, I thought. This active request for our presence was something I'd always stipulated as a prerequisite to our arrival anyway. It sounded perfect.

We cooked and ate the pig for breakfast, then set off with high hopes for this new treehouse, which was only a couple of hours' trek through the forest. Once again, when we got there, we were treated to the bow-and-arrow routine. They knew we were coming, had actually sent us a gift to invite us, so this was more confirmation in my head that all this was no more than a ritual. Eventually they put down their bows, came gingerly towards us and took the tobacco; the next thing we knew, we were being invited up into their treehouse for a smoke and a chat.

It was a small settlement, three men, five women and a sprawl of children. The eldest of the men was the first person I'd met. Called Wamufo, he was the one who had been most aggressive towards me in the stand-off and was the stockiest of the trio. Then there was Bomari, who had a broken front tooth and a ready smile. Finally there was the character of the group: Bofoko, truly a charismatic player; he was very tactile with lots of energy. We sat down with the three of them and, with Naftali translating, explained what it was we wanted to do. They were happy, they replied, to let us stay.

The men stayed up in the treehouse while the women and children lived in an adjacent ground shelter. They were always kept separate and constantly watched over. It seemed a lot of them were still being stolen by other clans, and the men needed to be vigilant. Unfortunately I was never able to get really close to any of the women on this trip. (Sadly our film reflected this fact.) For their protection and for hunting, the men carried bows which took a wide variety of arrows, with assorted sharp heads made from bamboo, hardwood or bone, depending on the prey: birds, pigs, cassowary, wallaby, fish. The biggest ones, made from bone, had huge carved barbs, which they told us were for humans.

For the first couple of nights – as had become the norm – I slept with the crew, who set up camp at the base of the tree-house. Meanwhile I was carefully watching our hosts. Early on, Naftali lent Bofoko a steel axe. His face lit up and he got to work on the base of a tree. But he got the movement all wrong. Stone axes are actually adzes, requiring a forward action rather than a sideways one. He didn't know I was watching, and this clinched it for me that these guys had never used steel before. They reacted interestingly to other Western stuff too: lighters, matches, fish hooks, clothing. It was clear from their slow and wondering reactions that these things were all alien to them. When someone lent Bofoko a mirror, he took it very politely, studied it for about ten minutes, looked at himself in it, made a face or two, then handed it back.

These people had heard about outsiders before, even if they hadn't met any. But I was sure now that they weren't faking anything. The wood of the treehouse was too roughly hewn to have been cut with metal implements; and the speed with which they could make a new stone axe demonstrated better than any words that this was something they needed and relied on.

On the second morning we got up at dawn and Tim and I joined our new friends on a hunt. Despite the thorns that littered the ground the men ran barefoot. They were incredibly fit and fast, racing along the track in the undergrowth. I was puffing and panting after ten minutes, just trying to keep up with them. They took their dogs with them, who chased and caught a wild pig.

It was fun; and also an excellent bonding exercise. When we returned to the treehouse we were breathless and laughing with the excitement of it all. They asked if I'd like to move up from the camp and stay with them in their treehouse ... which was exactly what I'd been hoping. Half of the house was unfinished, with two walls completely open save for a few support beams and struts. Only one-third of the floor was planked, leaving much of it as an open lattice of supports. It was relatively bright for filming and communicating, but quite chilly with no wind protection.

The platform was about twenty feet off the ground, and to get to it you climbed up a pole carved with circular steps, like a series of solid wooden cones pushed on top of each other. Some say these treehouses are so high to be above the mosquitoes; others that they're defensive. The Kombai have historically been terrorized by the Asmat people, who live just down the river on the coast and had once been famous cannibals and headhunters, needing a new crop of heads for each ritual and ceremony in their life cycle.

That evening I sat out on the veranda with Wamufo, Bomari and Bofoko and watched the sun sink through the trees. It was a tropical sunset: short and sharp and brilliantly coloured, for five minutes the whole sky glowing an intense yellow, orange and purple. It was a wonderful moment and I expressed to camera that it was as good a day as I could ever remember in the jungle. These people might not be the Korowai – but I meant it.

Naftali was staying down in the crew camp, so at times like this we had no language in common except gestures and smiles. But I was still able to start getting acquainted with our new hosts. This being my third trip, my sign language was definitely improving. But as dusk turned to dark it became harder to communicate. I could see only the gleam of their eyes and teeth in the dark, and any signs between us weren't clear. Though it was still probably very early, I decided to join them in lying by the fire and going to sleep, to start adjusting to their rhythms, living in the daylight, sleeping in the dark. I lay flat on the wooden slats of the floor, feeling the cool breeze on my body, looking out at the stars above the dark silhouettes of trees, hearing the strange rustles and squeals of the jungle beyond . . .

And not just beyond, as it turned out. The idea that these three tuned in to sleep with the natural rhythm of the day was another of my romantic notions. They were the noisiest companions I'd ever spent a night with, all my Marine and trekking experience included. Bomari kept up an intermittent chanting sing-song; Bofoko coughed and spluttered and cleared his throat so that I could hear every last drop of spluttering phlegm; Wamufo groaned and grunted and snored. There was no polite respect for would-be sleeping visitors. Everything was at full volume. And when they did sleep, it was never for long. One of them would always be up and about, tending the fire. Then another would get up to take a leak off the edge of the veranda, rocking the whole treehouse. I got the impression that none of them had ever had a full night's sleep in their lives.

I was awake with the dawn, barely refreshed. Bomari was still chanting noisily to himself (later that day we nicknamed him Bob Marley). Looking down from the edge of the veranda, I could see the crew camp below, their orange and green tents a few metres off from the base of the stilts of the treehouse. I knew that they had inflatable mattresses and bags and were no doubt sleeping like kings. I watched, enviously, as Kelly's cooks stirred and got the water on. Zips of tents were undone and cups of tea passed through. Then the smell of their breakfast drifted up as Tim and Jon finally emerged, bleary-eyed, into the light. By then I'd been up for well over two hours and had smoked about thirty roll-up cigarettes out of sheer boredom.

'Morning, gents!' I shouted down sarcastically. 'Sleep well?'

This daily contrast wasn't going to get any easier. That morning we headed off into the forest to source the staple of the Kombai diet – sago. The men felled a tree with a stone axe and then all the women pitched in, their faces splashed with white as they hacked at the fibrous pith inside. Then they mashed and strained it to leave a glutinous, starchy paste. This was collected in the sago palm fronds and then the water was drained off, leaving raw sago. It looks disgusting and it is disgusting, so dry that it saps all the moisture from your mouth. It's pure starch and not much else; I liken it to eating ground chalk. Of all the world food staples, it's one of my least favourite, though at the same time one of the easiest to cultivate.

It's almost impossible for a television programme to get across these mundane aspects of indigenous life. There's no fun in highlighting boredom or bland taste – it's just not good TV. Back home I get loads of cred for eating bugs and grubs and rats' tails and the like, when the simple truth is that if you've been eating sago all week, a locust is a real treat and in comparative terms tastes as good as a prawn.

Luckily there were other items on the menu besides sago. The next day the guys took me fishing. We started off spending a couple of hours collecting a poisonous root, which we then tied up into a bundle and took down to a stream a kilometre or so away. The women and children came too and set up camp for the day nearby. Now the guys dammed the stream with logs and stones, making a little pool. Then they mashed up the root – surprisingly hard work – and threw the resulting gunk into the stream: a series of white clouds spread slowly through the clear water, removing the life-giving oxygen. Soon fish began to float to the surface, asphyxiated. The men waded through the pool, pulling them out. Catching them looked easier than it actually was, as I discovered when I had a go. The fish might have looked comatose, but they wriggled hard when I tried to grab them. You have to scoop them out gently with both hands and somehow get them over to dry land. The other method the guys used was to spear them with an arrow as they floated.

It was a treat to have fresh fish that evening, doubly so because it wasn't sago. But as I dozed off on the hard slats of the treehouse floor, naked bar my shorts and happy at last with a full stomach, I was shocked to feel a hand on my waist. It was Bofoko's, and this clearly was no accident. I reached down and pushed it gently away. There was some heavy breathing and shuffling – worrying, as I knew he was naked apart from his penis gourd. After a minute or so I felt his hand again, further round my waist this time. I sat up, coughed, and stood to go and pee off the edge of the treehouse. Then I lay down elsewhere, using my camera case as a barricade. There was no denying that Bofoko had hit on me. Whether this was a private initiative or a feature of Kombai life, I didn't know. Although I wish never to be culturally insensitive, this was definitely the limit to my principle of living exactly like my indigenous hosts! Fond as I already was of Bofoko, I had no desire to shag him.

I spent the rest of the night on edge, half awake, not sure if I should expect a replay, but in the morning I acted as if nothing had happened and it was cool. Bofoko was an easy-going guy and we were soon back having meaningful sign-language chats, part of our unthreatening – if still tactile – relationship. He never made another direct pass at me, but life away from the cameras continued to have its Bofoko-related moments. Another night I woke to heavy breathing not too far away in the pitch black of the treehouse. I shut my eyes tight and tried desperately to get back to sleep, but it was no good. A short but excruciating while later, I was under no illusion that the resulting sighs and smells were more pleasant for Bofoko than for me. To top it off, I then had to lie listening to an all-too-obvious dry-leaf-mopping session. The BBC doesn't pay me *nearly* enough for this, I thought wearily.

As far as the cameras were concerned, however, Bofoko was a natural. He had no real concept of what television was, how could he, he'd never seen it, but he watched me interact with this strange machine and was soon playing up to it himself, jumping in and out of shot and behaving like a born star. I joked to the crew that he'd be on *The Tonight Show with Jay Leno* one day – I sincerely hoped that would never come to pass. (Ironically, he was one day, albeit on a video clip.)

Whether they had rejected imported goods in the past or not was impossible to know. Certainly in that settlement there was no evidence of any manufactured accoutrements. Wamufo's prized possession was an oyster shell, with which he would scoop up the juice of meat or fish. One day he let me use it, and watched carefully to see what I did. He nodded and smiled at me, as if to say, 'Well done, son. You know how to scoop properly.' It must have come from some sort of trade, because there are no shells in that area. But that was all I saw, the total extent of their utensils and tools: stone axes, some bamboo bows and arrows, and a shell.

Meanwhile, I was struggling with the daily diet of sago and was starving. Smelling the crew's dinner every night was killing me. And it wasn't made any easier by my three hosts having no concept of the rules I'd set myself. As far as they were concerned, if there was food going in the crew camp, just below the treehouse, they were going to have some too (and Jon could hardly deny them). So once again I was living a more 'traditional' life than anyone else; while Wamufo, Bomari and Bofoko were enjoying noodles and tinned beef.

It was at this point I had my one disagreement with Jon. Despite the odd crew snack, my three new friends were obviously feeling as hungry as I was; the next day they wanted to go out pig hunting again. Jon had already filmed a pig hunt, and didn't want to waste time filming another, so he asked if I might consider joining someone else doing another activity, to add variety to our film. But I was absolutely desperate for some meat. It's not fair, I thought. You're all sleeping in sleeping bags and eating three meals a day, and I'm surviving on a fistful of chalk. In the end I won him over: we went out and caught a rock wallaby, which made for a new scene for the film, and so everybody was happy.

We'd now been with this group for about a week and I still hadn't asked the big question: did they know of any cannibals, or had *they*, even, practised cannibalism themselves?

So that evening, my mood lightened by a bit of leaf-baked wallaby with mushroom and sago, we sat down together and Naftali and Kelly asked if they knew anyone who had ever eaten another human being. Slowly it transpired that at least one of them had. That they didn't immediately volunteer the information – as Britop and Yambu at Wangemalo had – only made me more convinced their story was genuine.

Wamufo ended up telling us about three people he had killed. All had been *khakua-kumu*, he said, which is their word for a man who walks alone in the forest and can harm people by casting spells on them. In their culture, he went on, it's not enough to simply kill a *khakua-kumu* and bury or cremate him, because his spirit may continue to do harm. They believe that a person's soul is contained in their head and stomach, and only by eating these body parts is the evil destroyed for ever. Often the limbs are cut off and the torso quartered, and the parts are placed at prominent places at the edge of the clan's territory to ward off other evildoers.

Wamufo had eaten two *khakua-kumu* from other clans. But the previous year, he said, his youngest brother had died; on his deathbed he had indicated to Wamufo who the *khakua-kumu* in the case was, a man from a neighbouring homestead within the same clan. Wamufo had then spoken to the clan elders and asked if he could kill this man. He was given permission and did so. He captured and tied him, threw him in the river and shot him repeatedly with arrows. Then he drank his blood mixed with the flowing water of the stream. On the way home, however, he decided not to eat his flesh; as a neighbour, he was too closely related. I asked if he would ever do such a thing again. If he had to, he replied, he would. 'If the *khakua-kumu* comes from another clan, I'll eat him. If he comes from among us, I'll give him to others to eat.'

The translation was third-hand, from Naftali to Kelly to us; the local language, then Indonesian, then English. I could follow quite a lot of it in Indonesian, but it was the earnestness of Wamufo's expression, the look in his eyes, his accompanying sign language, the quiet understated reaction of Bofoko and Bomari, that convinced me his story was true. I'd been living with them for a while now; we were beyond pretences. I must admit I was also excited. Here was a man I'd been sleeping next to for the previous six days, admitting he'd eaten other human beings.

Another night we asked the trio important questions of a different kind: where did they think their ancestors came from? What did they think lay beyond the jungle? Where did they think we came from? Anthropologists insist, rightly, that questions like this must never be leading. We were careful to stick to that rule. But what emerged was as fascinating to me as their lack of interest in my torch or penknife: they had no answers. They never thought about where they went when they died. This wasn't Naftali filtering; you could see from the shrug of their shoulders that it wasn't something that concerned them deeply. It seemed they just lived for the moment.

I asked where they thought I came from, but they displayed a similar lack of curiosity. Their translated reply was: 'We don't care where you've come from, because it's obviously crap! You can't climb trees, you've got no balance. We don't know what it is you wear on your body and feet, but it always seems to get in the way, it stays wet for ages and slows you up when you're hunting. You're too fat! We like you and think you're great entertainment, and we love having you here with us because you're different and that's interesting, but why on earth would we be interested in where you come from?'

Sadly we never caught this on camera – it was my favourite comment of the entire series. It came from one of the many conversations I had with the guys when it was just me and an interpreter. All their basic needs were provided for in their immediate surroundings. They showed no outward signs of desire for anything else, even our shiny-looking gear. In many ways their carefree life was enviable to me; certainly it afforded them much free time to play and reinforce family bonds. I couldn't help but think that this lack of need was at least part of the explanation for their lack of mechanical invention, because if one thing was apparent to me, it was that they were not short on intelligence.

Towards the end of my stay, they offered to kit me out in their traditional gear, with a lizard-skin strap round my head, a pig's-tooth necklace round my neck and a sago thorn through my nose. The actual insertion of the thorn through my septum was bloody painful, but I still loved this moment because, shortly afterwards, I had another gesture-conversation with Bofoko, where he said, in effect, 'If you come back to see us one day, and you still have the thorn in your nose, I will welcome you. But if you've taken the thorn out, you won't be welcome here.' (His acting-out of me going away and returning included the mime of a plane flying, complete with noise; they'd seen and heard planes overhead and must have known that that was how I'd got there.) For me this was both a justification of the premise for the series and a moment of genuine acceptance from my new friend. There had always been a risk that doing the nose-piercing would make me look like a wannabe tribesman acting out sensational moments for the camera. But Bofoko made it clear that it was much more than that. The thorn in my nose brought us closer together, so much so that if I returned without it, he didn't want to know me. I was touched.

Meanwhile, the hornbill beak they used as a genital covering simply wasn't ever going to fit me. They tried a gourd, but that was no good either. I would have been happy with a leaf wrapped around my penis, which is what we'd done at the first camp out of Wangemalo. But Bofoko was adamant that I should be exactly like them. He wanted to force my dick back inside my body!

'No way!' I was trying to say, even as the cameras rolled. But the translation was taking too long and Bofoko already had his hand on my foreskin. He didn't seem to be too bothered that I was verbally protesting, and I didn't want to rudely shove him away, so I couldn't help but allow this to happen. He took my foreskin between his fingers and rolled it up, so it was like a closed end. Then he grabbed the end of my shaft and squeezed it hard. It was as if he'd got a large sausage roll in his fist and had blocked one end. There was only one way my penis could go, and that was inwards. It was very odd. It wasn't painful, but I suddenly felt faint. Tim was right beside me filming and Jon was a couple of metres away directing. I could see his lips moving, but couldn't hear a word he said; it was as if my ears were full of cotton wool. My whole body was pouring with sweat and I felt completely disorientated. 'Sorry,' I blurted out. 'No way. I can't go through with this.' I had to lie down as if I was about to faint. With my penis half missing, I raised my legs to get the blood back to my head – not a pretty sight. Bofoko was laughing his head off. In the end he rolled my penis in a leaf. That was fine except that it wasn't secured in any way, so when I had to do a jumping dance the next day it kept slapping my gut. All a bit embarrassing, really.

The end came quite suddenly and unexpectedly. We'd all been out looking for sago grubs, and then filming a scene where the three men teased me by putting the wrong kind of maggot in my ear. We returned, cheerful as ever, to find a very spooky-looking guy waiting for us. He carried a bow and arrow and was wearing traditional Kombai headdress, with the cassowary feathers down, covering his face. He had a skin disease which is very common out there and made him look even more alarming. He was very polite but made it clear that he wasn't happy. It turned out that when we'd been at the previous homestead and sent out the three or four guys to see which one of the various treehouses we were going to stay in, the wires had got crossed – he and his people thought we were going to visit his place too. But now there was no way we could do that, even if we'd wanted to. We only had thirty-day tourist visas, and we needed to get down to the coast to film the Asmat people for a dramatic sequence which Jon wanted as a start to our film. A further detour to another village to meet another clan wouldn't be possible, and we certainly didn't want to introduce new characters and venues into the film at this late stage.

So with many translated apologies, we compromised: we invited the visitor and his people to a feast. After which we would have to leave, otherwise it would look like favouritism to our trio – clearly unacceptable to their neighbours.

Bomari, Bofoko and Wamufo slaughtered a domestic pig for the feast and my departure. It was a real honour. We ate and danced, in little groups in the cool shade of the trees. Then the porters from Wangemalo turned up and we packed up our kit and headed off. It was strange, I thought, as I prepared to leave. Of all the places I'd ever been, these guys were probably the furthest removed from what I took for granted back home: pots, pans, knives, cars, culture, knowledge of the outside world, science – everything. And yet I had never felt so much at home; or laughed so much or communicated as much without saying a word. When the time came to leave, I knew Bofoko would cry. He followed me, then sat down on a tree trunk and sobbed. 'Don't cry, don't cry,' I told him, standing with my hand on his shoulder, uncertain of what to say. It was very moving. We didn't use that footage in the end – it felt intrusive. Instead we used a scene shot a minute earlier, where they whistled along to our departure, and which I find equally sad and poignant.

This programme was probably the most difficult of all the films we've made, especially in the edit. It proved hard to mix all the interesting topics and storylines and hard to justify ethically. In all our other programmes, I can put my hand on my heart and say that our impact on our subjects' lives has been minimal in comparison to the other forces of change around them. In this instance the situation was more complex: I think we certainly changed these people's lives, even if just by leaving an emotional hole when we went. That said, I still stand by our decision to go there. A central goal of mine in making the series is to overturn preconceptions and challenge stereotypes in our world. Our hope was to portray these people in a human way; to demonstrate that they are so much more than 'Stone-Age, primitive cannibals' living in the jungle.

4. Stick-Fighters

The Suri of the Omo Valley, Ethiopia

TV images of dreadful famines – especially the one of 1984, which inspired Bob Geldof's famous Live Aid initiative – have left Ethiopia with a reputation for poverty and an association with scenes of starvation that they hate. Their country is, of course, so much more than a place where harvests sometimes fail. With the exception of the brief Italian occupation of 1936–41, Ethiopia is the only African nation never colonized. It's the oldest independent state in Africa, for centuries ruled over by a famous monarchy whose last scion was the Emperor Haile Selassie, the inspiration for Rastafarianism, revered by his followers as a deity. The country has some of the most ancient Christian churches and Muslim mosques in the world. Twice the size of Texas, it boasts a spectacular array of landscapes, from the mountainous highlands around the capital, Addis Ababa, to the escarpments and wide savannahs of the south. As for its population, Ethiopia is rich in ethnic diversity, with 83 separate languages and more than 200 dialects.

For our next *Tribe* programme, we planned to visit one of the lesser known of these tribal groups, who call themselves the Suri (but are known to outsiders as the Surma), who live a few days from the capital in the wild south-west, close to the border with Sudan. With a reputation for fierce independence, the Suri have historically remained wary of outsiders, having little time for colonizers, traders, administrators and soldiers, and maintaining continued defences against their neighbouring tribes, the Bume (or Nyangatom) and the Toposa, with whom they still have deadly conflicts. With high self-esteem and a strong belief in their own cattle-centred culture, the Suri are truly a people apart. Their women wear huge lip-plates, while their men engage in regular bouts of ferocious stick-fighting, both as a sport and as a historical preparation for aggressive self-defence. Anybody attempting to steal the Suri's cattle or encroach on their traditional lands can expect to be shot at with one of the AK-47s so ubiquitous in this part of Africa.

As I read about the Suri in preparation for my visit, I must admit that I was a little nervous. My only previous experience of Ethiopia had been an expedition with two good mates and six camels through the hottest desert in the world, the Danakil, where we encountered considerable hostility from the local Afar people and, for a few mad days, were held at gunpoint by a crazed tribesman trying to extort money from us – a lasting memory of the Horn of Africa.

At one point it looked as if we wouldn't make it out there at all. Michael Buerk had recently filmed and screened a 'twenty years on' programme about the 1984 famine. The programme had been highly critical of the current Ethiopian government, so the BBC were not popular there. We were informed that we would not be allowed in unless Ethiopia received a formal apology. Meanwhile, I'd managed to break my arm mountain-biking in the Alps, so I was sitting around in Cardiff with my arm in a sling as the argument raged on over whether or not we would be allowed access. The BBC would not apologize, and we all understood why: they felt they had been making an impartial news report. In the end, only the persuasive charm and dogged determination of our production manager, Lindsay Davies, sorted things out. She telephoned every embassy official she could find. As each department head politely apologized and passed the buck to another department, she calmly contacted the next official on the list. Eventually she went full circle until they all had no one left to pass the buck to. Exhausted, they agreed to allow us in. My arm was healing, and so off we flew.

After a couple of days in Addis Ababa, home to the UN's East African headquarters and – no coincidence – one of the plushest Sheraton hotels in the world, we set out on a four-day journey south. With me was James Smith, who had directed the Adi programme, cameraman Jon Clay (as per Gabon and Papua), and assistant producer Hannah Griffiths, the auburn-haired Scot who'd also been with us in Arunachal Pradesh. In Addis we'd met up with Zablon Beyene, an Ethiopian of Tegrain origin, who'd lived in London and had excellent English – our fixer for the trip.

As we left behind the dense, settled, agrarian landscape of the central highlands, the dirt road turned rougher and the vegetation wilder. The faces by the roadside became darker, the clothes more tattered and unkempt, the random friendly waves more frequent and the smiles broader. On our second day of travel we came off the high ground. The horizon opened up and the views grew longer as we bumped down into a wide and empty world of acacia-dotted savannah, broken by distant blue-green escarpments.

We drove on, arriving a day later at Kibish, the nearest on-road village to our final destination. It was dominated by a police compound with high brick and tin walls topped with barbed wire. For our own safety we were asked to stay within this compound: with all the guns around, we didn't argue.

The next two days were spent negotiating: with the local

police chief, the local authority head and, when they had satisfied themselves about what we wanted to do, with the chief of the local area. He was the *koromu*, the traditional spiritual leader: an old man of great dignity, dressed in colourful robes and wearing a crown of baboon fur.

The *koromu* spoke to us in a slow and measured manner, fixing me with the sincerest of gazes as he paused for Zablon to translate his words. 'My name is Black Bull. This is my village, my area. You come in peace and we are happy.' When we explained, through Zablon, that I hoped to stay with one of the village families while the crew camped nearby, he nodded forcefully at us, without a trace of a smile. 'It's right what you are talking,' came the halting, garbled translation, which had been made twice, passed from a local-dialect speaker to Zablon and then on to us in English.

'This is what I like and I really want. We'll come together and be one. You will sleep among us. We'll drink from one horn. We'll eat together.'

I matched the seriousness of the *koromu*'s expression with my nods. Then he added more. He spoke of how previous white visitors had just turned up to take photographs. They would drive by in powerful vehicles and not even stay a night before departing. 'We feel as if they look down on us,' Zablon translated. 'They don't want anything to do with us. We feel they think they are superior to us. But you have come to stay with us. To live in our house and drink blood with us. To be with us. This is what we want.' This was music to my ears. Like the stipulation from Bofoko only to return to his homestead if I had a thorn through my nose, I felt this was validation of our philosophy in the making of the series: to live with the people we were filming and experience everything, to humanize them and to show that we were equal.

Of course, as with all the tribal groups we intended to stay with, there would have to be payment involved. We would compensate these people for access to their lives, and there would be gifts as well. The *koromu* was not naïve. He knew that our white faces and cameras and vehicles would mean something concrete for his village. But at this point, no actual terms were discussed. I felt heartened: money aside, the *koromu* seemed genuinely delighted that I wanted to do more than just nose around and clear off.

The next day, we were in luck in another way too. There was to be a stick-fighting festival – or *sagenai* – a few kilometres back along the road we'd come in on. This was great news: it would add some colour and action to the opening of our film. We decided to drive there, to ease carriage of our cameras. Coming round the brow of a hill, we saw a huge and sprawling crowd on a wide-open green space. This was a taste of what we'd always hoped would be the climax of our programme and it was mesmerizing. Zablon led us down to where the fighting was taking place.

'What's the etiquette here?' I asked him. 'I don't want to upset anyone.' This isn't the sort of situation where you want to get things wrong, with hundreds of huge super-fit guys milling around, primed to the max with aggression, many with AK-47s. You could practically smell the testosterone.

'If you are just observing,' Zablon reassured me, 'everybody will be happy. But still, you have to take care, you know.'

I could see why. At the centre of the crowd were individual fights, with men charging each other with 2·5-metre-long hardwood sticks in a frenzy of strikes and parries that made fencing look like a kid's game. People were getting seriously hurt. We saw one man with blood streaming down his face; another lay on the ground, moaning and clutching his stomach. Some fighters wore colourful headdresses, or cloth head and neck padding; others wore knee-protectors made of woven reeds. But most used no protection at all and were all but naked. They had strings of decorative coloured beads around their necks and waist, but their genitals were uncovered and they were barefoot. This is seriously hardcore, I thought. If I was going to get stuck into this, I would be incredibly lucky not to get hurt.

We watched for a while. Victors were declared and hoisted on to the shoulders of supporters and paraded around. One winner wasn't a particularly big man, but clearly he was as hard as nails. As he was marched around by his cheering supporters, his face was completely devoid of expression – there was no way you could read what he was thinking.

With the *koromu*'s blessing, we set off the following morning on the final stage of our journey, the trek up the narrow bush track from Kibish to our chosen village of Regia. At this time of year, after the rains, the bush was thick and lush and green, the long grass interspersed with the acacia trees and thorn bushes so abundant in Africa. Regia itself was a collection of twenty or so huts on a hillside, all still made in the traditional way, with a conical straw roof reaching almost to the ground. Halfway between Kibish and the village there was a lovely grassy spot by the clear-flowing brook that is the Kibish River, which we all decided would make a great camp for the crew. As usual, I pitched my tent there for a couple of nights while we set up and got things ready. The *koromu* joined us. He had insisted that we be protected by armed guards against any thieving or attacks from outsiders, so he and they made their own little camp at the other end of this riverside site. The aggressive relationship between the Suri and their neighbours was all too real. I didn't seriously expect us to be attacked, but the ubiquitous presence of guns and gunmen made it clear that this was an altogether heavier situation than we'd yet encountered in the making of the *Tribe* series.

Security considerations to one side, my main concern now was how I would be received. What would these proud, clearly tough people make of me? But when we went up to the village proper and I was introduced to the family with whom I would be staying, my fears slipped away. One glance at my host Bargulu put me at ease: he had a wonderful sense of calm about him, a far-seeing, spiritual expression in his pale brown eyes. His wife, Nabala, was more down to earth, but equally welcoming, although initially I found it difficult to look at her – I'm ashamed to say – without staring at the huge clay plate in her lower lip.

These traditional adornments are worn by almost all the adult Suri women. When a Suri woman becomes engaged to be married, usually in her teens, she disappears from village life to live in her family hut. The gap between her front lip and the flesh below is pierced and gradually stretched. The stretching continues as successively bigger discs of clay are accommodated by the disfigured lip. Generally the two lower front teeth are pulled (or knocked) out to aid the process. The final size of the plate determines how many cattle the woman will receive as a dowry, so the more stretched her lip the better, and the more rewarded her parents and family will be. Nabala, who had married the son of the chief, had a lip-plate thirteen centimetres across, which had been worth a dowry of over forty cows. The origins of this bizarre tradition are not known. Though seen as a sign of beauty now, some say the disfigurement began as a way of putting slavers off seizing Suri women.

I was shown into Bargulu and Nabala's mud hut, which was built in two concentric layers under a low straw roof. The mud-and-dung walls of the round inner room were circled by a thinner outer wall. The entrances were at right angles to each other, so you had to crawl in from outside on your hands and knees, then round a quarter-circle in the pitch darkness of the narrow gap until you could see your way into the flickering firelight of the main room. It was pretty dark in there too, even when it was bright daylight outside, but I could make out two sleeping areas on each side of a central fireplace. They comprised smoothed-flat solid clay, a metre or so across, each with a thin cowhide cover. Pots and pans stood in the two-foot gap between the beds, with more at the back of the hut. The ceiling was covered with loops from which more pots hung.

That evening this tiny space was packed. Besides Bargulu and Nabala, there was my armed guard, Arbulla, not to mention numerous children and Nabala's charismatic friend Ndongele, who had a slightly smaller lip-plate than hers but a huge sense of humour. She was always laughing and quite often pissed as a fart.

I had to use the infrared setting on my portable camera to see them at all, it was so dark in there. A simple but amazing piece of technology, the bulb works in the pitch black and to everyone around just looks like a single red dot. But when seen through the viewfinder or the flip-out screen, the whole room lights up as if in daylight. This group was thrilled with the magical night view, squinting and giggling as they saw their faces lit up on the flip-out screen.

'I never knew my lip was so long,' cried Ndongele, as she saw what she looked like without her lip-plate (which she had taken out for the evening), presumably for the first time. To my eye, I can't pretend it was a pretty sight, a huge circle of stray lip dangling incongruously below a misshapen mouth.

Supper that evening was dry maize porridge with thick and lumpy sour milk, a staple for the Suri. I thought momentarily of the crew down by the river, sitting back around their gas stoves with beers and well-cooked pasta, and then forgot about them and got on with it. This food was hardly gourmet, but it was nutritious enough and, when mixed with the sour milk, much better than the starchy dry sago of the Kombai. After a little more chat and play with my camera, the women left for another hut and we guys lay down to sleep. Or rather, *they* lay down to sleep. We were three to a cowhide on each side of the fire. The hide didn't quite reach the edge, so I was half lying on the baked mud, pressed right up against the hut's rough mud-and-straw wall. Ants and ticks from the floor crawled all over me. On my other side was a tiny naked baby, as well as Bargulu's arm pushed up against the side of my face – he was snuffling and snoring right in my ear. I'm not usually a poor sleeper, but I wasn't going to nod off in a hurry in these conditions. I lay wide awake in the darkness, watching the firelight flicker on the ceiling, casting long oval shadows from the hooped utensil hangers. If I made the mistake of rolling on to my side, the space was instantly taken by Bargulu, and so I would be wedged until I could wrestle some space back from my grunting host.

Not that I was unhappy: my worst fears had evaporated. Suri culture did undoubtedly have its fearsome aspects, but Bargulu and Nabala were truly lovely, warm and welcoming – and the children were a delight. I lay there thinking, How dare I have thought I would have a hard time here? The reason we had encountered such hostility in the Danakil desert was because we were three kitted-up white men moving through at speed, not allowing time to get to know people or live on their terms. Here, now, I swore never again to worry about meeting new people. I was confident that provided I came in overtly as a true outsider (i.e. not part of a group that they have had any traditional hostility towards) and entered their settlements with humility and respect, it would be very hard to upset your hosts.

In the morning my companions were up at first cock-crow. Outside the hut the children lit fires in the dawn chill. These were not for us, but the cattle. There were several fires, so that each cow got a good chance to warm itself before the sun came up. I was seeing for myself the central role of the cow in the Suris' way of life. One of the key experts on these people, the anthropologist Jon Abbink, has described the Suris' cattle as 'virtually a part of human society ... the Suri do not see cattle simply as a material asset, but as the life-sustaining and meaningful companion *par excellence.*' Having warmed them with the fires, the boys then milk the cattle first thing, singing to them as they do so. Sometimes, as the days went by, I would see a boy drinking straight from a cow's teat.

So I had a good gourdful of fresh milk to go with the porridge that appeared once again for breakfast. Then my new friends had another local treat they wanted me to try – blood.

A cow was held by two boys while one of the men applied a tourniquet to its neck. Bargulu then picked up a small bow and fired into the thick, throbbing jugular with a specially adapted arrow – a sharp flat spear-like blade to pierce the skin, and two lumps of resin on either side to stop it going too far in. Blood streamed out in an arc under the tourniquet's pressure, to be caught in a big circular gourd. Once it was full, this was handed to me. There was a good two litres there, hot between the palms of my hands.

It didn't actually taste too bad. My immediate reaction to camera was that it was not unlike a nutritious shake, made with minerals and salts rather than sugar. My problem was that I had just eaten breakfast and my gut was already full. I did my best, but as the blood started to cool and get stringy it became increasingly unpleasant. I managed over half of the gourd, which must have been nearly a couple of pints in all. In the end I passed the gourd over to Bargulu, who picked it up like a pro and gulped the contents down, licking his crimsoned lips as he finished. The Suri very rarely eat the meat of their cows, so drinking blood and milk is a sustainable way of obtaining protein from their surroundings via their animals.

An altogether different traditional Suri drink is *gesso*, the thick local beer made from fermented maize, which we sampled later that day. The Suri drink *gesso* at any time of the day and get quite pissed on it sometimes. It comes in different strengths: some brews are quite weak; others seriously alcoholic. It's also drunk from a gourd, and one of the Suri customs is to share the drink, literally, so your lips are side by side with those of your drinking companion as you gulp it down. You're basically snogging the man you're sharing with – in this case Bargulu. I could feel his lips working away as he swallowed. And there was no let-up until he wanted to stop: Bargulu was lifting the gourd hard to keep the *gesso* pouring, while I was struggling to stop. He won, and the speed of ingestion made me very nearly vomit it all right up again.

Drinking blood was one thing, but clearly the central challenge for me with these people was going to be my attempt to take part in one of their stick-fighting sessions – or *sagenais*. After what we'd seen on our first day in Kibish, I knew this would be a tough call, but I was determined to take up the gauntlet. I really wanted to learn how to do it properly and then take part. I didn't expect to win a bout – or *donga* – but I wanted to at least try.

Which is not to say that I wasn't nervous. Inside, of course I was. And as we lay around outside the hut after our meagre supper, I took the opportunity to quiz Bargulu and the others about how dangerous they thought stick-fighting really was. Their answers were delivered in a frustratingly laid-back manner; it seemed as if getting hurt or even killed wasn't really that big a deal:

'Is it possible to learn the skill', I asked, 'to *donga*?'

'It is possible to learn.'

'D'you think I should fight?'

'Er . . .' – long pause – 'yes.'

'How dangerous is it?'

'The danger is one . . . maybe you lose your eyes or leg or . . . get killed.'

'And how often do people lose their eyes?'

'Maybe for one *sagenai*, two people or three people are losing their eyes, or leg or . . . get killed.'

I can't say this conversation inspired confidence in me. None the less, I started learning a few basic moves, practising under the supervision of Chagi, a bright young local we'd now taken on as a translator. He spoke excellent English, with which he was able to mock my attempts to learn to stick-fight. I'd boxed during my time in the Royal Marines, even making it to some tournament finals, but that meant nothing here. If there hadn't been such a risk of permanently losing an eye or testicle, my decision would have been a lot easier. But I didn't fancy sterilizing myself for the sake of TV.

Eventually Chagi considered me ready to take on a real live opponent, a boy of not much more than twelve. He trounced me fairly easily.

After a week or so in Regia word came that another *sagenai* was about to take place. This time it would be more interesting because a group of men from our village would be taking part. These were guys I'd got to know a little, so I stayed with them and watched as they went through their preparation. This begins the day before the *sagenai* with a ritual purging. They drink an infusion of the bark of a special tree mashed to a pulp and mixed with water. The mixture, known as *dokai*, is drunk to excess then vomited up by agitating the gag reflex in the throat with a stick. The water brings with it many of the body's impurities. Now they will eat nothing until the following morning, when they wash themselves in the river, drink blood, and decorate themselves with differing shades of brown river clay. The clay is smoothed on and the decoration is made by sliding the fingers through it to expose the dark skin underneath. Further body adornments are added: coloured or feathered headdresses, which clearly provide a little protection; strings of beads round the neck and waist; and woven reed knee pads. There was little doubt that this was a big showing-off opportunity and I asked Bargulu if the men were dressing up to catch the attention of the women.

'There is no point in stick-fighting without girls to watch us,' he replied with a gentle smile. Nabala echoed this: she had first met Bargulu, she told me, at a stick-fight: 'He was a good fighter. I liked the way he fought. He knocked down two or three men at each bout.'

Both the men and women of Regia now walked the couple

of kilometres or so to the site of the *sagenai*, a big open field on the edge of an adjacent village. Large groups of men from other villages were already there, strutting around and posturing in their undeniably aggressive way. They were naked, bar their decorations, and their lean, powerful physiques were fully on display as they parried with their thick sticks. The sexual suggestiveness of the occasion was unavoidable; the head of each stick was noticeably phallic, and the songs being sung were *very* graphic.

Looking more closely now, I was beginning to understand how the individual *dongas* got started. For a short period the men circled round each other, seeking opponents of a similar stature; then they would start with a couple of half-swings to test the water, and if both men felt they had found a match, they suddenly would throw themselves into the fight, hitting out with fierce fast strokes of their sticks. Cheers and shouts from the watching crowd matched the loud crack of wood on wood. Then one of the fighters would get a stroke past the parry and the stick would hit flesh, bringing a grunt and, quite often, blood. If one of the fighters was knocked over or backed out, the other would immediately declare himself the winner. The rules, Zablon explained, strictly forbade hitting a man when he was down. There were ten or more fights going on simultaneously, with many of the men around strutting in victory or parrying for the next fight. Even remembering my military days, this was the most hardcore display of male aggression I'd ever seen. It made milling and boxing seem decidedly genteel.

Away from the central mass of fighters, on the other hand, clearly this was a great outing for the locals (like a Sunday-league football match at home, James thought). Women went around in groups, watching the fights, checking out the men, saying hello to each other, drinking *gesso*, having a real day out. As the day progressed, people became drunker and rowdier. Champions began to emerge from the tight melee at the centre and were carried around shoulder-high by posses of men.

Throughout the day rifle shots had been fired. Usually nobody batted an eyelid: guns were often let off into the air in jubilation or showing off. However, as people got more pissed, some of these shots had a different feel to them. Once or twice there was a mass panic as a gun was lowered towards the crowds. The sound of this was amazing: like a ripple-effect animal stampede, with footsteps originating at a distance and very quickly getting louder and closer as the panic spread towards us and then past us, as people either hit the ground or ran for cover. Things had changed, Zablon explained. The civil war in the Sudan meant that guns were much more common everywhere in this region, and this sort of atmosphere in the afternoon of a *sagenai* was now fairly typical.

After the second such stampede, James made the decision to leave. He and cameraman Jon were getting understandably jumpy about the gunfire, and James felt that our presence as white Europeans with cameras might not exactly be helping. Personally, I wasn't so worried. I've been around guns for a lot of my life and I believe it's possible to sense the difference between a situation where you're a target and one where tempers are just running high. Yes, of course there were risks, but those risks were the same for everyone there. People do get shot, but I didn't think the odds were particularly high that it would be *us* that got hit. But I was in the minority: none of the rest of the team wanted to stick around, so we left.

Back in Regia I had plenty to think about. Having seen more *dongas* close up, I was now fully aware of how dangerous they were. Bargulu's talk about losing eyes or limbs or getting killed was no joke. But I was still eager to have a go, even if only out of pride. I started to practise more and learnt more moves.

The crew were now divided about whether I should actually take part in a *sagenai*. Originally this had been hoped for as the climax of the programme, and Jon thought I should take a chance and do it. James was less keen: for the time being, he was happy for me to continue practising, but he didn't want to be responsible for the casualty evacuation of his presenter. As for me, I was a little bit irritated that I couldn't just do it anyway, and instead had to follow some corporate safety protocol so far away from home.

In the meantime I continued to stay at Bargulu's hut and got to know the villagers a bit better. Besides Bargulu, Nabala and the charismatic Ndongele, I spent a lot of time with Chagi, who'd now become my main companion around the place, sometimes sleeping in Bargulu's hut at night so I could follow the conversation there. Even though he was teaching me how to do it, and training me, he thought I was crazy to want to stick-fight in a proper *donga*.

Apart from Bargulu and Chagi, though, I found it hard to bond with the men of my age in Regia. They were never actually unfriendly, but they didn't pay me any particular attention either. I was staying in the village, a guest of Bargulu, and that was that. I knew that until I'd fought a *donga* they would never even begin to accept me. This strengthened my resolve to at least try.

The children of the village, by contrast, wouldn't leave me alone. They were all over me. I would have a small black hand clasped around my index finger pretty much everywhere I went. If I sat down they crawled all over me, playing with my ears and running their fingers through my hair. Every evening they would get me out to the clearing by the acacia trees for a dance; then they would crowd into the hut and jump all over me. I positively courted their friendship. Although not deliberate, I have found it to be a natural way for softening up adults too. Even the hardest or coolest man can barely resist a smile when someone is making a fool of themselves with the village kids.

One day a goat was slaughtered and a fortune-teller was summoned to predict the future from the animal's entrails. The slimy pinkish innards represent a map of the surrounding area and the fortune-teller looks for spots or abnormalities which tell him when trouble or rain might arrive and from where. This, it became clear, is the Suris' deep underlying preoccupation. On the surface their cattle-tending life seems simple enough, but lurking beneath is their constant fear: defending their territory against the neighbouring tribes, in particular the ferocious Bume, whose name was always on their lips.

One day Bargulu walked me to the top of a neighbouring escarpment to show me the problem on the ground. From up here, we could see down across a wide wooded valley to the hazy bluish silhouettes of mountains on the horizon. There, Bargulu explained, was the border between Suri territory and Bume territory. Traditionally the two tribal groups had kept to their own lands. Since the recent wars in Sudan, however, guns had become plentiful and the Bume emboldened. A decade before there had been a mighty battle at the foot of the mountain, with hundreds of Suri killed, including women and children. And only three months before, a Bume cattle-raiding party had come right up to this ridge that I could see in the foreground. Much of the traditional Suri land now lay within the expanded Bume territories, including, to their great distress, their ancient burial grounds, a now all-too-distant knoll.

'We killed fifteen of them,' Bargulu told me, nodding in that calm, sage-like way of his. I've plenty of friends in the forces, and have heard war talk on many occasions, but it was hard to square the gentleness of my friend's expression with this talk of slaughter. But this was the world the Suri were in. These struggles over tribal lands had been conducted in Africa for ever; but the advent of the AK-47 had made everything so much bloodier.

Another *sagenai* was imminent and I was still practising my stick-fighting, continuing my daily lessons with Chagi. I was determined to take part in the next *sagenai*, even though I would be running a big risk.

James, however, wasn't happy. One evening, at the end of the day's filming, he told me he'd made a decision. He didn't want me to take part in a *sagenai*. It just wasn't worth the risk. I could appeal to Steve back home if I wanted, and maybe go on practising with Chagi until then, but that was it from him.

In retrospect, I should have just accepted the common sense of his decision and packed in my training. But my pride was at stake. Where was my say in all of this? I wasn't just doing this programme to live with and like the locals, but to show, I'd thought, every aspect of their lives.

'But how is this going to appear in the film?' I asked. 'We can't just say, "The director won't let me fight because he thinks it's too dangerous." That's going to sound ridiculous.'

James agreed that that wouldn't work. 'Maybe you could say you realized how dangerous it was and decided not to do it.'

I was unhappy with that. It wasn't true: I wanted no TV lies about pretending to do things we hadn't, or setting situations up to make them look harder than they were. But also, I didn't want to come across as someone who would wimp out of something like this – I'd been a Royal Marine Commando, for Christ's sake! I might well turn out to be rubbish and have all hell kicked out of me, but I'd never ducked out of anything physical before, and I didn't want to start now.

So it was a bit of a tense time, not helped by the fact that even as I was standing my ground on this, I was genuinely scared. I had seen for myself how ferocious the *dongas* were. There was no way, with a mere couple of hours' training, I was going to measure up to these huge, super-fit men with five or ten years of practice behind them.

Hannah and Jon tried to come up with compromise solutions. Maybe I could just have a set-up fight with one of the local guys? But I wasn't happy with that either. It wouldn't be the same as actually taking part in the *sagenai*, with 600 people watching and all that adrenalin pumping.

In the end our dispute was solved for us by the *koromu*. A couple of days before the big *sagenai* that I was preparing for, he appeared suddenly on the edge of the field where I was practising with Bargulu, and told us to stop.

'That's enough,' Chagi translated; not that it was hard to work out the *koromu*'s meaning from his stern expression. 'No more stick-fighting.'

I protested, but he was adamant. He didn't want me to take part in a real stick-fight, he went on. I might get a broken finger, a broken arm or a bad head injury. Or I might lose a finger completely; or break a leg. 'As king of this area,' he told me, 'I would be blamed.' I could go to the *donga*, he concluded, but only to watch.

The whole thing was caught on camera. At first I thought it had been set up by James, but in fact it was one of those wonderful moments in documentary-making when the camera is rolling as something significant happens. And when I quizzed him later, James swore blind that he'd had nothing to do with the *koromu*'s decision. Secretly, I was relieved. I had the perfect get-out clause. I could hardly go against the diktat of the king.

Even though I could no longer take part, the guys from the village did try and make our final *sagenai* special for me. We got to the fight early, before anything had begun, so they took ten minutes out to dress me up as if I were a warrior. They put on the wrist and neck and waist bands and the knee pads they wear. Then they gave me a stick and all got round me and started singing. I was one of the gang for a short while . . . though only while they got ready themselves for their own big fight.

It was quite something being in the middle of this. I could smell their sweat and fear and excitement. It was like the captain's brief in the huddle before a rugby match, a big psyching session. Then we came down through a clearing, where they stopped for a moment to take all their gear back from me, and suddenly we were on the edge of the field where it was happening.

I looked up the slope ahead of me and it was like the famous scene from *Zulu* – the decorated heads and torsos of all these stick-fighters coming into view over the brow of the hill. It was an amazing moment which I'll always remember. Then they started sprinting towards each other. But it didn't continue as you'd imagine in a movie, with everyone charging and the sticks coming out and people falling over. It was more elegant than that. They were more loping than running, but still very fast; then, as they came close, they almost instantaneously paired off and three big circles of men formed. There were about twenty pairs in each of these three circles. Everyone, it seemed, wanted to be the first pair to fight.

I stood and watched in rapt admiration. But I was glad that the *koromu* had, in the end, banned me. At the very best I'd have made a fool of myself out there. As it was, I was able to take in all the activity on the fringes: Nabala and Ndongele selling *gesso* to men who'd finished their fights, as well as getting tipsy on their own brew; other women openly admiring their successful men; all the posturing and flirting that was going on. The Suri clearly still need their men to be strong and protective, and the stick-fight is proof of those qualities.

The next day we prepared to leave Regia. Before we left we were addressed by the *koromu*. 'We are one,' he told us, with a slow gravitas that gave the words a significance beyond their simple translation. 'We all have ten fingers. We have two eyes. We have two ears. We have one stomach. We are all one. Remember me.'

It was a powerful moment, and once again, completely natural. This was just how he responded when I went to thank him and the village for being so hospitable and gracious during our stay.

As he looked at me, it felt like he meant it from the bottom of his heart. And I felt sad, as I left him and his ineffably dignified son Bargulu, that the Suri still had such a struggle on their hands just to stay put, that their place in the world was still so vulnerable. Why did the Bume have to harass them so? Wasn't there some way, in the twenty-first century, that these deadly local squabbles could be sorted out and this seemingly endless cycle of attack and counterattack halted?

I didn't know it then, but within a year I'd be back in the Omo Valley, searching out the answers to these questions.

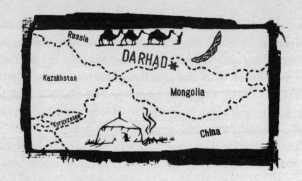

5. Frosty Steppes

The Darhad of the Darhad Valley, Mongolia

Outer Mongolia is a place I have fantasized about since I was a child: like Timbuktu, the very name seems synonymous with the ends of the earth. Nowadays, of course, it's not so remote, being relatively easily accessible by air in the far south-eastern reaches of what used to be the USSR. Soviet control ended there in 1991, but the heavy stamp of the recent Communist past is still very much in evidence. Our intention with this trip was to take part in the traditional autumn migration – or *naduul* – of a family from the Darhad Valley, who move their homes and livestock to fresh pastures four times a year, categorizing them as 'transhumance' rather than nomadic people. The *naduul* we hoped to witness was from the autumn encampment on the steppe, up through the mountain passes to find warmer, less snowbound winter pastures on the shores of Lake Hövsgöl, a 160-kilometre-long inland sea.

I had a new crew for this programme: Steve Robinson, James Smith and Jon Clay were all hard at work in Cardiff, either editing existing programmes or preparing for the last one of the series. This time I was in the hands of Graham Johnson, an older, more experienced director who has won awards all around the world for his films, many of which are about remote indigenous peoples, particularly in northern Canada. A jovial, silver-haired character, who plays in a jazz band back home in Suffolk, Graham was to bring a different, altogether more cinematic style to this programme. With us too was Willow Murton, who had been one of our researchers in Cardiff from the beginning of *Tribe*. Willow grew up in west Wales on her family organic farm before going to Cambridge to read languages. She's highly intelligent and very thoughtful and a great person to have long philosophical conversations with, as well as being game for a laugh when the occasion requires.

From Seoul we flew north to the capital of Mongolia, Ulaanbaatar – an extraordinary place, as ugly as sin, a mass of drab concrete tower blocks left over from the Soviet era. All the hot water in the town is piped from one central boiler building: if you live near it your water is so hot you have to leave your windows constantly open; but at the far end of the pipeline it is miserably cold. There are many other reminders of Communism: great squares where you can easily imagine the Red Army marching through, and streets wide enough for tanks, now jammed with traffic. On the outskirts is a large encampment of the big round felt tents – or *gers* – that Mongolians traditionally live in. I used to call them *yurts*, but that, we discovered, is just a Russian word for 'tent'.

In Ulaanbaatar we met Kent Madin, our fixer for the trip, an American from Colorado who had set up a horse-trail business out here. With him was Cinbat, a kindly, round-faced man who was to be our translator. Cinbat is a Mongolian who grew up in rural Mongolia, but who now lives half the year in America, where his daughter is an ice-skating prodigy.

We flew from Ulaanbaatar to the northern city of Mörön, then drove to the town of Hatgal on the shores of Lake Hövsgöl.

To get to our next destination of Rinchinlhümbe, Kent had organized a picturesque trip up the lake on a boat run by the tiny Mongolian navy. In the early afternoon the navy guys dropped us off at one of Kent's tour camps, a couple of wooden chalets in a lovely spot where a river flowed into the lake. Here we met Nimhu and Nimdala, two local cowboys, who were there to escort us on our ride up over the Jigleg pass.

I had managed to reach the age of thirty-five without having been on a horse for more than a couple of hours, so was excited to meet Fred, my steed for the journey, and learn how to mount and dismount, and get an idea about trotting and cantering before setting out on my first serious ride the next day. Fortunately Fred was good-natured and friendly, a fine horse to learn on; I managed to keep my seat and had soon mastered the 'choo, choo' command that got Fred moving forward, first at a trot, then a gallop – highly exhilarating, as I felt totally out of control. Later that afternoon, I joined in with some traditional Mongolian wrestling, at which I was less successful. I won one of three bouts with Cinbat, but luckily wasn't asked to do battle with Nimhu and Nimdala, who were both fitter and obviously far more skilled than me.

In the morning we set off up through the woods of the valley; in the autumn sunlight the leaves were turning brown and golden and the valley was empty, still and indescribably beautiful. This was a very different landscape to the jungle environments of the first three *Tribes*, and as I rode, taking in the fresh air and scenery, I almost felt as if I were on holiday. I was certainly having a great time with Fred, wondering why I'd never got into horse-riding before. My style was atrocious, and I was still bouncing around a fair amount, but I stayed on and was now learning how to use my reins, knees and feet to increase my speed and steer Fred left and right. The two cowboys were herding a group of wild horses along with us, and when we got up to more open grassland, I felt confident enough to go way out in front with them, going really fast, pushing them on. Mongolian horses, Cinbat had explained, do in fact run wild for most of their lives, out with the herd on the open steppe. Once every few years, a horse is caught, retamed and used for a season before being allowed to go free again. It made, Cinbat thought, for a very different kind of horse to the highly strung animals found in Europe, who are broken in early and enclosed in a stable or paddock for most of their lives.

When we stopped that evening to camp, I realized that in all the excitement I had managed to shed my saddlebag. Luckily Nimhu had spotted it and picked it up, saving me a sixteen-kilometre ride back to fetch it. With a twinkle in his eye, Cinbat took his chance to tease me on camera:

'And what was your mistake today, Bruce?'

'I don't know . . . I stand up in the saddle too much?'

'Tell me about your saddlebag.'

'That's really unfair,' I said, laughing. 'I like your style.'

So then I had to explain how I'd lost my saddlebag.

There was more humiliation for the novice in the morning, when Fred ran off as I was saddling him up. Willow had come over and offered me some hand cream for my rein-chapped hands, something I'd never used in my life. Needing both hands to apply the cream, I'd put the reins on the ground for a moment, also using the opportunity to retie my gaiters, and Fred took his chance. I chased after him, but he'd gone. I walked back, embarrassed, to find Graham's camera trained on me.

We rode on up to the top of the pass, where we stopped for a short time to pay our respects to the *ovoo*, which is a sort of wigwam made of sticks, to which lots of odd bits and pieces have been attached: prayer flags, scarves, torn and fluttering banknotes. *Ovoos* are always found at the tops of passes, and when you come to them it's traditional to leave a gift of some kind, like money, before walking or riding round clockwise three times. This appeases the spirits and brings good luck. I tried to get Fred close to the *ovoo*, but there was a marshy area all around where previous circumnavigators had ridden and walked; Fred was having none of it. It became a battle of wills, which Fred, unsurprisingly, won. I dismounted, did my three circuits on foot, and left a dollar note.

As we came down the far side of the pass we found an enormous white, six-wheeled, ex-Russian army truck waiting for us. At the wheel was Mishig, Kent's business partner, who was to stay with us for the rest of our time in the province. A short stocky guy, he had great style, wearing a Stetson, dark glasses and, quite often, white gloves. Mishig was a vet by profession, and a key figure in the area; an ex-governor, he was very much the big local entrepreneur. He used his huge truck to go round the valley spreading news, seeing to animals, trading goods and acting as a local messenger and go-between. He knew the name of every person in the valley and was massively respected and loved by everyone. He had already been hard at work preparing for our arrival and even had a family in mind for us to stay with. We were very lucky to have him on side. With him was the crew's cook, Maggie, who looked like an off-duty 1970s pop star, in lurid shellsuit, moonboots and spandex. This, we were to discover, is high fashion in this region.

We camped that night with them, and in the morning they followed us down on the final approach to the little town of Rinchinlhümbe, which was like something out of the American Wild West, all wooden houses with high wooden fences surrounding the backyards. Ex-army trucks shared the dirt streets with ponies, which were tied up to posts and in corrals at every corner. At the centre of the town were a sprinkling of concrete and wooden buildings from Communist times. There was even a podium for public speeches, with the Soviet red star still painted in the middle of its balcony. Mishig had arranged for us to stay at a guesthouse on the edge of town.

We were well in time for the *nadaam* – a traditional Mongolian festival. I'd heard a lot about these flamboyant public games and was full of anticipation. I'd decided that I would not take part in any of the activities, but would instead be viewing them as a tourist. I think Graham was a little disappointed that I wouldn't be wrestling, but I pointed out that I hadn't even met my family yet – it was a bit too early to try and get stuck in. I have a healthy fear of public humiliation and didn't fancy my chances much at all. Furthermore, I like to be comfortable with the people that I'm participating with before I join in; I'm acutely conscious of being watched by people saying, 'Who does he think he is?' How much better to be invited to join in by my hosts, rather than arrogantly just strutting up with a camera crew in tow, expecting to be allowed to take part.

The next day I was glad of my stance when I saw the wrestlers. All eighty-odd competitors in the knockout were wearing the traditional Mongolian wrestling shirt, which has sleeves, neck and back, but with the whole front open to expose the navel and chest. Added to that are tight, coloured Y-fronts, pointed skullcaps and high boots. It's surely the weirdest costume ever conceived.

I likened it to some Jean-Paul Gaultier-designed spaceship marshal's uniform from a futuristic gay skin-flick.

I could just picture my puny white body in such an outfit. Cinbat explained the historical reason for the unusual attire. It dates back to a time when a woman once entered the event and won. The humiliation of the men was acute, and so the bare-breasted costume was devised to put off any future female entrants. The actual fighting turned out to be great fun to watch, and our two cowboys, Nimhu and Nimdala, were stalwart participants. Nimdala – the older, stronger one – did incredibly well, battling his way into the quarter finals and ending up third.

Besides the wrestling, there were two horse races for animals of different ages: five-year-olds in the morning and seven-year-olds in the afternoon. The horses were ridden by children between the ages of six and twelve. The tiny kids wore peaked caps and coloured capes; many had no shoes and plenty rode bareback. The race was one straight twenty-four-kilometre dash to the finish in town. The horses had been taught not to stop, no matter what happened, and a steed that has lost its jockey is still in the running – traditionally, it can win the event. As the racing pack neared town the crowd picked up on the shouts of the young riders and abandoned the other events to run over to the finishing line, standing on fences or their own mounts to get a better view of the approaching racers. The winning horse was greeted with wild cheers and then named *Tumay ekh* or 'Winner of ten thousand'. Meanwhile, its owner won another horse – no small prize – while the victor itself had a poem recited in its honour. The last animal in the pack was also sung a song – not to humble it, but to encourage it on for next year.

Around these central activities, there was also singing and dancing and even a chess tournament. The singing was mainly the preserve of little girls and old ladies, clearly enjoying their chance to get up in public with a microphone – to my untutored English ears, it sounded like high-pitched wailing, but everyone seemed to be enjoying it. It was clear that the *nadaam* is a great opportunity for people from the outlying rural areas to get together and catch up, much like a big fete at home, complete with screeching feedback from the announcer's sound system. Mishig was keen that I give a speech, so I dutifully introduced myself and said where I was from – not that anybody took a blind bit of notice. I'd been practising a few lines of Mongolian, and even tried a weak joke, but most people just carried on their conversations, oblivious to the amplified background din.

Nadaam over, we said goodbye to Nimhu, Nimdala and, just as sadly, Fred. Mishig had decided it would be better for me to ride a horse belonging to the family I'd be staying with. After a couple more nights at our guesthouse, finalizing our plans, we boarded Mishig's big white truck and lumbered off across the open grassland of the steppe to find our family.

Even though he didn't speak any English, with the help of Cinbat's translations I was getting to know Mishig quite well by now. He was critical of the old Communist regime and pretty right wing in response. He didn't even believe in the idea of a welfare state; it removed people's self-sufficiency, he said, and made them lazy. He believed that on principle people should pay for their schools and doctors. Interestingly, this hardline view seemed quite common among many of the people I met.

Our drive out was interrupted frequently with calls on various family *gers*, as Mishig delivered medicine or checked on sick or wounded animals. Wolf attacks are common in this remote area, and we saw evidence of this at one of the *gers* we stopped at: two savagely attacked and mauled foals.

Finally, at the end of a long day, we arrived at the settlement that would be our home for the next month: two *gers* set up by a permanent wooden cabin. In one lived our family. As we jumped down from the truck, the family group came towards us, all smiles in the evening light: father Batbayer and mother Puruhan, and their children Purusuran (sixteen), Delgilmoron (nine), Batana (four), and baby Bachdelgin, not yet one. Next door, in their own *ger*, lived Batbayer's parents Banzarich and his wife Densmaa. Purusuran had been adopted from Puruhan's sister, in part to help look after Delgilmoron, who had suffered a stroke at a young age and needed constant care, as she was not able to form coherent words or stand up. The family were wonderful with her – they included her in everything, took her everywhere in her wheelchair or pushchair and showered her with love. Although she couldn't speak, her frequent laughter suggested she was a very happy child.

I shook their hands, repeating my name, then bent down to greet the stern-faced little boy Batana, little realizing what a bizarre and territorial relationship I was going to have with him over the coming month.

Mishig had brought another *ger*, for himself, Maggie and the crew, which we erected that evening, about twenty metres away from the family's. The *gers* are beautifully made, a thing of wonder as they go up. One person holds up a central wheel while the others fix long poles into it like spokes, which fan out to the edges of the walls. Then a concertinaed, curved lattice wall is positioned, and covered with sections of thick white felt, to keep out the bitter cold. The temperature fluctuated madly during our stay; it was often sunny and warm in the day but could easily drop to minus twenty at night.

Each *ger* has a stove at its centre, which stays lit much of the time. There are rugs on the floor, homely pieces of furniture – chairs and a table and cupboards – and pictures on the walls. It's all very traditional, but also makes use of modern hi-tech equipment where it's useful. Batbayer's *ger* had solar panels on the roof for electricity, and there was a portable satellite dish for the television, which they had enough power to watch for an hour a night if they wanted to – not that Mongolian TV's one channel was that inspiring, featuring blank-faced news-readers and government stooges, endless programmes of dancing and judo competitions, appallingly dubbed, prehistoric Hollywood B movies, and, for some strange reason, countless shampoo commercials.

That first night I stayed with Mishig and the crew in the new *ger*, and we called round to the family with a gift of the local vodka and a bottle of twelve-year-old Scotch I'd bought at Heathrow. The vodka went down well, but you could see from their wincing expressions that the Laphroaig wasn't quite to their taste. Our communication was more with smiles, nods and facial expressions than with talk, but Cinbat translated a generous welcome from Batbayer, saying how happy they were to have me to stay, and glad that I was taking an interest in their lives. I was happy too: I could see from his and his wife's glowing, friendly faces that I would be made very welcome. This is no exaggeration: perhaps it was all the exercise they took, or the contrast between the cold exterior and the hot fireside, but their faces really did seem to exude warmth – and Batbayer, in particular, had the smiliest expression.

By now I had learnt to apologize in advance in case I made any cultural faux pas and to ask for my family's help in correcting me. And, as it happened, I'd already made a mistake. When I'd taken out my gift of whisky and said, 'This is for you, we'll have it later,' and placed it on the ground, what I *should* have done was hand it straight to my host, Batbayer, looking him in the eye as I did so. It was then up to him to pour a slug into their beautiful silver-plated drinking bowl, which he must give to the most senior person present. Then a blessing would follow. With eye contact maintained, the bowl had to be passed back to the host, who would then refill the bowl and hand it in turn to the second most senior person.

We had similar fun with the snuff, which also came out that evening. Luckily Cinbat was on hand to guide me this time. On receiving the snuff bottle, you take it in your right hand, turn it round and look at it before taking snuff. If it's a particularly beautiful bottle you should notice that and say so. Then you remove the cork, take the little spoon between your right forefinger and thumb, transfer it to your left hand, then sniff the snuff. It was quite a little ritual and it took me a couple of attempts to get right.

After my usual couple of days with the crew, I moved into the main family *ger*. Batbayer had suggested I stay with his father, Banzarich, and his wife. There would be more room there and it would be quieter, he said. But I was keen to get into the thick of family life, for all the noise and lack of privacy that entailed. We all ate, chatted and slept together, crashed out on rugs on the floor. How the parents ever got a quiet moment to themselves, let alone a private one, is a mystery. Even the outside harboured no hiding places – not a bush or bike shed in sight.

Though I got on very well with Batbayer and Puruhan,

bonding with their children was, for a change, going to be much harder. The adopted niece, sixteen-year-old Purusuran, kept herself to herself, and would only return my smile with a very brief one. Delgilmoron could only communicate through gurgles and smiles; she normally sat in her pushchair by the stove. As for stony-faced little Batana, he was truly a force to be reckoned with: four going on fourteen. Batbayer told me it was typical in the families he knew for the children to be allowed a free rein to be kids until they were seven, and then they were expected to help out. In little Batana's case, he had started to be a working family member already. To him, play was copying his father and learning the skills of life on the steppe. If Batbayer was out collecting goats, little Batana would be with him, running around pulling on their tails and trying to help. When his dad was chopping wood, he'd be doing it too, with a smaller knife and smaller logs, but chopping wood he would be, and the shards of timber would all be collected up like his father's and gratefully received in the family home by his mother. When Puruhan was cooking, he would be right beside her, replicating her every move. He rarely smiled, and never at me. I had no obvious skills to copy: I got the impression he thought me a bit of an idiot.

Batbayer's sixty-nine-year-old father, Banzarich, was a wonderful character with an intriguing outlook on life. In stark contrast to Mishig, he looked back on the Communist years with affection. He proudly showed me the medal he had received from the state for being a competent bull herder, an inscribed gold circle hanging from a gold-edged triangle in maroon and blue. These days, he said, there was nobody to tell you what to do, whereas in the old days your life was mapped out; people worked harder then and got their skills to a higher standard. As he told me this, he gestured over towards an axe handle that a neighbouring boy was carving and fitting to a blade. 'The quality of the work these days is rubbish,' he scoffed.

Never having travelled to an ex-Soviet country before, I

found his attitude fascinating – and felt a bit ashamed that back in the cold war years I'd allowed myself to be brainwashed into accepting that Communism was universally hated by all. For Banzarich at least, the old system – as far as it worked in the Mongolian steppe – had clearly brought many good things.

I joined in with the daily routine, waking at five in the morning for a breakfast of milky tea, bread and the very hard cheese that was one of their staples. Then it would be out to help where I could. It was an interesting contrast to my earlier trips, where I'd always been the centre of attention, with people watching and hanging around wherever I went. Here they didn't give a damn; I was there to help, so they showed me what to do and I got on with it.

As usual I wasn't very good at most of the necessary activities, but I did my best to get stuck in. Every day was different in the corral, but some tasks were always the same: first off, the milking, which meant taking the calves from the pen where they were kept by night, one by one, to find their mothers. As soon as they nuzzled up to the teat and started to drink, they had to be pulled off, led away and tied up, while Puruhan got to work milking the now-lactating cow. Once they'd given a bucket-load, you could then let the calf go back and finish off its breakfast. Then you'd go and find the next calf and take it to the next mother; and so on. After milking we had some new chore, often maintenance in preparation for the upcoming migration, when everything has to be in perfect working condition. In previous *Tribe* programmes, local activities would often stop to let me be filmed at work; but here there was too much to do. Graham followed me around, filming where he could.

As well as bread and cheese, Puruhan made flour noodles, which we often ate with lamb, usually served up as meatballs. Batbayer's method of slaughtering the sheep was a new one to me: he pinned the animal down, made a slight incision in the abdomen, then stuck a hand up through the intestines, through the diaphragm and round past the lungs and heart to find the vertebral column. Then he hooked a finger round the media sternum – where the vital blood vessels and nerves are – and sharply pulled. Apart from at the first incision, the animal wouldn't flinch. Once the nerves were ruptured, death seemed to be instantaneous and painless. For a moment the creature's eyes would bulge wildly, then the animal would go limp. Extraordinary.

Even as the regular daily work went on, preparations were being made for the big move. The oxen were haltered, the yaks tethered and saddled – in itself no small challenge. They had been wandering around the pasture freely for three or four months, and the last thing they wanted was a wooden saddle on their backs; then, even as they jumped and jostled, we had to hook the harness back through the septum in their noses.

If the family's life was hard, it also seemed beautifully straight-forward. Puruhan had met Batbayer, she told me, when she was in high school:

'He looked good, and he thought I looked good, so we went out. Our parents approved, so we got married when I was twenty-one. My parents gave us some animals and so did Batbayer's. So when we started life together we had a hundred animals of our own.'

Had their courtship been as straightforward as this translation of her story made it seem? Perhaps it really had. And watching their happy companionship each evening, with the family around them, it was hard not to feel that this simplicity had a lot going for it.

As daily life went on in and around the *ger*, occasionally travel-ling tradesmen would appear offering goods and services. One day a truck arrived with necessities that could only come from outside: boots, clothes, supplies of flour and rice, as well as crucial pills and drugs. It was a bizarre sight, this giant colourful market stall marooned in the middle of nowhere. Puruhan produced a ready stash of cash, made from selling sheep, to pay her bill. In this family she was responsible for the sheep and goats while Batbayer was in charge of the larger livestock.

On another day, a TV repairman appeared out of nowhere to fix the satellite dish, which had gone on the blink. He arrived very late in the evening, with a female assistant. We were already lying out on the floor, trying to get to sleep, and in the silence we all at once became aware of their approach. First came the sound of the vehicle, then stumbling and crashing, then sniggering and singing, then the little *ger* door burst wide open. Even though the TV guy was visibly the worse for wear, once he'd got the TV working again – which took all of five minutes – Batbayer hospitably brought out some vodka and bits of bread and cheese to entertain them both, even though he was clearly exhausted at the end of a long day and wished, like the rest of us, to crash back out and get some sleep.

Eventually the boozy pair headed off back into the night. No sooner had I fallen asleep again than there was another commotion. People had arrived outside and there was the sound of urgent talk. I lay on the floor, drugged with tiredness, wrapped in the warmth of my blanket, wondering who it could be this time. I assumed it was something to do with a wolf-attack. As always, I didn't want to be a nuisance or get in the way, so I decided to stay put unless someone called me; nobody did. Batbayer rode off into the night with Purusuran and the rest of us were left in darkness.

In the morning it became clear what had happened. There had been, Cinbat explained, a terrible family tragedy: Puruhan's niece, the sister of Purusuran, had killed herself. Batbayer had gone to join his relatives and take his adopted daughter immediately to be with her original family. That evening he returned for his wife, even as other family members were beginning to arrive from elsewhere to help.

I went over to the crew tent to discuss with Graham and Willow what we should do about this unexpected crisis. Cinbat and Mishig explained that both Batbayer and Puruhan were OK with us staying and carrying on filming. I thought about it long and hard, but knew that no matter how much I might try to be of use to them at this difficult time, it was obvious that we were really nothing more than a hindrance. There was no question in my mind: they needed time away from us and the cameras.

So we took off in Mishig's truck and drove back to Rinchinlhümbe, where we did a bit more background filming while Willow got to work with Cinbat on translating the footage we'd already recorded. This is a behind-the-scenes job that takes up a great deal of time with each programme, but is absolutely crucial and must, of course, be done on site. Quite apart from the potential difficulty of finding a Mongolian speaker back in Cardiff, the translations of what people have said to us often throw up insights that we need to act on in the filming.

After a week away, we trundled back over the frozen steppe in Mishig's truck. As soon as we saw Batbayer and his family again, I was glad we had given them space to deal with their tragedy; they now seemed genuinely ready to welcome us back. Teenager Purusuran was no longer with them; she had gone back to live with her real mother, for the time being at least. We offered our sympathies again and then the subject was dropped. A dreadful and unusual thing had happened – suicide, Mishig explained, is very rare in that community – but they weren't going to dwell on it in our company. We were back to the normality of the hard daily round. The time for the *naduul* was fast approaching, and the preparations had to go on.

Back at the beginning of our stay I'd seen the damage that wolves could do to the livestock. As we'd driven up that first time from Rinchinlhümbe with Mishig we'd seen, at one of the *gers* we stopped at, two horribly savaged ponies. There had been much talk around the fire about how the wolves hunt in packs at night, and not always to kill; sometimes they'll just attack and maim a horse or pony before moving on to the next one. In this area alone, 200 out of every 300 newborn foals are lost to wolves, Mishig told me – a remarkable statistic.

A recent attack on some horses at a nearby *ger* had prompted the decision among the people of the area to have a wolf hunt. It amazed me how quickly word got out. There were no mobiles, walkie-talkies or telephones up here, yet when we all turned up one morning at the allotted place, there was a healthy gathering of hunters, twenty or more.

As we sat and waited for the full complement, I got chatting to one of the local characters, a man famous for having over a thousand head of livestock – pretty much a millionaire in local terms. He had a brand-new white jeep and an equally smart blue fleece. Edging over to join us and – fairly obviously – get in the camera frame, he grinned broadly as he offered me snuff from a beautifully carved stone bottle.

He was so keen to be in the film, I felt confident in asking him a difficult question. Given that the Soviet collectivization had ended only a decade or so before, and numbers of livestock shared back out to the herders had been strictly controlled to perhaps a hundred per head, how had he managed to build up such a huge herd in such a short space of time? Cinbat delivered the question straight-faced, but I could see the beginnings of a wry smile at the millionaire's otherwise deadpan answer.

'I do it,' Cinbat translated, 'by hard work and being concerned about my animals. I try not to give them to the wolves. I stay up working most of the night and even lose sleep thinking about them.'

Wow, I thought, that's pretty focused and industrious . . . until Batbayer explained the truth a little later. The millionaire had come from a rich family. When the Soviets had introduced collectivization in the 1970s, he had made private arrangements with local families to distribute his herd, on the understanding that if and when things returned to normal, he could have his animals back again; and for their trouble, he would give them a percentage of what he had, in effect, lent them. So when collectivization ended in the 1990s, he had been able to restore his herd quickly to what he'd had before.

Once everyone had gathered, we mounted our horses and rode off towards the dense woods that ran up the lowest slopes of the mighty mountains all around us – wolf country. Here we split into two groups: the men with the guns rode on ahead, to form a long line beyond a chosen clearing; the rest of us got right in among the trees, dropping off a horseman every hundred metres or so. We waited at our individual posts for a signal, then started trotting in a long extended line, whooping and cheering as we went, hopefully driving any lurking wolves out of their lairs and into the line of the guns.

This was how it worked in theory. In practice, it was all more haphazard. On more than one occasion my horse bolted in the middle of the wood. It would get spooked by something and shoot off through the trees, branches and twigs breaking in my face. Once I saw a huge head-height bough looming. As certain death raced towards me, I tugged hard on the reins; to no avail. The horse thundered on through the crackling undergrowth. It was too late to lean forward or duck – I leant right back, yanking on the reins as I stared skywards, and managed to stop the animal just as the rough bark of the bough pressed against my upturned chin.

Not content with trying to kill me that way, my horse kept falling over! Once, we were all in a line crossing a boggy patch of ground one after the other. The bog had a skin of ice just thin enough for the horses' hooves to break through. It was treacherous and I did feel bad for my poor steed. As he sank in deep, right up to his rump, I patted and encouraged him. Then, as we squelched along behind the others, he simply leant to the left and fell over, and just lay there on my leg, so that I was trapped and sinking into the freezing bog. No other horse was doing this. Everyone else looked down at me and pissed themselves laughing. I had to concede the funny side, but it wasn't so amusing when he kept doing it in the middle of the woods, when we were all alone and I had no one to share the moment with. Where was my lovely Fred?

We had five or six long drives through the woods; but at the end of the day we'd got nothing. One of the old hunters explained, as we sat for a short while on the steppe drinking a post-hunt shot or two of vodka, that wolves are very smart animals: 'They think like humans and can outwit us.'

It wasn't until our second day out, a few days later, that we finally caught one. I'd been out with the beaters most of the day, then I'd moved round to be with the guns for the last drive, so even though I didn't see the actual kill, I was close enough. Five separate shots rang out as the wolf ran up the clearing – and then silence. After all this hard work, it was a rewarding moment for the hunters. The man who had hit the wolf was wreathed in smiles as everyone congratulated him. Then we all gathered round to look at the victim. As I studied the mass of sharp white teeth in its gaping snout, I could see why these creatures loom so large in these people's lives. In some parts of adjacent Siberia, it's taboo to even mention a wolf by name. The language translates as 'him with the dangerous mouth'.

A few days after the second hunt we went to meet the local shaman. The Communists may have killed almost all the lamas and other religious figures, but some shamanizing survived underground. The need to believe in something still looms large in this beautiful world of vast steppe and mighty mountains, dark nights, bright stars, huge moons, ravaging wolves and raging blizzards. Puruhan was more Buddhist in her beliefs, but for Batbayer shamans and their animist world of spirits were undeniably real.

The particular shaman he wanted us to meet lived a good two hours' ride away. I had imagined that the spiritualist might be something of a recluse, a Mongolian version of Jorsing's *miri*.

But when we arrived at his *ger*, he seemed to be a completely regular guy, dressed in the same traditional attire as everyone else, with his wife and family all around him, ready to welcome us in for tea, bread and hard cheese. We sat with him for a while as Batbayer asked questions he wanted the spirits to answer. How was the migration going to go? What did the future hold? Then the shaman went to one side of the big tent and casually and visibly donned his outfit. His magnificent headdress consisted of a wide headband, from which sprouted a mass of tall and colourful feathers, with a front protrusion rather like a table-tennis bat coming down to cover his face; on its flat surface was a crudely painted red-lipped face. Around his torso was wrapped a tasselled cloak in a mass of colours, mainly blue and white, but with bright strips of green and yellow and red in the mix. Two family members stood by to assist him.

The ceremony began without flamboyance. The shaman picked up a large shallow drum and started to bang out a regular rhythm. He held his head right inside the drum itself, next to the tight skin where the percussion must have been incredibly loud. This continued for some time, until he was visibly acting differently and apparently lost in a deep trance. Then he began to dance in a very exaggerated way, his body thrashing wildly around the room, his plumage swirling through the air in a kaleidoscope of colour, so that he looked like a huge crazy jungle bird, trapped in this tiny space. Eventually he fell back with a dramatic gesture – his whole body pivoted from his feet without his torso bending at all. He would have landed on me with some force had not his two helpers anticipated this movement and positioned themselves in the exact position to be able to catch him. They had moved into place some moments before, and I was watching their preparations as much as I was following his moves. They then lowered him gently until he was writhing around on the floor, foaming at the mouth, muttering to himself and making weird choking noises, almost as if he were trying to be sick.

His incantations were repetitive and a bit of a garble, but his helpers seemed to understand them. At some times they would light a cigarette and pass it to him, at others they would offer him various alcoholic drinks, as each spirit requested different refreshments as payment for their advice or sacred knowledge. Though his assistants did their best to help, most drinks were spilt down his chest as he continued to writhe. Finally, still lolloping clumsily around the place, he was helped back into his everyday clothes. Once he was re-dressed, as if by magic his eyes sprung open again and it was all over. It was a fantastic performance.

He sat with us for a while, calmly drinking tea and telling of what he'd seen and experienced. When he beat the drum, he explained, the spirits heard it across the valley and gathered on his roof. 'When I'm in a trance,' he said, 'the spirits communicate in signs. If they are angry, they send images of wolves threatening our livestock. By signs like these, I can understand what the spirits are telling me.' He had spoken directly to four spirits that evening, he told us.

Batbayer sat nodding and taking it all in. He was happy with the answers the spirits had given to the shaman, that his journey over the mountain pass would go fine and the immediate future held no serious worries for him.

'We rely on our shaman and ask him to remove any problems we may encounter during our migration,' he told me.

How much he and the others really believed in it all was hard to tell. 'It gives you the confidence to think everything will be fine if he says so,' was the more subtle way a wizened old friend of Banzarich's put it later. 'It's just a matter of reassuring yourself because you need to hear it.' Mishig and Cinbat were with us too and went along with the whole performance. But I got the feeling from the expressions on their faces that they were more sceptical than Batbayer.

As for the shaman himself, he was moving to Ulaanbaatar. It was hard for him to make a living any more in this remote rural area. In town, he said, he would have more clients. He was also angry because he felt that many of the town shamans were bogus and were getting rich on false pretences.

Every day the mountains had been getting a little whiter, the icing-sugar coating of their peaks spreading further and further down towards the golden-brown larch woods below. The ice on the ground was getting thicker; now you could walk on it without slipping through. The *naduul* was imminent and Batbayer and Puruhan's preparations were approaching their final stages. The yaks were harnessed and saddled, stamping and bucking as they got ready to move again. We crossed the valley to help collect sacks of salt-lick for the animals to use through the winter. Then crates and saddlebags appeared and were packed up. Batbayer had slaughtered a sheep, to provide meat for the journey, while Puruhan baked special biscuits. We were almost ready to go.

One of the men we'd met on the hunt had some Bactrian camels. Quite apart from looking great, these huge hairy beasts provide a much better platform to film from than a horse; they're higher off the ground and their forward motion is so much smoother. So, with Mishig's help, we arranged to add the camels to our family's caravan. Graham's film of the migration would be all the more spectacular as a result.

I, meanwhile, was trying to get stuck in and be as helpful as I could. The tying of knots and strapping of boxes and bags to the sides of camels is something I've done plenty of times before – during my crossing of the Ethiopian Danakil desert, for example. But here they had a completely different method from that of the African camel hands. Every time I'd try to tie something, Batbayer or one of the others would come over and say, 'No, no, not like that.' Once again, I felt a bit useless until I mastered it their way.

Finally the day came when we were ready to leave. The mysterious system of steppe communication was at work again, as we were joined at dawn by numerous helpers from other *gers*. Very quickly the tents came down and were stacked away. Then the children were loaded into open, padded crates that would sit on the sides of yaks. Then Banzarich's sister-in-law was made comfortable in a wheelless ox dray – she sat there smoking, surveying all before her with a wonderfully impassive expression. There was no great commotion, no shouting or running, just people quietly getting on with their allotted tasks. At last, totally without ceremony, we were off, a huge herd of mixed animals heading in a straight line along the edge of the mountain.

At the front were the horses, trotting along without baggage; they were the wildest of all our animals. Then came the yaks and oxen, laden down with crates and bags; at the back were the sheep and goats. We were up on horseback, but any guiding of the animals seemed unnecessary: they already knew the way. It was all beautifully quiet, just the sound of hooves on hard ground, the rustling of legs in the long green-brown steppe grass, the occasional whinny of a mare from the front, or the bleat of a sheep or goat from the back.

After five hours on the trail, we stopped to make camp at a place that had clearly seen many a migrating herd before, complete with ready-made wooden corrals for the sheep and goats. The yaks had their bags and boxes taken off and were tied up by long leads to wooden poles. The horses were left to their own devices. I thought it seemed like only half a day's journey, but it was important, Batbayer explained, that all the animals had time to graze.

In just a few fast minutes, the small travelling *ger* was erected and a fire lit. We were soon inside, sitting drinking tea, chewing cold ribs and munching bread and hard cheese. Batbayer told me I'd looked sad on the ride. No, I replied, I was just thoughtful: the sheer beauty of the spectacle had affected me deeply.

On the second day, we were up early. Now we turned right off the steppe and up through the pass over the mountains. The trail narrowed as it cut through the mountain's thick skirt of woodland. The loosely advancing herd bunched up, four abreast, to make a kilometre-long caravan of animals – a fine sight from my saddle halfway back. Then the trail got steeper, there were freezing streams to cross, and the air was noticeably cooler.

Like the famous river crossings of the Serengeti wildebeest during their migration, you could see that no one animal wanted to be first into the icy water until the pressure from behind forced them. Then there was a sudden surge and they all struggled to swim across, bleating and screaming from the pain of the cold. It's common, Mishig told us, to lose animals when they ford such freezing water. Families who were not travelling with elderly or disabled family members, would generally take their chances with the cold and do their migration later, when the streams are an iced-over solid surface.

After another long morning's ride we made camp again, in a clearing at the forest's edge. While we were unloading, corralling and tying up the other animals, the horses were noticeably skittish. This woodland was an area where there were wolves, Batbayer said, and they could sense it. He and the other men were also worried about the look of the sky. The brilliant blue of the morning had been replaced by lowering grey clouds. 'Usually when it's like this it starts snowing,' he said. 'By afternoon there'll be a storm in the pass.' This was the thing they feared most: a white-out. Animals and men had died up here in blizzards in the past. Graham, Willow and I were, to be honest, in two minds. Our overriding desire was the safest and easiest journey for our friends in the family, but mixed with that were our TV heads. On the one hand a whiteout would make for dull filming as we really wanted to see the peaks and the pass. On the other, what magnificent drama, a wonderful conclusion to our film – and we really wanted deep snow. To cover all possibilities, I recorded a little piece to camera where I looked nervously up at the darkening sky.

But by the morning the clouds had cleared and the sky was a glorious blue again. Batbayer's relief was obvious on his face. We pushed on up the pass in the bright sunshine, the animals making tracks in the crisp white snow. It was steep now, and Mishig's truck, which had been following at the back, could go no further. Graham and Willow, meanwhile, had gone ahead on horses to get a good view of the animals approaching. Poor Graham had to climb to his final filming position on foot. On watching the rushes back later, I had to laugh – he was all over the place, stumbling and breathing heavily into the microphone.

At the top of the pass there was another *ovoo*. We paused and dismounted to make the traditional three circuits. As we walked round, making our prayers to the spirits for Past, Present and Future, something remarkable happened: po-faced little Batana, who had been sparring with me from day one, reached up and put his warm hand in mine. Acceptance at last! It was funny how with this family, it had been the children who had taken the longest to adjust to my presence.

Our journey was by no means over yet. The track along the top of the pass was the most treacherous part, with bogs to either side and sheer drops not far off. Now we horsemen were working hard, cantering off to the sides to bring in stray cattle, helping others who had got stuck in the mud. I could see why Batbayer had been worried about the weather – this would be no fun in a blizzard.

We were in the saddle for much longer that day, but finally we came to the end of the pass and saw down to the other side. There were the snow-free brown grasslands of the winter pastures, with Lake Hövsgöl gleaming its deep cobalt blue in the distance. We rode down the gentle slope and into the valley and made camp at the base of the mountains that night for the last time. Sadly, in the morning we were going our separate ways: Batbayer, Puruhan and the others heading on down to set up their *gers* by the lake; the crew and I going back over the pass to find Mishig and Maggie, then driving back to Rinchinlhümbe and Ulaanbaatar, before flying home.

The relief at seeing the pastures was all too clear on our family's faces. All had made it across in one piece with no major dramas. The bitterly cold winter would now be spent in the area by the lake where the wind is so strong that the snow never settles and the animals can always graze.

Batbayer had said I looked sad as I rode, and it would be a lie to say I didn't feel more than a few pangs of melancholy leaving my wonderful hosts in that beautiful place. I won't get sentimental and say I don't enjoy my hectic existence at home, but there is a deeply enviable serenity about their lives. I tried desperately not to over-romanticize, but I couldn't help but think that some aspects of their community and its wonderfully generous habits, their hospitality and way of sharing, put my cynical, materialistic life to shame. Puruhan had talked about her ambitions for little Batana: getting him to school so that maybe he could, in her words, 'improve himself', become an engineer or a doctor. But part of me hoped he would carry on the family tradition.

'What makes you happy?' I asked Batbayer, in our final chat on camera before we headed back.

He smiled. 'It's very simple: there's the work I have to do, and the peace in my mind.'

'Stress-free living?' I suggested, then listened as Cinbat struggled to translate 'stress'. But he couldn't. It seemed he didn't know if the word even existed in Mongolian.

6. Dreams, Trips and Reality

The Sanema of the Orinoco Basin, Venezuela

We decided to make a programme about the famously fascinating Yanomami people of the Venezuelan Orinoco Delta
– specifically the Sanema, one of their sub-groups, who live
deep in the jungle, on the Caura River, near the border with
Brazil. This new episode was being directed by Jon Clay, with
Tim Butt as cameraman – it was the same tight, mobile team
as I'd had in Papua with the Kombai. As for the Venezuelan
side of things, we were using Emilio Perez: a chubby, fun guy
with experience both as a guide and in television, Emilio had
been to the UK and had worked with Jon at the famous Natural
History Unit at BBC Bristol. To complete the team, Emilio
had recruited a young Spanish-speaking German woman, Angela
Lehner, to help out with the translations on the ground.

Since the modern world made contact with the Yanomami
in the early 1950s, they have been one of the most investigated
of all indigenous groups. Napoleon Chagnon, an American
anthropologist, spent nineteen months with them in the late

1960s and wrote a bestselling book, *The Fierce People*, which stunned the scientific community by his finding that Yanomami men who had killed other men were more likely to find wives who would bear them children (implying therefore that human beings had a genetic disposition to violence). This kicked off an anthropological debate about whether Chagnon's analysis was fair; by the 1990s the criticism of him and his methods was such that he had been charged with misconduct and banned from ever visiting the area by the Venezuelan government. He was accused of exposing the Yanomami to outside infections, of trading goods for taboo cultural information and causing conflict between villagers, while one of his colleagues, Lizot, had come under fire for allegedly abusing young boys. In the meantime, however, many other anthropologists had followed Chagnon's lead in studying the Yanomami.

Whatever the truth about their temperament, it's hardly surprising that they've been much investigated. Most of the adult males are shamans, who use hallucinogenic drugs on an almost daily basis. They have an extraordinary relationship with a spirit world which encompasses everything around them: trees, rocks, water, animals – everything has a spirit, and not always a benevolent one. They see dreams, tripping and reality as all equally valid and sometimes merging. The universe has four layers and human beings have more than one soul. I'd been fascinated by the masses of research notes about these people, all of which I'd read voraciously; now I couldn't wait to meet them and see for myself.

After a few days in Caracas, we flew south to the little town of Ciudad Bolivar, where Emilio had hired no less than three light aircraft to carry the team and all our kit on the next stage, deep into the jungle. These were tiny planes, each with its own macho, big-bellied pilot, brimming with attitude, smoking fat cigars and making all-too-predictable sexist remarks. Mine got on my nerves more than a little, but I didn't want to risk any screw-ups, so I just looked out the window at the huge swathe of green jungle below and kept my thoughts to myself.

Anyone will tell you that the South American jungles are vast, but you have to fly over them to truly appreciate what that means. The thick green canopy goes on and on for ever, broken in this case only by the great silver curves of the Orinoco River, which starts at the border with Brazil and snakes down to its many-tributaried basin on the coast, 1,100 kilometres away. As in Papua, it's not hard to imagine how indigenous peoples could have lived isolated from outside influences for so long in such a place.

After a five-hour flight south, our three planes touched – or rather bumped – down on the grassy airstrip at Canaracuni, a village of the Ye'kwana, another tribal group who have historically had a close, indeed dominant, relationship with the Sanema. Having been skilled rivermen, the Ye'kwana took to trading with tribal groups up and down the various rivers in this part of the forest, latterly developing a successful relationship with the larger outside world. This gave them a head start in obtaining goods, and they now supply tools and medicines to the Sanema, who work for them in return as hunters and labourers. The Ye'kwana no longer live a completely traditional life. Their buildings are made of brick with flat corrugated-iron roofs; they have a school and a clinic, a football pitch and television.

After a night in Canaracuni we got on the river in two long dugouts. We were heading downstream and so hardly needed the outboard motor. Sections of smooth, slow-flowing water were punctuated with rocky rapids, through which our boatmen steered us expertly. Dense foliage overhung the river's surface. Apart from occasional squawks and cries of jungle birds, it was exceptionally still. I began to feel that we had at last got to where we'd intended to be: deep in the remote Amazonian forest. Round one corner we came upon a crashed plane, tilted over and rusting by the riverbank.

I sat at the back of one boat with Julio, our Sanema translator, practising the Sanema word for hello − *ma-kit-o-pa-swa-hil-e*, something of a mouthful − and trying to work out how I would get round another difficulty: supposedly, you are not allowed to use the name of a Sanema person in their presence.

After three or four hours we pulled into the riverbank and moored up. Emilio was waiting for us. He had gone ahead the previous day to make the crew's base camp and had cleared what he thought was a suitable area, before building what was almost a wooden house, complete with kitchen. It was way over the top in plushness and size. It was also positioned a good twenty-minute walk from the Sanema village where I would be staying. This was a problem: I wouldn't easily be able to grab the crew if something interesting happened that needed filming, and Jon and Tim were rather pissed off with the trek back and forth by the end of our stay. But it was too late to move it now, so we dumped the food and cooking equipment and most of the camera gear and carried on downstream to the main Sanema settlement.

The first we saw of the village was three small children waving from the top of a steep bank, where green undergrowth sprawled down over the orange-brown riverside mud. There were shouts and other, older people appeared. Some wore Western T-shirts, others were naked to the waist, dressed in shorts or slip-like red loincloths.

'*Makitopaswahile!*' I shouted as we scrambled out of the boat and up the bank. It was definitely the longest, most awkward 'hello' I'd ever used, but it earned me a resounding '*Makitopaswahile!*' in reply. Julio the translator introduced us to a short, stocky guy called Sosa, who did all the talking and seemed to be in charge. I assumed he was the *pata*, or traditional headman, who in Sanema society leads, but doesn't rule, the local people. There was no problem about uttering his or anyone else's name, it transpired; in addition to their forbidden Sanema names, they all have Spanish ones which are acceptable to use.

The village proper was at the centre of a wide jungle clearing, with tall trees encroaching all around. A string of huts surrounded a broad area of cropped grass which resembled an English village green. To one side was a big circular hut, with a conical thatched roof and tables and benches inside; this was the communal meeting place. After exchanging greetings and looking around, we moved in here and sat down, myself and the crew facing the men of the village, the women watching from the perimeter, standing, sitting on stools or lounging on hammocks. I delivered my usual spiel about wanting not just to observe but to take part in the life of the village – to be treated as a family member and not a guest; I explained that I was particularly interested in how they see the world, the shamanistic side of Sanema life.

Sosa was still obviously the main man. 'If you want to know about shamanism and the spirits,' he replied, 'then you should train to be a shaman. We can teach you how.'

Before leaving for this trip, I'd spoken to the eminent anthropologist Marcus Colchester, who has written extensively on the Sanema. He had told me they might offer me this training, and now I was excited that they had done so so early. It would give me something to work towards and provide our programme with a structure. (And unlike my Bwiti experience in Gabon, I felt a little better prepared this time.)

We had just begun to discuss how the village had been settled in the same place for twenty years ... when suddenly one of the villagers appeared from his hut and started dancing around next to us. He wore a red loincloth, a double string of white beads around his neck, and not much else. He was holding a small aluminium cooking pot, while he muttered and chanted – or rather groaned – to himself in a crazy-sounding, gratingly sing-song voice. His top lip and chin were covered in gooey black snot and had I not known different, I might have thought him mad. But I knew this was quite normal behaviour in this place; he was shamanizing, communicating with the spirits of the forest. I'd seen it on video back home, but up close and personal it was something else. I couldn't concentrate on what was being said because my eyes kept being drawn to him. Sosa followed my gaze and the conversation soon fell apart. Nobody else batted an eyelid.

The man chosen as my host was Eloy, a solemn-looking character with a monk-like pudding bowl of black hair over a sleepy face. It transpired that *he* was the *pata* – although Sosa had done most of the talking so far, he was in fact a visiting chief from another village.

We crossed the green to check out Eloy's place – my new home. It was an oblong hut built of traditional materials. The walls were thin wooden slats and the roof matted bark. Beams of bright daylight shone through on to a rough dirt floor. Sitting by a small fire inside was Eloy's wife, Todlioshoma, a small, dour woman whom I soon learnt to call 'Mama', because she'd instantly adopted me as her son. In the hut with them lived Mama's father, a blind old man who always seemed to be dribbling, and a little girl, Juliana, who I assumed to be their daughter.

After my initial few nights in camp with the crew, I moved up to Eloy and Mama's hut. I was to sleep in a traditional hammock, made up of long, two-centimetre-thick strips of a wet green tree bark, tied head and toe. It had no cross pieces, and so it was extremely easy to fall through the strips. As I struggled unsuccessfully to lie in it, the villagers gathered round to laugh. You have to get your head and feet on to each end, grip hard with one hand, then tense your whole body up in an arc between your heels and the back of your head, then use your other hand to spread the strands under your back and bum before you can relax into it. This is not easy, especially with the whole thing swinging from side to side. The tenser you are, the more the hammock swings. And if you only get three or four strands in place before relaxing, they dig hard into your arse or shoulder, like cheese wire. Then if you move a millimetre the wrong way, you'll fall through. It was a nightmare. Sensibly, most of the villagers seemed to sleep in an upgraded model of hammock, made from natural woven fibres, which at least are criss-crossed in a lattice. Mine was the only traditional one I saw during my entire trip.

My first night was even more uncomfortable than I'd imagined. Not only was the hammock a nightmare, but no sooner had I finally drifted off to sleep than I was woken by the same chanting and groaning we'd heard from the shaman in the communal hut. Barely two metres from me, Mama's father was shamanizing loudly while he seemed to be asleep – and as dreams and reality are all one to the Sanema, I could hardly tell him to shut up. It might have been a culturally intriguing experience, but to me, tired and uncomfortable in my hammock, this racket was no lullaby. I lay, sleepless, forced to listen to what sounded like the grinding whine of a moped constantly changing gear while going up a very steep hill.

No sooner had I got up the following morning than Mama handed me a big wad of tobacco to put in my mouth, under my lower lip. This is made up of leaves that have been softened by the fire, then rubbed in soot from the fireplace. It's an acrid taste, like a mouthful of charcoal dipped in petrol. I hadn't eaten much, so it gave me an instant high, and woke me from my sleepy stupor. There was no question of taking it out of my mouth and putting it to one side: Mama was adamant that I should keep it in. If I was going to live the life of the village, I must copy the other men, all of whom constantly had a black wad stretching their lower lips. I made the mistake of swallowing some of the toxic black saliva rather than spitting it out; it burnt my throat and the bitter taste lingered for more than an hour. Mama didn't care: I was told to keep it in.

Mama had rapidly understood the concept behind my stay, and soon had me working hard around the house, cleaning, collecting water and making the fire. She was the bossiest of all the hosts I'd had on any expedition so far. Cassava, also known as manioc, was the main staple here. Known in Spanish as *yuca* (not to be confused with the spiky Mexican yucca plant of the Agavaceae family), the manioc variety grown here needs heavy processing to strain out its dangerous quantities of arsenic. This is a laborious task which Mama wasted no time in assigning to me. The white tuber is peeled, then grated, then strained in long woven baskets to leach out the poison. The resulting mush is then ground to a powder and cooked. One favourite use is to bake it on a griddle over the fire to make a kind of flat bread.

I fared better, however, than poor little Juliana, with whom Mama was strict to the point of harshness. On more than one occasion I saw her grab a stick off the floor and beat Juliana. As their guest, I was unsure of what to do. I was trying to fit in with their life, and clearly this was a part of it; but at the same time, from the perspective of my culture this bordered on child abuse. It was something we discussed a lot, down in the crew camp.

I had thought Juliana was their daughter, but then I discovered the truth: despite being prepubescent, Juliana was Eloy's second wife. Her father had been Mama's brother: her parents died in a hut fire and so she had been absorbed by her closest kin. This didn't excuse Mama's cruelty towards her, but it certainly explained it.

'I was the one who told Eloy to marry the girl,' Mama told me. 'I knew I would not have more children. When I am old she will prepare the manioc for me.'

Little Juliana giggled about her situation when we interviewed her. Did she like Eloy? Jon asked.

'Yes, I like him. That's why I do what he tells me to do. But sometimes he treats me badly. He throws things at me and tells me to sleep on the floor. If he treats me like this when my breasts are large I will run away to another village.'

A perceptive child, Juliana understood that puberty would

bring another kind of relationship with her husband, but she was too young to understand what marriage would really mean. I felt sorry for her, destined for a life that had nothing to do with love or even physical attraction. Eloy was already in his late thirties. By the time Juliana reached puberty, he would be – by Sanema standards – an old man.

Eloy was quite a strange character who spent most of his time in his hammock. He was weak compared to his wife, and despite being the chief, he was bullied by the charismatic Sosa, who regarded himself as a more powerful shaman. At one point the two men fought about it. Both were tripping in the communal hut, when Sosa declared himself a better shaman than Eloy would ever be. Eloy objected, and Sosa threw him to the ground to make his point. It was a minor tussle, but it was noted by everyone as a successful show of power.

Sosa had offered to initiate me as a shaman, but first I had to understand, he said, what shamanizing was all about. So Mama painted my face and upper body with the traditional red lines and dots. Along with the feathers and furry pom-poms and fluffy white down on your forehead, these are supposed to make you look like the forest spirits – known as *hekura* – and therefore attractive to them. Then I put on a red loincloth and joined the other shamans – four-fifths of the men in the village – in the communal hut.

To get into the right frame of mind to communicate with the spirits, the men take a drug they call *ebene* – also known to the Sanema as *sakona* – made from the dried sap of the virola tree. The sap is collected, carefully simmered down to a sticky residue which is allowed to cool, mixed with leaves, ground to a powdered snuff and then blown (by another shaman) up your nose through a hollow green bamboo shoot. It contains a compound called dimethyltryptamine (DMT), one of the most powerful hallucinogens known to humankind. Other forms of tryptamine are found in psilocybin mushrooms and other plant sources used by other cultures, including, historically, some in northern Europe. One of the common reported hallucinations is of small fairylike beings. This could explain the *hekura* spirits which the Sanema see and talk to, once they reach an altered plane of consciousness. In their mythology, taking the drug allows the spirits to come to them and start singing through them.

This wasn't the occasion to take lots of *ebene* and get seriously intoxicated (that would come later), but to get in the mood I accepted the offer of a couple of snorts of the snuff. Again, it was pretty grim. But I felt the high gradually and, looking around, I started to feel more in tune with the crazy-dancing, chanting men than with the other straight-faced watchers, Tim and Jon included. Sosa took time out to explain to me what each song meant. This one was the armadillo spirit; this one the anteater; and this faint one here, the tortoise spirit. 'He is small, and often ill. His voice is not clear.'

The next day, in answer to my questions, Sosa elaborated. When the shamans are in a trance, they do indeed see the *hekura* spirits as tiny beings, two centimetres or so high, which occupy all animate and inanimate things, from trees and streams to animals and humans. A powerful shaman can invite particular *hekura* to occupy him. The spirits crawl in through your feet or arsehole and up into your chest cavity, then hack away at the foliage which they believe to be there. Then they string up a little hammock between your ribs and start to sing. This is the song you hear coming out of the mouths of the shamans. The more spirits he has in his chest, the more songs a shaman has and the more powerful he is: because he can then ask his *hekura* to go and perform tasks for him – even fight off the other, evil spirits who might bring illness or death.

This was how the village seemed to be; the men spent most afternoons shamanizing, taking *ebene* and talking to the spirits.

Meanwhile the women got on with running the place. Not only did they cook and look after the children, they also went out to collect manioc from the little gardens and fields they'd carved out of the jungle, made flour, spun cotton and made thread, wove baskets, gathered nuts, fruit and honey in the forest; they even chopped and carried the firewood.

One day I joined them in this task. Perhaps the gathered women were startled by the novelty of a man at work, because they just sat around watching me. It was only when it came to carrying the logs back that I realized how strong they were. I've carried baskets on my head before, but for some reason today it was unbearable. It was like having my head in a clamp, the weight screaming in at my temples. I seriously thought I might burst an eardrum; I had to keep stopping to release the pressure. If only it had been a rucksack I would have been fine.

The most obviously productive work the men got involved with was hunting. And even this wasn't an exclusively male activity. After a week or so I joined a small party on a three-day trip into the jungle. As well as Sosa and his wife and child, there were Franco and Paulino with their wives, and Paulino's brother José, who came alone.

There were no guns in this village, so we took bows and arrows and knives. The bows were nearly two metres long – almost as tall as a man – as were the arrows, which were beautifully made from straightened reeds, each with a sharp sliver of bamboo as the tip and broad feathers in a spiral at the other end. Both tip and feathers were intricately bound with a fine natural thread and finished off with resin.

We walked for a number of hours, then set up camp in the jungle. Sosa, Franco, Paulino and José got to work building a lean-to, a sturdy structure of cut branches lashed together and covered with broad flat leaves, in case of rain. The uprights were robust enough to string a hammock from. The guys found a termites' nest and used that as kindling for a fire, which acted as a smoky mosquito repellent as well as keeping away any unwelcome animals, such as jaguars.

In the morning we set off in pairs, looking for animal tracks to follow. This was more interesting than the sit–up–a–tree hunting technique of the Adi in India. I went with Paulino, whose company I enjoyed. He was a sweet, gentle man who had decided, unusually, not to become a shaman. The spirits had warned him against it, he said.

'So what about me?' I asked. What did he think of me being initiated?

'You will become a shaman,' he replied in his soft voice. 'And when you return home many ill people will come to you to be cured, because you will be a powerful shaman.'

It was a generous answer; though it did make me wonder – as I had with the Kombai – what his conception of my home might be.

Paulino and I weren't having much luck with the hunt. We'd found a couple of tracks in the mud and followed them assidu- ously through the undergrowth, but they'd petered out. Then we heard voices and the crackling of a fire – Franco and his wife had found an armadillo's den. They'd tried to dig it out but it was too deep, so they had decided to smoke the animal out. Using the ever–useful dried termites' nests, they built up a fire in the den's entrance and resealed the burrow with a mud wall, leaving a small hole to allow the fire to oxygenate. Using a broad green leaf, Franco was now fanning this opening. You could see the fire glowing inside, its smoke billowing down into the tunnels of the den. It took some time, and much taking it in turns to fan, but eventually, when the whole den had filled with smoke, the armadillo had nowhere left to hide and surfaced to make his escape – only to find a fire in his front hallway, and beyond that a mud wall, blocking his path. At this point you could hear the poor creature clearly, coughing and scrabbling, unable to get past the fire, choking to death. It was a horrible sound.

Eventually the guys dismantled the wall, cleared out the

embers and reached into the hole to drag the dead beast out. It was nearly a metre long, with a piggy snout, a fat pink underbelly, a hard, scaly brown back and a pointed tail. We ate it that evening, baked over the camp fire. Surprisingly it tasted rather bland – like smoky chicken – but had the advantage of coming with its own scaly plate. After we'd eaten, we discussed the day's hunting. I asked Paulino if this was the norm; was the jungle always short of wildlife?

'Our grandparents caught a lot of animals,' he replied, 'because they dreamt with the animal spirits. For example, they dreamt of the tapir spirit, and the next day they caught a tapir. But now the outsiders have come and told us to stop dealing with the spirits. So we catch fewer animals than our grandparents.'

When pushed, he gave another explanation: 'Now the animals live far from the village,' he said. 'They left because we hunted their families. When we were always on the move we killed many animals. But the Ye'kwana told us to stop migrating and now the hunting is poor. When our children grow up they will find very few animals. We rely more on our crops now.'

This was a different type of overhunting problem from that experienced by the Adi, with their overuse of newer hunting technology, specifically the shotgun; traditionally, they had left tracts of their territory as hunt-free zones to allow their prey to recuperate. The Sanema, however, had always been nomadic, so they had never needed to adopt this method – they would simply move their whole village when the prey density was depleted. Now, because they wanted to be in close proximity to their goods and medicine providers, the Ye'kwana, they had settled in their current location for twenty years, with consequent depletion of animal stocks.

Later that evening there was a bit of a scrap in camp between Paulino and his brother José, over Paulino's wife Oima. José had been making suggestive remarks to Oima from the moment we'd set off, even in front of Paulino, so I'd thought it was all just banter. But now José had clearly gone too far: Oima screamed and slapped him. So then he got upset and slapped her with the side of his machete. Unsurprisingly, a fight kicked off. The problem seemed to be more with José not respecting the girl's objections, rather than with any idea of infidelity as such.

I am always wary of asking questions about sexual relations. If at all possible, I prefer to get my information from the anthropological studies of experts who've lived with a group for many years and know their typical behaviour well. I always feel that starting a conversation about sex might send the wrong message when I haven't yet gained enough trust; such interviews are always best conducted in the company of only men, or only women. But it is intriguing: different cultures can have widely varying attitudes to sex. The raucous Adi teasing had been an example of that. Here, infidelity was both tolerated and common, it seemed.

When we returned to the village, Eloy and Mama had fallen sick. Traditionally, illness would have been seen as the work of evil spirits, to be cured by the healing powers of the shamans. Now, to combat modern ailments, the Sanema use modern medicines too, which they rely on the Ye'kwana to provide. So we went upriver to visit the clinic in Canaracuni. Here Eloy and his wife could receive treatment from the resident Ye'kwana medic. It was strange to see my hosts in this other village. Eloy walked round staring at his feet, almost scared to catch anyone's eye. Even bossy Mama, who was so confident back home, had an air of subservience about her when talking to a Ye'kwana. I wondered how much worse it might be when they didn't have a film crew following them round.

The relationship between the two tribal groups looked to be well established. Wonderful people though they were individually (our medic, for example, was thoroughly charming and efficient), as a group the Ye'kwana seemed to be more than content to keep the Sanema in this dependent position. Kuyajani, the NGO set up to look after the interests of the Sanema and

Willow and Graham

Nimhu (left) and Nimdala (right) with another contestant (middle)

(top left to right) Banzarich, Densmaa, local boy, Purusuran, Bachdelgin, Puruhan
(front) Batana, Delgilmoron

Heading off to wolf country

Little Juliana

Nutted, and not the only one

The Sanema of the Orinoco Basin, Venezuela

Sosa trying in vain to teach me his *hekura* song

The DMT trip gave me a new perspective on my natural surroundings

Something out of the Bible

Such wells collapsed on occasion,
potentially killing anyone in it

The Ibex being chastised – note Lokirimor being held down by three of his friends

Songs for my big day

Marks of respect for one's male relatives

Some of Suri's female relatives, including Kaira (left)

The seemingly simple act of ploughing proved almost impossible to this first-timer

Nude gymnastics

Ye'kwana in the wider world, has a strong voice, given the new apologetic climate of Venezuelan politics. But apart from a sprinkling of Sanema, the Ye'kwana have taken on the role of representing the Sanema in this organization. Confused by and perhaps scared of the complexities of such politics, the Sanema have gone along with this. Not that this was as bad as the relationship between some indigenous groups in this area and the outside world. In Caracas we'd heard stories of tribal representatives living it up in their local towns, squandering the governmental and charity donations on wine, women and song, while their friends and families deep in the forest thought their representative was working hard on their behalf. It was a complex situation, and never clear-cut.

Despite their reliance on the Ye'kwana, traditional ideas about illness hadn't been entirely eradicated from the Sanema. Mama told me about a period in recent history when a neighbouring tribe, the Waika, had been responsible for killing many Sanema. Because of the Waika's magic, she said, the Sanema had fallen ill and died. But the disease she attributed to the Waika was almost certainly something brought in by Westerners, the traders and gold miners who had invaded the area in the last twenty years, since the gold rush of 1987. (Mindful of posing a disease threat ourselves, Steve and I had made the decision at the start of *Tribe* to get inoculated against any potentially dangerous diseases: not just the usual stuff like typhoid and hepatitis A and B, to protect ourselves; but also measles, mumps, rubella, polio and other diseases which pose little threat to us, but that we could potentially pick up at an airport and carry unwittingly into a tribal community.)

Our day in the Ye'kwana town over, we piled into the dugout canoe and headed back into deep jungle. No one spoke as we glided downriver, and I gazed at the tall trees reflected all around us in the water. The next day Mama was back on her feet. Sleepy Eloy took some days to recover.

*

Throughout my stay with the Sanema, the shamans' presence dominated. They were not like the Mongolian shaman, out in his *ger*, to be consulted on special occasions; or even the Adi's *miri*, a more constant presence in the village. Here, shamanizing was the central activity, practised almost daily by many of the village men, at the core of these people's lives and beliefs.

The shamanizing men repeatedly asked whether I had yet dreamt about *hekura* spirits; or better still, been given a spirit song in my dreams. In their system, where dreams are reality, that would be just as good as little spirit men turning up on Eloy's doorstep. Sosa in particular kept on at me about this, and was disappointed when I told him that I hadn't. I suppose I could have lied but, as always, I wanted this to be a genuine experience. Who knew – perhaps one night soon I would be given a song. Sosa, meanwhile, had been dreaming about me. He had seen me, he said, among the *hekura* spirits. He had jumped on my chest and I hadn't woken up, but I had still been surrounded by them.

My full initiation didn't happen until the end of my stay. I was told not to eat for twenty-four hours; by the time we were ready to start, I was starving. The morning was quite relaxed, but around midday I could sense that people were starting to talk about the coming events. Mama led the proceedings, refer-ring to me throughout as her son. She stripped me down and gave me another bright red loincloth to wear. I hesitated for a second, not because the cloth neatly parted my bum cheeks, but because this one had been lent by Sosa – a decidedly sweaty chap. Mama wrapped it round my hips a couple of times, then between my legs to cup my genitals. (Over the course of the coming day – much to the amusement of Tim and Jon – this big red nappy kept coming loose, and I never could quite master the method for keeping it tight while high.) Next Mama painted me with swirls of red on my body and face. I had feathers tied to my head and arms and fluffy down stuck on my forehead, using banana sap as glue. Finally I had some pom-poms on sticks placed behind my ears and arm bands, giving me a very effeminate appearance. Then I was taken to the central hut, where *sakona* was already being snorted and the shamans were beginning to chant.

As my stomach was completely empty, the effect was immediate when I started to take the snuff. This time I didn't stop at a couple of snorts. At first I felt very light-headed, and soon I became dizzy. All around me was madness: everyone screaming and shouting and running in all directions, reciting their *hekura* spirit chants. They knew I needed to go deep this time, so pretty much every time anyone else had a snort, I was given one too, like a groom being primed with booze on his stag night. Everyone made sure I was the most nutted. Before long my nerves began to twitch and my head was swirling round – not a particularly pleasant sensation. From time to time someone would come within a couple of metres and leer at me, as if they could see right into me. Some would come and lean on each other and discuss the state I was in, bringing their heads really close to look into my face as if I was an inanimate object. Sosa kept pointing at me like he was aiming a pistol.

I thought if I closed my eyes I might be sick; but keeping them open was like having multicoloured lights shone on me. The other shamans danced around me, chanting, and I began to have crazy visions. The shamans became holograms, as if a 3D image of each had been imposed on top of their existing forms. I could see straight through them and these new auras.

Then – suddenly – I got it. I went into a wild mental spin and saw everything differently.

All the faces had changed dramatically and the background of trees and tables and chairs had altered to simple patterns of colour and light. The dancing shamans had become *hekura* spirits themselves; they hadn't shrunk, but they looked like magical beings, with their feathers and finery and movement, while their previously terrible grinding chants had become the most enchanting ethereal songs. They were a mix of pixies, lepre-chauns, fairies and forest spirits, all at the same time. Something clicked in my head and everything made sense; I could under-stand folklore of old. If there was a parallel universe somewhere, or even an alternate level of consciousness, I was on the brink of it at that point. And now the faces dancing around me knew it too. They nodded and winked at me in a different way. The chanting and dancing continued, but there was a new level of acceptance.

This seemed like a single moment, but it might well have lasted quite a while. I was beyond any comprehension of time. By now I was carrying my own tin pot of snuff, grabbing handfuls of the stuff and snorting it like Al Pacino in *Scarface*. It was still an unpleasant sensation to take it, but I wanted to go deeper into this magical place I was visiting. I knew this was my only chance to do it, so I wilfully went as far as I could. But my euphoria didn't last. A massive tide of nausea welled up in me and I could no longer hold it all together. I stumbled outside, temporarily blinded by the bright sunlight. I fell to my knees and vomited copiously.

I remember muttering to myself, 'My God, what is happen-ing? This is a very strange place.' As soon as I'd said it, I knew my journey on to that other plane had ended. I was aware of the crew again, enough even to hope they'd caught my words on film. I stayed there for a while, recovering, while the madness continued in the hut just a few metres away.

My deepest desire now was just to get away and lie down. I felt ashamed that I didn't want to stand up and sing with the other shamans; but I owed it to my new friends to at least try. Sosa had had his 'real' dream about me, in which I'd encoun-tered *hekura* spirits. I should now be coming out with a mantra of my own, surely! But it wasn't happening.

Finally I mustered the energy to join in, so I made my own chant. I repeated some names in a rhythm, but it didn't impress Sosa at all. It obviously wasn't in the right tongue for *hekura* spirits. I felt I was missing the point, as I had with the Bwiti elders back in Gabon, before I'd realized that all they wanted to know about was the shapes. In the end I simply started repeating Sosa's chant – I didn't know what else to do. It seemed incredibly difficult: their vocal range is extraordinarily versatile. They were using all kinds of sounds – from the lips, tongue, mouth, stomach and throat – and I could hardly do it at all. After what seemed like an age of not getting it even vaguely right, I finally got to something approaching Sosa's song and he was happy – ecstatic in fact, hugging me and grinning. Jon and Tim filmed all this, and later they told me they'd been in hysterics because it had always been so obvious what he'd wanted me to do, but I was just so nutted I couldn't see it.

Once I started chanting Sosa's song I realized the power of that too. It was a mantra. If said over and over, it tripped you into a deeper state of trance. I could feel myself slipping away again into another place. I didn't notice that I was singing, just that my head was becoming blurred, the resonance of the sounds I was making was shaking the core of my body and my senses were spinning out of control. And then I was off again on a magical, mental journey. Looking round at all the shamans chanting their different *hekura* songs, I now realized why the songs were so powerful to them.

We had started at about ten in the morning, and continued all day. Perhaps the oddest thing that happened was around mid-afternoon: I suddenly found I was very horny. This was bewildering. When I began working on *Tribe* I was aware that there was a long history of outsiders getting involved with local people during their travels. It's not a good idea. Visitors are always in a position of power and any sexual encounters are bound to be exploitative to some degree. But this drug was a powerful aphrodisiac. Interestingly, it wasn't the obviously beautiful women I fancied, but those who'd painted their faces in a certain way. (One of the prettier girls in the village wandered by without face paint and I didn't give her a second glance.)

Here in the hut were women who'd suddenly become complete babes. You dirty little minxes, I thought, as I realized that this was unadulterated flirtation on their behalf. I wanted to grab one and run off into the bushes; it was very primal. This face-painting was clearly designed as a come-on, something I'd not have discovered had I not taken the drug. Somehow, though, I maintained my professionalism.

Towards the end of the day, I had a powerful urge to go outside and commune with nature. It was a sensation I'd felt very strongly with my *iboga* experience too. The forest seemed so much more alive than normal; I could hear things more acutely. Visually everything was heightened too, as if I could distinguish every layer of foliage stretching off into the distance; I could see so much more detail, and colours were so much more vibrant. Nature seemed truly alive and there to be cherished: our green living planet with which we were messing so dangerously.

I had had an incredible time with the Sanema, and my initiation gave me a lot to think about. As I lay there at the end, off my head, on the edge of the forest, I felt a wonderful sense of oneness with the world. I had no desire to hate, chop down a tree or fight anyone ever again. I felt a profound love for all humankind. Even as I felt this, I was thinking, 'Shut up, Parry, you knob! If your old Marine mates could hear you now! All this soft talk of love and peace and understanding. They'd so take the piss.' But that was the point. My experiences over the past year had just added to a long process of change, that had seen me move from being an indoctrinated, institutionalized Royal Marine Commando to where I was now. No wonder such substances were banned back home. Along the journey I'd learnt to see things in a new light, realize that our way of doing things back home isn't the *only* way. I'd seen at once both how fragile and how strong culture can be, and how easily we're all influenced by our own. I'd learnt to see other points of view without simply turning off because they didn't fit in with my own preconceptions. Tolerance and understanding were the two words that kept coming into my head at that moment.

Take this drug, for example. The initiation trip I'd just had had been an extraordinary and incredibly positive experience, yet I had been brought up to think of such an activity as illicit drug-taking at its worst. *Sakona* snuff was just the kind of dangerous, mind-altering substance I'd been warned off, both as a child and as a young man, as our society had successfully taught me to despise such things. I knew, of course, that all drugs are dangerous. They need to be treated with caution and respect – not forgetting caffeine, alcohol, tobacco and sugar. But these Sanema have a culture of shamans who know the right doses, how to monitor your progress, and ensure that you are to a greater degree protected. This had been true of the Babongo in Gabon too: with them I was always looked after and the whole village had ensured that I never spiralled off into a bad trip. For them, such substances were part of their culture, and a necessary, life-enhancing part too.

As I lay in that jungle clearing, it dawned on me how prejudiced my previous deep hatred of so many things had been; starting at home and reinforced all my institutionalized life. I am a product of my society and culture as much as these indigenous people are of theirs. This applied to so many other things I'd experienced in this past year.

And with each episode of *Tribe* that I'd made, another realization had been growing stronger: I knew that I would never fully understand what it was like to truly live within another culture. How could I ever know or believe that dreams, trips and reality were the same? And if I couldn't understand it, how could I ever judge it?

I then looked at Tim and Jon and thought about the team back in Wales. It had been a difficult yet profound year for all the people involved in the making of the series. We had no idea how the viewing public would take it, though expected some sort of backlash from the anthropological community. But I didn't care any more; my bit was all but finished. I was knackered.

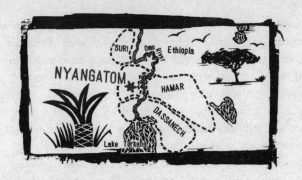

7. The Yellow Guns

The Nyangatom of the Omo Valley, Ethiopia

I was back in Africa again after almost a year away from *Tribe*, all set to get stuck in to a second series. So much had happened in the eleven months since I'd been in Venezuela with the Sanema – not least that the first series had been broadcast and suddenly my whole life seemed like a runaway train.

Meanwhile, thanks to the surprise success of the series, the BBC heads wanted *Tribe* back on screen as soon as possible. To meet our new deadline, the next three programmes would have to be done in the same geographical location. Series producer Steve Robinson knew only one person could pull off this difficult feat for him – James Smith, who'd made the Adi and Suri films. James accepted the challenge and decided he wanted to go back to the area where we'd stayed with the Suri: the Omo Valley in south-western Ethiopia. We would begin the new series by revisiting our old friends, before heading off to meet their sworn enemies over the mountain – the fearsome Bume, or Nyangatom, as they are also known.

Alongside James on this extended three-month trip were cameraman Jon Clay, veteran of Gabon, Papua, Ethiopia and Venezuela, and Willow Murton, our long-time researcher in Cardiff, who'd been with me in Mongolia. New to the gang was researcher Jane Atkins, ideal for this job as she'd lived in Africa and knew Ethiopia well. We'd recruited the same wonderful Ethiopian fixer, Zablon Beyene, who had made things run so smoothly with the Suri. It was a great team.

Four days out of Addis Ababa, we started to see tell-tale signs that we were coming into Suri lands. There were cattle-herders with big white grins, naked but for a tartan shawl, waving from the roadside; men with big droopy earrings, women with lip-plates. Suddenly we all felt apprehensive: this was the first time any of us had revisited a *Tribe* location. How would we be received?

As we slowed down to ford a river, a group of kids playing in the water gathered round, laughing and chattering. Then: 'Bruce! Bruce!' one cried. I didn't recall his face, but he certainly remembered me. Then another kid came up and wanted to lift up my T-shirt and look for the scar on my arm. When they saw the special marking the Suri women had cut into my shoulder with razor blades they started going mad, dancing around and laughing and shouting 'Bruce! Bruce!' and wanting to shake my hand.

Ten kilometres further on, we arrived at the town of Kibish and the familiar sight of the police compound, shimmering in the mid-morning heat. I could hardly believe we were back. Luckily James and Jon were ready with the cameras, because I was greeted like the prodigal son. One of our old guards in particular just couldn't stop grinning and saying my name. James and Jon were included in this big welcome and many asked after Hannah.

Unfortunately my old translator and friend Chagi was no longer living in the area, so Zablon found a Suri–Amharic speaker and we set off to meet our old friends in the nearby village of Regia, where I had stayed before. We were told that a new dirt road had been cleared all the way to the crew's old campsite by the river. Why? We were soon to find out. On arrival we saw the whole area was covered with tents. What did this mean? Had the success of our programme turned Kibish and Regia into tourist attractions? But no, we were told, it was a French TV crew, who'd been there filming for a month. I knew the success of *Tribe* had spawned a host of similar productions in the UK and America – was this as a result of us? We gave them a wide berth for the time being and headed up towards the village. On the way we came across another group of locals. They too were excited to see us. People swarmed round, touching me and checking out my scar.

'*Chalai! Chalai!*' they cried. Then, 'Bruce! *Bruchai!* How are you? Where have you been?'

While this was all happening, out of nowhere a Land Cruiser appeared, revving and hooting its horn. One of the French film crew, presumably. Willow and Jane went over and explained that we'd just arrived and were trying to catch the moment on film.

'Could you wait five minutes?' Willow asked. 'We're doing some filming. It's a really important moment for us.'

The driver had wraparound shades under a mane of hair. 'This is our patch. We'll see what the chief says about that,' he shouted. Then he drove on through, honking on his horn as he sped down to the tents, scattering locals everywhere.

As we stood in amazement at this rudeness and inconsideration, we spotted some of my old family. My heart leapt. Bargulu came over to me, smiled and shook my hand, his demeanour as dignified as ever. We did the traditional Ethiopian bow, touching alternate shoulders from side to side, then he surprised me with a hug. Next up was his wife Nabala, her extrovert friend Ndongele, and finally the *koromu*. It was so good to greet the dignified old leader, and I told him how his 'we are all one' speech had touched so many people back home;

indeed it had become the unofficial strap line for the whole first series.

James and Jon were getting lots of attention too. Everyone wanted to hug Jon while he was still filming with his big camera. We walked up through the sorghum fields to the village, to find yet more familiar faces.

'You are my friend!' cried a man I had practised stick-fighting with, baring his teeth in a huge grin. We set up a computer outside Bargulu's hut and showed everyone our film. It was bizarre: half the village was there, sitting on animal skins, in a few neat rows, shouting and laughing as they recognized themselves on screen.

'That's me! That's me!' cried a child.

'Look, there, that's my hand,' said another.

'My father looks like Haile Selassie on screen,' said the *koromu*'s son, to laughter.

Afterwards I asked Bargulu how things were. I started with the traditional form of greeting between friends. How were the cattle? Had there been rain? How were the crops? A couple of the cattle had died, Bargulu replied, but the rains had been good, the crops in the fields where I'd worked before had been good, the health of the village likewise. Regia men had been doing well in the stick-fights and there had been only minor battles with the dreaded Bume.

'And what about this French film crew? Have you had lots of visitors since we left?'

No; it seemed that they were the first Europeans the village had seen since we'd departed, over a year before.

That night it bucketed down with rain. I lay in my sleeping bag in the police compound in Kibish, worrying about the morning. Our return had gone so well, and Bargulu and the others had clearly loved our film, but today we had to break the news to them that our plan was not only to now leave again, but to go right into the territory of their sworn enemy. I didn't want them to find out about my visit to the Bume third-hand.

Somewhere deep down I felt sure that Bargulu would understand. I wanted his blessing, but letting him know would be tough.

The next afternoon, back in Regia, we kicked off our meeting with a couple of presents. Bargulu and Nabala seemed thrilled with framed photos of themselves, showing them to the other villagers with pride. Then came the difficult moment.

'I'm planning to walk down the Kibish River and into Bume land,' I told them. The joviality and laughter halted instantly, and there was silence. I could see Bargulu was upset. Not angry – that wasn't his style – just seriously worried for me.

'To visit the Bume is unthinkable,' came the translation of his solemn words. 'They are very bad people. Even if they see a small child, they will kill it. Since I was little I've known them as enemies. If you go there, we will consider you dead. They will kill you.'

I listened intently as he and others expressed their concerns. But even with my silence they knew that I *was* going. I didn't have to say anything; they could read my eyes. Eventually Bargulu simply said, 'I know you must go. I give you my blessing.'

Our next destination, a few days' walk away, was confusingly also called Kibish, though this was located deep in Bume territory. Presumably both villages were named after the river that joined them, which changed from the clear bubbling stream of the lush Suri hills to a dry river bed as it entered the arid plains. This difference in landscape and cattle pastures was such an important feature of the story of the two battling tribal groups that I'd originally wanted to trek down the river to show the difference graphically. However, the Kibish River cut straight through some battlegrounds where men had been killed just a week before. Although *I* felt safe enough about that, James wasn't keen. The BBC being the BBC, we had safety protocols to follow, and heads would roll if I was injured or killed – the main head in question being James's. Then Bargulu also asked us to go by vehicle. I didn't argue.

We said our farewells and bumped off down the narrow dirt road towards Bume territory. We were all excited about getting down there and finding out for ourselves what the Bume were really like. However, stopping for a few minutes in the next little settlement of Tulgit, we ran into an American missionary called John, whom we'd heard a lot about on our previous trip but had never met. It was a shame we were heading off, he said, because today was the big *donga sagenai* – the last stick-fight of the season. And in the evening the elders would announce the rite of passage called *rawra*, when senior adult males are made into a ruling group of elders, a ceremony that happens only about once every twenty years. As well as the French film crew we'd seen, there had been a German film-maker hanging around, John said, hoping to catch this rare event.

We were torn. Our new film wasn't about the Suri; but on the other hand, if we had a chance to catch this ceremony it might make for incredible footage. There was another consideration: things were changing so quickly in this part of the world, this could well be the last time the *rawra* ever took place. We decided we wouldn't lose anything by picking up a couple of local militia guys and going down to the *donga* field to see what was going on.

But as we approached the turn-off, our little convoy was confronted by a Suri armed guard. I was in the second vehicle, but I could see him shouting at Zablon and the women in the Land Cruiser up front. It soon transpired that he was under orders to keep us away. Orders from whom? Bargulu? The *koromu*? No, the film crew had paid him, and they had specifically mentioned us in their instructions. If that was true, then it was ridiculous. Zablon was furious and drove on regardless, taking the poor guard with us to save his face.

We sped on down the track, only to be stopped at the edge of the woods by more armed guards, this time in a little huddle. One of them even recognized me and smiled as he shook my hand. But they were adamant that we couldn't proceed. From here we were close enough to hear shouts and the crack of stick on stick through the trees. Did this other crew think they owned the entire show? Can you own an event and people? Zablon was on the warpath and the guards were becoming physical.

We could easily have outmanoeuvred them, driven back 500 metres and walked in through the woods another way; or entered the bidding war and paid a higher fee. But we decided not to bother. Zablon had a long, heated discussion, but we calmed him down and agreed that we would rise above it. We'd already filmed stick-fighting in the last series and this was not *our* way of operating. We would leave them to it.

We drove down off the hills towards the Bume, through fields where hidden boulders lurked treacherously in elephant grass that was taller than our vehicles. It was burning hot, and by the evening my arm, dangled out of the window, was scarlet with sunburn. We spent the night in the HQ of the Omo National Park, a protected tract of land where game still roam: hartebeest and gazelle, warthog, ostriches and a mass of other bird life. You wouldn't see such a wonderful sight anywhere else round here – the massive increase in guns had made sure of that.

The next morning we were finally out of the vehicle. It was so nice to be on foot again. Zablon and I and cameraman Jon and an armed National Park guide hotfooted off across the biscuit-brown scrub, Zablon setting a decent five-kilometre-an-hour pace.

We walked on until the sun sank in the sky, then set huge and crimson across the plain. The African darkness descended rapidly. You forget how bright the stars are out here, far away from the light-pollution of home. We had a fine view of Venus, looming unbelievably bright and large.

We woke at 4 a.m. and decided to get going while it was still cool. As we paced through the darkness, Zablon taught me the local greeting – '*Adjok*' – in case we encountered any wandering herdsmen. Slowly the sky grew lighter, wisps of pink cloud appeared high up, then there came that brilliant African yellow glow before the edge of the sun appeared over the distant hills. Now our route lay over bare brown earth dotted with dry green bushes. Here and there were stalagmite-like termite mounds, crazy sculptures of dried mud, towering above us. There were also some wonderful plants that looked like bonsai versions of baobab trees, topped with huge pink flowers. Eventually we came in sight of the Kibish River itself, marked out on this barren landscape by a double line of trees. As predicted, it was bone dry. What a contrast to the fast-flowing stream I'd sat beside with the *koromu*, just a couple of days before. Down here the Kibish flows for just one month each year, in the December rainy season.

We arrived at the village that James had chosen for us at almost exactly the same time as the others arrived, bringing with them our new translator Soya, a bright-eyed and energetic young guy who'd learnt his English from missionaries. They had collected him from nearby Kibish town, where they had stayed overnight while sorting out final bits and pieces for the crew camp.

Our first meeting with the Bume on the sandy river bed was wonderful. The women were strikingly beautiful, with dazzling white smiles, shiny jet-black skin and sculpted, high-cheekboned faces. They were adorned with a fine array of heavy-looking necklaces, bangles and earrings, with a different lip-piercing from the Suri: they puncture the skin below the lower lip and insert little screws and other decorative pieces. As I'd always hoped and believed, far from being in any way ferocious, they were in actual fact charming – they were even a little timid. James filmed from afar as I tried to shake hands with the children. Every time I lifted my hand, they backed off en masse, as if some invisible force emanated from my fingers. Soon enough, though, the bravest of them stepped forward to shake my hand, then one of his mates, then they all wanted to do it, till even the smallest of them had found the courage.

Now we walked up to the village proper, a sprawling oval of huts surrounded by a wall of piled-up, dried thorn branches. The huts were entirely traditional in design, beehive-shaped, and beautifully made from woven twigs. A small, low oblong door at the front was their only entry. Zablon had gone off to locate the chief and talk about our proposal to film and negotiate a payment for our stay. In this case, as well as money, we had brought many items including sacks of the coffee husks which they use for their traditional drink. All went well, and after some time I was taken to meet the chief and sit with him in the compound, next to his central mud hut. Ajam was a tall, lean, athletically built man whose face and torso were covered with lines of ritual scarring, which I knew signified the killing of enemies: half the chest for one death, a whole chest for two, half the back for three, and so on, until they move on, apparently, to scarring your wife. I immediately wondered if he had killed Suri – perhaps even relatives of Bargulu and my other friends.

This alarming scarification was offset by the chief's warm eyes and welcoming body language. Our every request was met by a high-pitched, Eddie-Murphy-style shout of acceptance, accompanied by a flick of his wrist. We were then introduced to his entourage: a posse of young, very solid and good-looking armed guards, and a group of older men, who were equally friendly. It would be fine, it seemed, for me to live in the village, and for our crew to camp nearby. With a nod from Ajam, the guards led us to a site about fifty metres away from his hut, on the west side of the dry river, which actually put us in either Kenya or Sudan, depending on who you believed – not that anybody is bothered much about borders in this lawless area. Ajam insisted too on tripling our armed guard, from two militia to six.

We pitched camp in this beautiful spot, under the shade of a vast tree, watched by a group of curious villagers as we cleared the ground and erected tents and mozzy nets and set up tables

and chairs, making ourselves at home. As well as myself and
the crew, there were all Zablon's people too: the guards and
cooks and drivers. We sat back as dinner was cooked – and
served! It seemed to be a feature of every trip I went on with
James that we were always exceedingly well looked after. I
realized that the crew had a hard job to do and they needed
their downtime, but sometimes it was laughable how comfortable we made ourselves. But I didn't complain as I retired to
the comfort of my tent and totally-over-the-top foam mattress
that Zablon had provided for each of us.

I had a lie-in the next morning, then stayed in the crew area
to help finish set up the camp. At 5 p.m., when it started to
cool in the late-afternoon light, we returned to the village with
the cameras to resume filming.

I was struck now by how closed and fortified the village
was. There were probably thirty huts in the one large compound,
surrounded by this piled-up wall of thorny branches. Here and
there were narrow openings to let the human inhabitants pass
through. When not in use, these gaps would be closed by a
huge wedge of thorns that could be rolled out of the way on
exiting, then rolled back into the gap again and secured in place
on the inside by a tied stick. A pot or pan would be balanced
on top of the stick, which would clatter and fall, alerting the
villagers, if the wedge was tampered with from the outside.

Before we entered the village, Soya put me right on a potentially disastrous faux pas. To camera I had been happily calling
these people Bume, as the Suri did, but it turned out that this,
in local dialect, meant 'the smelly ones'. We all knew that they
were also known as the Nyangatom, but I had no idea that
'Bume' was so rude.

At this time of the evening there was plenty of activity going
on around the huts. Women were grinding corn and kids ran
around playing. While those men who we saw around wore
T-shirts and other bits of Western clothing, all the women were

traditionally dressed, naked under the heavy swathes of beads around their necks, with cowhide skirts beneath. We did some filming, then went to say hello again to Ajam. He sat in his compound with his impressive machine gun, proudly polishing it with a black feather. He had been given it as a reward for several years' military service in the Sudan.

Zablon wanted to leave further negotiations till the morning, so we spent another pleasant evening in camp. The next day the news came that things had gone well. The villagers had been informed of our project and had given their consent. As we ate lunch in camp, we heard a great shout. It was the Nyangatom blessing ritual – my arrival was being formally sanctioned. I had a final wash and shave and said goodbye to lasagne and beer. Then, in the late afternoon, we headed over to the village.

We sat in Ajam's compound while one of his three wives prepared husk coffee in huge calabash gourds. This was then passed to Ajam, who took a mouthful and sprayed it all over me – a ritual blessing, apparently. Nice. Then it was my turn to spray him.

'From now on you are my son,' Ajam told me through Soya. 'I will treat you as my son and I will tell all the villagers that you are my son and you can take part in everything here. If you do this, people will really appreciate it. But if you don't look after the goats properly, if they haven't grazed enough, I will punish you, like my son.'

'Thank you,' I replied. 'I will work hard to be a good son for you.'

At last light the crew departed. Zablon stayed a further twenty minutes. Then I was left alone with Soya and Ajam and his family. Supper tonight was sorghum porridge, made from ground sorghum powder and goat's milk. There was a huge stodge of it at the bottom of a large calabash gourd and a massive wooden spoon – the size of a salad spoon – with which to eat it.

'Perhaps I should eat with my fingers?' I said to Soya, thinking I'd never get the thing into my mouth.

'No. You have to use the spoon. We all use spoons here.'

With Soya translating, Ajam and I sat among his watching entourage, talking late into the evening. Even if Soya's spoken English wasn't the best, he certainly understood well, so we were able to talk about Ajam's concerns at length: how hard life was for his villagers; how little food there was at that moment; how the best grazing for the cattle was up by the more fertile Suri land, but it wasn't safe for them to leave their cattle there because they would be taken by the Suri.

'I want peace with the Suri,' Ajam told me. And then: 'If an outsider were to set up a school for Nyangatom and Suri children, then we could make peace and farm together.'

I thought of Bargulu's portrayal of the Bume as child-killers and rapists and wondered privately if they could ever trust each other. But for the time being my philosophy had proved true, for me at least: that if you get people on their own land on their own terms, treat them with respect and humility, they are always welcoming.

The chief now offered me a choice of three huts to sleep in. There was laughter and big cheers from the entourage when I chose the nearest one to his, which happened to belong to his third and youngest wife, Naqua. But in the end, after more long discussions with Soya, it was decided we'd sleep outside on a cowhide under the stars.

Naqua had an infectious smile and was truly beautiful and cool. She kept asking me if I was really going to do the things I'd said I wanted to: help with the cattle and wrestle and stick-fight. I got the feeling she didn't believe I was up to it; she howled with laughter when I said yes. I loved her instantly.

It wasn't a great night's sleep. Outside, the children of the village danced late into the night, noisy and unchided. Then the lightning storm that had been flickering on the horizon moved closer, accompanied by a sudden wind which whipped up the topsoil of the overgrazed land into a dust storm. I covered my face with my hands but I was still sandblasted. Finally, heavy spots of rain pricked our skin and we shuffled into Naqua's hut before the downpour. Lying on my cowhide on the hard dirt floor, listening to the thunder and lightning overhead, I definitely felt back in tribal living. After a fitful bit of sleep I was woken early by a persistent howling, like a hundred babies crying. It was the young goats in the compound, a pre-dawn chorus I was to get very used to.

My first day with the Nyangatom was pretty chilled. I was taught how to sling my purple tartan shawl over my shoulders and given a wonderful shepherd's crook by Ajam for my new role as goatherd. Then the chief and I strolled off with his son Capa to the pastures. Along the way I kept up a long dialogue with Ajam, as he told me in detail about the scars on his body, how he'd got them from killing enemies from the Turkana tribe on a cattle raid. He gestured first to his left shoulder, covered with neat rows of protruding oblong scars – 'This one is for a Turkana' – then his right – 'This is for another Turkana. If you kill an enemy, you spill their blood, and it will enter your body and kill you, unless you protect yourself. To do this you have to cut your own body and let your blood out. That is why we have scars.'

Out at the goat pastures the gentle pace of the day continued. As the animals grazed around us, we sat under a tree and talked about Ajam's childhood – a more fertile time, he said, before the overgrazing and desertification of the land today. Eventually it was time to milk the goats. The young boys herded them up, then the women got to work.

'The goats haven't got much milk because it hasn't rained for a while,' Naqua told me. Last night had been the first proper downfall they'd had for ages. If the rain continued, there would be lots of milk.

I had a go myself, using techniques I'd learnt over the years.

Naqua screeched with high-pitched laughter and gestured: 'Try hitting the udder before each tug, that will bring more milk out.' Then as I did that, there was more laughter: I was overdoing it. 'That's enough, that's enough.' The poor goat was having a terrible time.

As we worked, Naqua told me what happened when food was scarce. 'If there is a shortage, we look for fruit and other foods. Then we eat the goats and cattle. But killing them is a last resort. Finally, when it rains, we'll sow sorghum again. Without rain we go hungry. When it's really dry we only drink blood, from the cattle – the children too.'

Lunch was more sorghum porridge back at the compound, during which Ajam showed me an unusual use for his lower lip-piercing, closing his mouth and squirting water through the hole like a water pistol to wash his hands. Afterwards I joined the older men for a nap in the elders' hut, about 150 metres beyond the village's thorn enclosure. Crouching down to enter through a very low doorway, I found all these old boys laid out stark naked on their tartan shawls. There was saggy black old skin and hairless balls everywhere. One guy had what looked like a miniature hip flask jutting out from the piercing in his lower lip. They barely moved all afternoon. I'm not sure they even noticed me. Like most of the tribal groups around here, all Nyangatom men are divided into different age-sets: each has a different name and differing roles within the community. These old guys were of the oldest age-set – the 'Elephants'; below the Elephants were the middle-aged Birds and below them the youthful Ibex.

After an hour or so's welcome snooze in the heat, Ajam woke me to go back and give his goats their daily drink. The water came from a big well; the surface of the water was about two metres across within a much larger hole in the ground. It needed a spot of maintenance before we could proceed. I was allowed to clamber down into it to collect sand, which had collapsed from the walls, and scoop it out. Then we repaired the step down. Finally water was passed out into our trough with a beaten-up metal cooking pot. We shooed away any goats that weren't Ajam's, then let our animals drink. They guzzled the water from the trough as fast as we could fill it.

Now the kids had a drink too, crouched over the trough just like the goats. A bit parched myself by now, I got on my hands and knees and joined them. To my surprise, the water was cool and pleasant, if a bit muddy and full of grass seeds. I had to laugh at myself when, after my first attempt, one of the boys showed me his simple technique: by blowing down on the water first, he eradicated any seeds and scum from the area in a circular ripple from the centre.

The next day I met three of the men who were nearer my own age – the Ibex. This age-set is the warrior group of the tribe, young and strong and fit. I felt ridiculous wandering around with my traditional shepherd's crook and shawl, like something out of the Bible, while they wore T-shirts and carried AK-47s.

We walked out about three kilometres to the edge of their territory, beyond which is that of the Turkana, their tribal enemy. Here they loaded their weapons – and this was not just for show. One of them had the same heavy scarring on his body as Ajam.

'You killed a man?'

'Yes.'

As we sat in the shade of a thorny acacia tree, he explained how he had been not only scarred but also renamed after his first killing – Lokirimor: 'the man who killed Suri'. The Nyangatom used to be one of the smallest and weakest tribes in the Omo Valley, an easy target for their neighbours. But these sophisticated weapons, acquired before their enemies, have given them the means to fight back and settle old scores. As I knew from my previous trip to the region, they had all too recently driven the Suri right back off their traditional lands.

The second Ibex was called Locho. Tall and elegant, he was

known locally as a bit of a rich kid, as he owned 250 cattle and 16 donkeys. He was the most unassuming of characters and very kind and gentle in manner, with a great look – a huge green comb stuck into his cropped hair.

The unofficial leader of these three herders was Challis. He wore a smart new black and red T-shirt with a tartan shawl slung like a kilt around his hips. He was buzzing with enthusiasm, laughing and nodding along as, with Soya translating, Lokirimor told me stories of their battles. One episode twenty years ago had passed into Nyangatom legend.

'The Nyangatom crossed the river,' said Lokirimor, 'and went up into Suri land. They hid themselves in the bush. When the Suri appeared they surprised them and killed many, many of them. More than six hundred Suri were killed at that time. The blood flowed like a river. We even killed Suri children.'

That was in 1986. The massacre, he explained, was in retaliation for earlier Suri atrocities. The Nyangatom had since stayed in the area, occupying the captured Suri land to take advantage of a valuable spring and the better pastures.

Now Challis chipped in, grinning as he talked. 'If there are many of us we will kill them. Take their guns and celebrate in the village. The elders will bless us, saying, "Kill them before they kill you."'

The saddest thing for me about this ongoing cycle of violence is how similar these people are to the Suri. They live in the same territory. Livestock is their main means of subsistence. They have similar ritual scars. The next day I was even invited to drink blood again.

It was the same procedure as I'd seen before, up in the hills. A sharp arrow to a cow's jugular made the dark crimson liquid spurt out into a waiting calabash. But then something new: the guys stirred the warm blood with a stick, round and round in the gourd, until a congealed, spaghetti-like mix started to form under the frothing red surface. This was then pulled out and kneaded, ready for eating, while the remaining blood was shared around. I gulped mine dutifully – *not* my favourite meal. Then, like a good guest, I joined in eating the congealed spaghetti mess.

'It's a bit like all the hair and goo you find at the bottom of the bath plug,' was my uncharitable assessment to camera.

Later we drove Ajam up to a low, stony hill from where he could point out all his land on the ochre, tree-dotted plain below. It was a dramatic moment as he gestured round with his long, sinewy arms. He pointed to a distant knoll and talked of a huge massacre of the Suri, the same battle Challis and the others had told me about. It was then that I had a shocking realization: Bargulu had pointed out the very same landmark to me a year before. It was an ancient Suri burial ground, and he had explained passionately that they were waiting to get it back, because it was so important to them as a tribal group.

Ajam reiterated his call for peace. Like the Suri, the Nyangatom talk of peace and killing with equal enthusiasm, but in reality are pursuing only one of those courses actively. Both groups contain great leaders and wonderful people but the enmity runs deep. Water and pastures are depleting rapidly with climate change and overgrazing. Growing populations with such limited resources will only increase the intertribal pressures. Governmental intervention from Addis Ababa could only improve things if done with respect and sensitivity. As ever when feelings run so deep, it was hard to see how either side would have the foresight to forget their past grievances and take an independent initiative on any talk of peace.

As each day passed I got on better with my new Ibex friends, Challis, Locho and Lokirimor. I was thrilled about this, because up with the Suri, as with most of the groups I'd lived with so far, I'd bonded with either the elders and chiefs or the children. The men of my own age had usually left me pretty much alone. These three had now become the best friends I'd yet made during the filming of a *Tribe* episode.

In the cool of the afternoon we got down and dirty with some wrestling. We found a shady bit of dry river bed and prepared for a competition in the sand. Challis had invited a whole group of Ibex along, including some I'd not met before. There were few takers for the scrap at first, but Challis soon whipped us all up. Topless bodies leant towards each other, hands clasped to grip each other's back from behind, your left arm over their right. Then you tussle. The first man thrown to the ground loses, and the best of three or five fights wins.

I watched the first two bouts, then Challis asked me to take on the scarred Lokirimor. He was a skilled opponent and won the first bout easily. Not that it mattered, because the whole occasion was very good-natured and my attempts to stall him were met with big cheers. I won the second bout but lost the third even more resoundingly, and sat back with the crowd, totally knackered.

They weren't going to let me off that lightly. A little later I was called up again, this time to face a guy more my size. A good grip on your opponent's buttocks was clearly good for lifting and turning . . . and mine were firmly in his hands. I lost the first bout again, but on the second he fell over almost immediately. It was an obvious fake-out, so I insisted on a proper rematch. He put up a good fight, but I was still able to throw him to the ground. He retired to cheers as if I'd won. What a laugh.

I invited the whole Ibex gang back to the crew camp to watch the video rushes of our bouts. It's always nice to let everyone see what we've been doing and – provided we have the battery power – we do it as often as we can. Sometimes it can work against us, because people can become self-conscious when the camera is rolling, but we considered it only fair to show what we were doing with their images as and when we could. They loved seeing themselves, of course.

I took the opportunity to have a refreshing cup of tea, to soothe the sore throat and headache that had been with me for the last couple of days. My firm no-crew-food rule, which had begun back in Gabon, was entirely self-imposed, a reaction to Steve's repeated offers of sustenance during my first hungry weeks living on potatoes with the Babongo. I had turned him down then because I felt that once the food gates were open, it would be much harder not to keep topping up on crew goodies and I'd miss out on the experience of properly living like the locals. Now I was seriously thinking of being softer on myself; everything else on this trip was more televisual, and so long as I felt I was bonding, surely it was OK to have the occasional off-screen snack? James thought I was completely mad with my strictures. He saw no problem in me allowing myself the occasional meal or drink in camp, just so long as 90 per cent of the time I was with my hosts. So later that evening I had a beer – it tasted great.

Ajam and the elders had agreed that as well as living with them I could be initiated into the Nyangatom as an Ibex, in a ceremony known as *aripaknek*. The next day the process would start with the sacrifice of a cow and a goat, followed by a feast. Challis and I and the gang began in the morning by collecting fresh green branches from the trees around the village. These were easy to tear off with one hand. We laid them round the big pile of dry firewood just outside the village.

Then it was off to meet the day's first victim. The doomed cow stood under a tree with a rope around its hind foot. I was given a three-metre metal spear with a remarkably sharp blade and asked to make the first stab. I refused. Not because I was squeamish or thought I couldn't do it; there was just no need for me to do it, especially when there were many more skilled executioners to hand.

So the spear was handed to one of the Ibex men. He took a stab at the cow's left side, but it seemed to make little impact. The cow just stood there, squirming and looking miffed, while a little blood dribbled out from the wound on to its hide. Nothing was happening, so our guy took the spear and jabbed it expertly back into the original wound, thrusting it deeper and moving it around. There was a hideous squelching sound – some key organ being finished off – and within a minute the beast was flat on its side, eyes rolling wildly as it gave up the ghost.

A fire was now ablaze at the centre of the circle of greenery. Bits of cow were passed over for cooking: legs, stomach, ribs, the head with the horns intact. The elders used their own little wooden stools to sit round the leafy table – they took them with them wherever they went, it seemed. The beef was for them; we junior Ibex had to wait for the second animal to be killed today – the goat.

Challis led a dance and I tried not to think about how hungry I felt, the scent of cooked meat drifting across in the woodsmoke. Grabbing me, he led a procession of prancing Ibex towards the elders. We sang and danced in single file, like a conga, two or three separate snakes in total, with lots of posturing with guns and the occasional shot. I joined in as best as I could with my spear, though I don't think I looked particularly threatening. Finally we came to rest in the centre of the elders' semicircle, sitting on our own stools, with our backs to them.

Now two or three of the elders stepped forward to address our group. There was no simultaneous translation, but I realized a lot of the talk was about me, as I recognized my new name – Lokorlam (which means 'colourful fruit', and is also the name of the village) – being repeated often. Later, when Willow and Jane had done the painstaking translations that are a key part of the vast amount of background work that is done on location, I read what they had been saying:

ELDER: From this moment on, there are no more bad things.
MEN (*chanting*): No more!
ELDER: Let good things prevail in our clan.
MEN: Prevail!

ELDER: Let Bruce have a good spirit.
MEN: Let it be so!
ELDER: Let him live with our clan.
MEN: Let him live!
ELDER: Let Lokorlam do good things for our clan.
MEN: Let him do!

And so on, for some time. Then there was a lot of horn blowing, more running around in congas, then the tone of the elders became audibly more scornful.

ELDERS: You young boys have become so spoilt. You always drink alcohol and never look after the cattle. You are so scared you don't even take out the goats. It's the children that look after the goats now.
   Our clan is getting weaker. Because you young men are selling your guns. If you don't have guns and cattle, money will not be able to get you brides. What's going to happen to our clan if you keep doing this?

These sorts of taunts were soon driving a couple of our guys crazy. They were up on their feet, running around pretending they were up for any challenge with a 'Bring on the enemy, let me show them!' kind of posturing. Lokirimor completely lost it, and fell into a fit, almost like epilepsy, which required at least three others to restrain him. Challis told me later that it was not uncommon for everyone to rush off as a raiding party after such a chastisement from their elders just to prove their worth.

There would be no raids today, though, so after this frenzy of taunting and reaction was over, everyone backed off to chill in the shade. The elders, too, retired under a tree. Now I was invited over to be blessed. A pan of sweet red liquid was passed round: watered-down blood, sweetened with sugar. One of the old boys stuck his face in the pan, sucked up some liquid, then sprayed it all over me with his mouth. Then it was another's turn. They were pretty ancient, these elders, and it was clearly an effort for them to muster up the energy. I helped them by putting my face in close, barely fifteen centimetres from their quivering lips to receive the fine spray.

When each in the circle had finished and I was splattered with blood, I got up to leave. But it wasn't over yet: apparently I had to return the blessing. The elders sat there and I took a big mouthful of sugary blood-liquid, then let them have it. Help! I'd clearly overdone it. The whole company were wiping their faces in complete disbelief, wringing their hands as they looked down at their bloodstained clothing. Soya was trying hard to tell me it was all OK, I hadn't made a massive faux pas, but all I could hear behind me were bemused mutterings from the old boys . . .

The women were harder to get to know, until something happened the next day that allowed me to bond with them. It was around lunchtime, and I'd nipped back to the crew area to get a fresh battery and tape for my Bruce-cam and had ended up chatting with James. One of the women ran up to us and told us something was going on back in the village, so we hurried over to find Jon, camera in hand, pretty much the only man left in the place. A Turkana raiding party had been spotted near the area where the village goats were grazing, and a small boy had raised the alarm. Every man had gone to the front line, not only from our village but from every village around – 400 people all told.

James wasn't keen on my taking sides in a battle, and I agreed. With the men gone, the women seemed to come out of themselves a bit. Soon enough we were all laughing and joking, and they were trying to teach me a completely incomprehensible dance. It looked as if all you had to do was jump up and down and clap, but clearly I was getting it wrong. They were howling with laughter at whatever slight nuance of movement I'd missed.

Then a cow's tail on a hand loop was brought out, and they showed me what I was supposed to do with that: something like pointing one elbow while the other is raised bent above the head. I was clearly still miles off doing the right thing, so I decided just to swing the tail round my head like a dead cat. This was the final straw for the women, who by now had all collapsed completely. Even Ajam's toothless mother joined in with a high-pitched cackle.

Early in the evening the guys returned. The news was good: no shots had been fired, no goats or sheep rustled. It had been a successful defensive operation – or maybe even a false alarm. It emerged that the Turkana patrol who'd kicked the whole thing off had been out trying to recapture some of their own livestock, about 600 goats and sheep that had been stolen by a group of Nyangatom a couple of days before. *A couple of days before?* That was when we'd been here. Nobody had told us about *that*.

Challis was excited about the day's excursion and admitted he'd known all about the previous raid. Had he not been with us, he said, he'd have gone on it himself. I asked him how going on raids fitted in with his professed desire for peace. His answer, of course, was that the raid was a legitimate retaliation. A previous Turkana raid had claimed a thousand of their livestock.

Challis wasn't at all political. He was highly intelligent, a big character and a natural leader. He'd never been to school but had fought in Sudan – a typical local Nyangatom man. So it was interesting that he came up with the same stock answers as Ajam. When I asked him directly whether the traditional scarring made him more attractive to the women, or if there was kudos in having killed, he was equally diplomatic. He repeated the stuff about the scarring being essential to cultural tradition: after taking on the soul of a defeated foe, one must let blood to avoid sickness ... And so on.

A couple of days later Naqua was altogether more frank, as

I asked her questions while we filmed her doing domestic chores. I'd been trying to copy her grinding sorghum with a pestle on a flat stone and my inept efforts had brought cries, wails and laughter. I thought I'd take advantage of the jovial mood to get her view on the deeper motives behind the young guys' raiding of livestock from other groups, and how ingrained all this is in their culture. Her answer was revealingly simple.

'It's good to be a killer,' she told me. 'A man who fights is a real man. A woman would be proud of him. If she had to spend a night away from the village, she'd feel safe with him. A man without scars is a coward. A real man has scars.'

Now it was the day of the emergence of the new moon, and the big annual ceremony where the precedence of the age-sets is reinforced: the Elephant elders first, then the middle-aged Birds, and finally the young Ibex. The sons of the Ibex had not been given a class name yet. Cattle would be slaughtered and their meat offered ritually to the older groups by the younger. I was all set to observe and join in when required. The day began with dancing, our usual conga snake, gesturing and posturing our way over towards the village compound where two sacrificial bulls awaited their demise.

At this point James informed me that the ceremony was going to be centred around me. The translations of earlier footage by Willow, Jane and Soya always took time, and as a result we were generally a few days behind real-time events. Sometimes we don't pick up on small details and nuances of things that people have said until much later, even back home in the edit suite. So James had only just discovered that today's events were in fact the final part of my initiation – my *acad-amdam*. And because it was *my* initiation, *I* was expected to make the sacrifice and the ritual offering. Wow! That changed everything – they wanted me to kill an animal.

This was a departure from all the previous *Tribe* films, where I'd observed ritual slaughter but had never done it myself. My initial reaction was for me to do it but not use it in the film. Logic told me that as soon as I directly participated in such an emotive, controversial activity, the focus of our home audience's attention would shift – from learning about the ritual and the tribal group, to wondering whether or not I should have got involved. James, however, felt that we should film the sacrifice, as the offering of the meat from the Ibex to their elders is central to the whole *acadamdam*. He suggested that I symbolically gesture with my spear and let someone else do the actual killing, a compromise that had been offered by the locals when they had seen my dilemma. But I wasn't happy. If the killing was going to be in the film and I was going to have to discuss it later, then I should enter the argument at the place where I felt most comfortable, and that, in this instance, was that I had no problem with the slaughter of animals in such a way and in such a setting.

James finally agreed and I was handed the spear. Things were turning out quite differently from how I'd expected the day to go. I could already imagine the mail from the animal rights activists. So Challis and I and a big camera and half the village descended on the cattle enclosure, to find a white bull and a brown bull that someone had forgotten to tie down properly. Seeing our horde arriving, the two bulls dashed for the thorn fence in a bid for freedom. For one wonderful minute I thought that my victim had escaped, but both bulls were chased by fit strong Ibex and hit with sticks until they made their way back into the slaughter pen. Now they knew their number was up – they were jumping around with fear in their eyes, jittery and manic.

This was now a very changed situation from the well-organized, speedy slaughter I'd envisaged, and was turning into something I really did not wish to be a part of. It didn't look good for me *or* the cattle.

The white bull was lassoed round the front left foot as Challis got in to do his stuff. His thrust with the long metal spear was well aimed and the animal was soon on its knees. My bull, seeing the fate of its colleague, made another bid for freedom. I followed the Ibex gang out of the village with my spear, secretly hoping that someone would see fit to shoot the bull. But the guys chased it back and lined it up ready for me. It was only as I got close that I noticed what a fine set of horns the thing possessed, and what an exceedingly pissed-off look it had in its eye. It stomped the ground with its tied-up foot, checking out this little white man waving a spear over the corpse of its mate.

The villagers hurried me over to within striking range. The frantic animal jumped in my direction. I prepared to land my blow.

'No!' came a cry. 'It must be on the right side.'

This was all getting too much for me now. I felt for the poor animal. As quickly as I could I repositioned myself and thrust the spear. But it was too far back, so I had to try again. It was horrible and I really didn't want to go on with it. Fortunately, with the next hit the animal fell. That was it: I'd done my best and everyone was full of compliments.

As before, the dead bulls were roughly butchered and the hunks of meat carried to the central fire: horns, tail, stomach and even hooves, in slow succession. The huge pile of wood had soon sunk down to a mass of glowing orange embers, perfect for barbecuing. The cooks sweated in the heat and smoke, turning the meat with long sticks. Meanwhile the elders had gathered at their semicircular leafy table.

Once they had eaten, I and the Ibex took our places at the centre of the ring. The women sang and danced in my honour. Then, as the guys chanted around me, mud was rubbed on my chest and legs and there were wild shouts and gunshots. We then trooped off to the river bed for the slaughter of a goat and our own Ibex feast.

This was great, the culmination of weeks of games and battles and bonding. I really felt like I was one of them, sitting there, laughing and joshing as the light grew ever yellower and the shadows of the thorn trees lengthened around us. It was hard to believe that my new friends were the sworn enemies of the people in the hills I had also come to love. The tragic reality of the situation was brought home nine months later when I found out that my good friend Locho had met his death at the hands of a Turkana raiding party. Now, on the day we left he had insisted on accompanying us down the Omo River to our next destination, even though his wife had just given birth to their first child that morning. It was a thirty-six kilometre trek to where the Hamar lived, and he would have come all the way had I not sent him back. I can only hope his son will be part of a new generation that won't be at the mercy of this endless cycle of violence that currently plagues the tribes of the Omo Valley.

8. Leap of Faith

The Hamar of the Omo Valley, Ethiopia

The main Omo River is wide and deep, unlike the dried-up sand bed that was the Kibish in the Nyangatom lands, by Lokorlam village. There was no bridge, ford or any other way for our vehicles to make the crossing, so Zablon had organized a fleet of tiny boats to ferry all our gear across to a new set of vehicles on the far side. Zablon and I then came back to film our passage once more in a traditional dugout canoe: to set the scene for this second episode of the Omo trip, as well as make clear to our viewers that the territory of the Hamar people was very different from that of the Nyangatom – green, wooded and relatively lush.

After a few days' R & R in a safari camp down the river, Zablon, Jon and I continued the journey on foot, while James and Willow went ahead in the vehicles to check out villages where we might stay. As well as sticking to my original plan of trekking, we were also looking for footage to give a further sense of contrast to the dry Nyangatom lands: views down the green valley, random encounters with Hamar people, and so on. We were soon rewarded: herds of cattle and goats came past at intervals with the usual herder boy or two beside them, keeping them on the dusty track with a stick. The girls we met were beautiful with short braided hair dyed orange with ochre, and gorgeous adornments all over: necklaces and earrings of red, yellow and blue beads over shawls and dresses of black, white and crimson fabric. The men were equally colourful. Most had red and black *kikoys* round their loins, bright beads around their necks and long white feathers protruding from skullcaps or headbands on top of their heads, while one or two were dressed up in a hotchpotch of European clothes: hats, jackets and waistcoats that had somehow made their way down to this remote part of Africa. Looking more closely at the women, I saw that many of them had badly scarred backs, a consequence of the extraordinary local tradition of whipping, a prelude to and part of a Hamar initiation rite where young men leap over a row of tethered cattle – something we were hoping to both see and film.

We camped that evening in a dry river bed; Jon in his tent, and Zablon, me and Jon's porter under a bivvy sheet I'd bought. I dined on rehydrated spaghetti, listened to music on my iPod, read a book and slept blissfully under a mosquito net on an inflatable mattress. Such luxury – there'd be nothing like this in the hut I would soon be staying in!

A day later we had reached the little town of Dimeka, close to the village that James and Willow had decided was the right place for us to stay. It was Saturday, market day, and the place was packed with people, vibrant colours everywhere. Sprawling fruit stalls, stacks of ochre pots, locals resplendent in beads and *kikoys*. Among them were European tourists with baseball caps and safari hats, slung with heavy cameras, bartering for gifts and photographs. I avoided the hypocrisy of being upset or cynical about 'other' visitors sharing our 'off the beaten track' experience, but instead was interested in the strange dynamic that the Hamar have built up with tourists over the years. Indeed one could almost say that 'bull-jumping', as it's erroneously described by most tour guides to add hype, is in many ways now a sponsored event, with the tourists being invited along as the financial backers.

James introduced me to Korka, a skinny guy in a tight stripy top, with an absurdly large Nazi U-boat captain's hat on his head. He was from our chosen village and a fantastic character, a local wheeler-dealer type who I knew would instantly latch himself on to the crew. Almost every community we'd visited has one of these charismatic helpers who always appears on the first day or so, trying to get in on the action. Often they start off trying to be with me in front of the camera, thinking that's where the rewards are, but they soon realize their error and discard me and my discomforts and head straight for the relative luxury of the crew camp. They almost invariably end up living in the kitchen.

Korka was clearly one of these guys and I loved him for it. I also met Gallo, our new interpreter, an educated young Hamar man with a thin moustache and a wispy pointed beard surrounding a huge white smile. I warmed to him immediately; as usual, Zablon had done well. Gallo arrived in a Western shirt and trousers and then, without any request from us, disappeared and came back in traditional vest and *kikoy*, looking completely different, totally the part for village life.

I savoured what I thought might be my last cold soft drink for a while at lunchtime, then Zablon, Jon and I trekked the seven kilometres on to the village with Korka and Gallo. James and Willow had gone on ahead in the vehicles, so we arrived to see the familiar orange tents of the crew camp. I decided to leave checking out my new home till morning, so set up my tent and hammock in camp and sat drinking whisky with the crew. Korka brought over a few villagers, who seemed very friendly and cool. Poor James got cornered by an enthusiastic, not to say amorous, bunch of girls trying to sell him stuff. There was singing and merriment well into the night and we discovered that by good fortune there was to be a cattle-leap and initiation in the vicinity the next day.

The ceremony took place the following afternoon, on the edge of a wood a kilometre or so from the main village. The young man whose special day it was was called an *okuli*. His jumping over a row of tethered cattle was a rite of passage that marked his becoming a *charcolai* and then a *maza*, one of a group of initiated males who roam together as a pack until it's time for them to be married; they are forbidden to eat wheat or sorghum, and are only allowed to visit family and the village for ceremonies. In the morning, the *okuli* and his father are ritually washed in the middle of the village, then the tight plaits on the *okuli*'s head are undone and his hair is brushed out in a wild Afro style. Before he does his jump, a ritual cross is painted over the *okuli*'s upper body with dung from the cattle. His female relatives on his father's side, meanwhile, present themselves to be whipped by the *maz*. They are not supposed to show any pain. To them, the whipping is an honour, a sign of their devotion to and love for the *okuli*.

I had read all about this extraordinary custom in my research notes, but nothing could prepare me for the frenzied reality. In a little grassy dell close to the wood, the girls shouted and screamed and blew little tin trumpets as they danced madly round the waiting *maz*, each of whom held a long flexible branch in his right hand. Far from being forced into the whipping, the girls seemed to be actively soliciting it. This wasn't just for show – it was a good hard whack they wanted. Several of them would gather round a particular *maza* and taunt him into action, even fighting among themselves to get the best hits:

'Whip me first!'

'Do it, do it again!'

'Today's our brother's special day, so don't stop us from being whipped!'

'You're not man enough to whip me – you're a coward!'

'You only whipped me once!'

'One more time!'

The translations of their cries, which I read later, didn't surprise me. It was clear enough from the crazed expression in their eyes that they were up for what they were getting. Another aspect I noticed (that the translations later confirmed) was that the *maz* initially seemed reluctant to get on with the whipping. This may have been play-acting, but being provoked into action by the girls was clearly part of the ritual:

'I don't want to whip you.'

'You must go and eat your lunch before we whip you.'

'Are you insulting me?'

These were the sort of things the *maz* were saying before they got started; once they did, it was culture shock at its most extreme. I found it hard to stand by and watch the sticks lacerating the smooth backs of these young women, making deep, bloody welts in their dark skin. As to what I should say to the camera, it felt like I was going to be damned no matter what: for being either culturally insensitive or an insensitive male. One time I turned to camera – after one particularly persistent girl was demanding a whipping – and said, 'She's asking for it!' which was obviously meant literally and not in the way it *might* be taken. Thankfully James never used that particular piece of footage, or else I'd probably be single for the rest of my life!

It may be hard to believe, but all around this violent central spectacle was the loveliest festive atmosphere. People were dancing, coffee and sorghum beer were being drunk, there was laughter and singing. In the late afternoon the *maz* turned their attention to rounding up the animals for the second half of the ceremony: the cattle-leaping. Even though these were not the full-grown bulls of tourist legend, but cows and bullocks, they still had impressive horns and were extremely frisky. The newly whipped girls added to the frenzy, dancing in a circle round the animals, waving knives hung with bells as the *maz* made shooing noises. Finally the *maz* moved in to line the cattle up, one grabbing the horns and lower jaw, another the tail. More than once people lost control of their animals and got dragged off across the grass rodeo-style.

Eventually they had ten cattle side by side in a jostling row. The *okuli* was ready, naked apart from the cross of dried reed around his torso. He took a short run up, but then stumbled on top of the cattle. He'd messed up, but avoided falling between them, so tried again and this time managed to leap then dance over their backs to jump off on to the ground at the far end. The run was repeated in reverse, then twice more. He'd done it, and saved himself from the humiliation of being whipped by the women, the punishment – apparently – for those who fall to the ground. Now his dried-reed torso-wrap was torn off him and he was taken to one side to be blessed by the women. Now the party could get going properly.

The young men and women lined up in rows and danced, a kind of jump-dance with a lot of very obvious flirting going on; individual girls kicked the heels of men they liked the look of in the line, then broke away for a five-second private dance, with a fair amount of suggestive thrusting. Gallo explained that this would all get more intimate as the night wore on. The *okuli*, meanwhile, was taken off to be ritually shaved then smeared with a mixture of butter and charcoal, after which he'd become a *charcolai*. A week later he would graduate to being a *maza*.

The dancing looked huge fun, but having not moved in with a family yet I still felt very much the voyeur visitor, so I walked back with James, Jon, Zablon and Willow to our camp by the village. Our heads were full of the extraordinary events of the day – and once again we had much to talk about that evening around the fire.

I was making the most of still being in the crew camp, eating three lots of eggy bread with ketchup for breakfast. Then it was off back to the village with Gallo to be introduced to Suri, a young guy who would become an *okuli* in a fortnight's time. James's plan was that I should spend time with him in the run-up to his cattle-leaping ceremony, and hopefully join him in attempting to jump the cattle myself. We filmed him giving me the traditional invitation to his cattle-leap, a piece of straw tied with ten or so tight little knots. Each knot represents a day; you untie one every morning until there are none left and then it is the day of the ceremony.

Suri certainly looked the part: young and fit, with the front half of his head shaved ready for his initiation. He was friendly enough too, but became completely silent when the camera was turned on him. I was working hard, asking questions about his forthcoming cattle-jump and not getting much back:

'I've seen the cattle-jump and the walking across the cattle. How do you train for that? . . . It looks quite difficult – d'you have any practice?'

Without the crew in attendance we'd had a decent chat, but now I needed almost to give his answers for him: 'The next time you do that will you promise to show me, so I can see you train?' and so on, getting in return only a blank nod and an empty smile. It was a shame, because it then felt like I was being pushy when in reality he'd already suggested these things himself off camera.

The search was now on for a suitable family for me to live with. Ideally one related to Suri, so I might get to know some of the women who were going to submit to being whipped on his big day. Korka invited me to stay, and that would have been fine except that his wife had a twelve-day-old child; it wouldn't be fair imposing me on her as well. Suri's other uncles were nice enough, but James wanted me to be among the women. We went back for lunch in camp, undecided.

Later that afternoon things took a turn for the better. Korka and Gallo took us over to meet the village chief, an old guy in khaki shorts and a faded khaki hat. He had several names, it seemed, including one just for visitors – Koroboco. I was invited to call him Lalombai – the name, apparently, of the cow he had jumped years ago in his initiation ceremony. He had two wives who sat to one side, Mary and Ika. I delivered my now regular patter about how I hoped our presence in the village wasn't an imposition and so on. He smiled and nodded and replied in words that Gallo translated:

'We welcome our guest and are happy to receive him. Let him bring peace whenever he visits. You are good people, we welcome you all. Do what you have come to do, no one will disturb you. There are no problems here.'

We retired for a third night in camp feeling that we were slowly getting there.

And in the morning things did at last start to fall into place. The chief introduced us to his eldest son, Jamu (meaning 'first-born'), a fit young guy not yet initiated. He wore a thick necklace of black and red beads, feathers in his hair and metal bangles on his wrists. He seemed easy-going and totally up for being in the film. The plan was that I would stay with him in the hut of the chief's second wife, Ika, a squat, rather muscular young woman with beaded hair like a helmet down to her shoulder blades. In a nearby hut lived some of Suri's female relatives, who were due to be whipped on his big day, so hopefully I could get to know them a bit and try to find out their opinions on the whipping ritual.

To mark my moving out of the crew camp into the village proper, the gods rewarded us with a storm of biblical proportions. A powerful wind whipped up from nowhere and tugged at our tent flaps. This was followed by torrential rain, splashing down hard and pooling on the ground. If this kind of thing was a regular occurrence, it wasn't hard to see why this area was so lush and green.

When the rain had passed over I took my basic kit over to the village and moved into my new abode. With Gallo trans-lating, I began to explain about wanting to be treated as a member of the family, not as a guest. Ika took me at my word, setting me to work grinding sorghum straightaway, rubbing a smooth stone over the grains on a larger flat stone to reduce them to white powder. In Hamar terms this is women's work, and the surrounding crowd of villagers laughed their heads off at my attempts to get it right. At sunset I was taken out to bring in the sheep, goats and cattle, which turned out to be the easiest job in my *Tribe* experience to date, as the animals just strolled straight back to their pens on their own. Then I fixed some fencing on the hut, to the delight of the watching chief.

Supper followed inside the hut. Sweet, delicious goat's milk, accompanied by heated-up sorghum flour, which was dry and unappetizing, coagulated into little damp balls at the bottom of a big circular gourd. Following that was a concoction called *farsi*, a thick local beer, sour and fizzy and full of bits: truly a miserable broth. Ika mixed it with boiling water before drinking it, and although Gallo told me it was a traditional local staple, I wasn't rushing for seconds. I could see that any surplus weight I'd put on in the crew camp was going to fall off rapidly in the coming week.

We sat with the children, watching the sun set outside. As before on my nights in tribal huts, the kids were entranced by the infra-red setting on 'Bruce-cam', seeing their bright eyes and grinning faces appearing on the flip-out screen, when otherwise it was pitch dark in the hut. We had our usual fun with that, then I was shown my sleeping arrangements: flat, crisp cowhides on the floor, and for a pillow, a little wooden seat shaped like a toadstool. To cover me I had only my poly-ester stripy shawl. It was no surprise that I hardly slept a wink. Outside a full moon shone bright; the village cockerels responded to this near-daylight by crowing all night. Dogs barked. Right in my ear Gallo snored loudly. After comfortable nights 'camping' on the inflatable mattress, this 'homely' floor was painfully hard, and cold as well. My gut was churning from some ailment or other and producing chronic amounts of wind. Farting in your brand new quarters is never, I guess, good etiquette, so a couple of times in the night I felt so bloated I got up and crawled outside into the lunar landscape for a blissful tirade of releases.

In the morning, the village's new recruit was set to work. My first job was ploughing, something I'd never done before. Jamu lined me up with the yoked oxen and the plough and I got going. What a disaster! I was all over the place – such seemingly simple traditional activities are actually incredibly skilled. A lot of pressure has to go through the bit in the oxen's mouths, and the tying of the plough to get the angle of the blade has to be just right – too little and you just scratch the surface of the ground; too deep and you bury the plough. Meanwhile, the poor ploughman is trying to keep control of the varied stresses on the rope ties and moving wooden parts, quite apart from the oxen themselves. I soon realized that a straight line would be totally beyond my ability, with or without a bull whip. After two hours I'd done maybe twenty lines, had broken one plough and several ropes. I decided to call it a day.

Next up was pot-making with Ika – another skill that clearly was going to be beyond me. Ika collected the clay herself, she told me, from a particular hill quite a way away. As she had no wheel, she had to put her pot together from flat slabs of clay, which she rolled and kneaded into shape with expert fingers, before building them up slowly into an open bowl. It was true craftsmanship and lovely to watch, even though by now I was all but nodding off from last night's lack of sleep. I struck a deal with her to help her try to sell her finished pot in the Dimeka market. The rate, she said, was five *birr* for locals, fifty *birr* for tourists!

None of this activity was helped by the plague of flies that hovered round the village, landing on lips, ears, eyes, arms, hands and feet, making it impossible to enjoy any quiet moments at all. After lunch I tried to get an hour's kip and eventually managed to lay myself flat out in the hut, *kikoy* over my face to escape the infuriating buzzing and tickling.

The following morning James, Zablon and I went to see another cattle-leaping ceremony in a nearby village. I went on foot with Gallo and Jamu, but when I arrived, once again I didn't feel a part of things at all. As I walked out into a crowd of people in my *kikoy* and bracelets, there wasn't the warm 'Bruce, Bruce!' of previous encounters in the Omo Valley, and I felt self-conscious and excluded. It was understandable, as they were having their big special day, and who was I to interfere with an intrusive film crew? Perhaps too, I thought, the *maz* had been watched by one too many tourists, so the sight of another intrigued white man held no interest for them – especially one kitted out in their traditional clothes. I realized I was going to have my work cut out to get to the level of intimacy that would make me feel comfortable and also make for a good film. After negotiations with James and Gallo, it was agreed I would stay over with the *maz* the following night.

After a good night's sleep we headed off to Suri's hut. No sign of our main man, but several women were practising dancing in the dirt area outside the front door, shouting and singing and blowing their noisy little tin trumpets as they danced around in a circle. Today they seemed less shy and I was able to ask them a few questions about the cattle-leaping ceremony and the whipping. Their answers were fascinating. They firmly believed that women were less important than men, and that they were honouring their relative by allowing themselves to be beaten. A family is seen to be strong, they told me, if a girl can invite and accept a lot of painful whipping. To my repeated question of 'Why?', we kept coming round in circles to 'It's our culture.'

'Why don't you whip the men?' I asked.

'We do if a man doesn't jump the cow correctly.'

'Why is jumping the cattle so important?'

'Because it's our culture.'

Back to square one. I found it frustrating that I would never really be able to get to the root of this story. I knew that eminent anthropologists such as Jean Lydall had devoted their lives to such questions, learning the language and spending decades with these people, so it was a little arrogant to think that I would uncover anything new. But the medium of television demanded answers. As a result my questions were often shamefully thematic and leading.

Next up was a visit to the other side of the village and the matriarch of Suri's family, his grandmother Alo. She had the same orange-ochre braided hair as the other women, with beads like cowrie shells strung over her wrinkled head. Round her neck and over her breasts was a long, loose piece of leather, a cross between a scarf and a waistcoat. As head of Suri's family, Gallo explained, she had spiritual as well as practical responsibilities and was an extremely important figure in the community. Without her approval, I wouldn't be able to join Suri in the cattle-jump. We sat with her and watched as she performed a naming ceremony on the newest young baby in the family, taking a bunch of fresh green foliage and brushing his head with it. Sitting with her afterwards, I asked what she thought of the whipping of women and got similar answers as I'd had from the younger girls: 'It's our culture' was what she told me, and there was no probing with such a senior and respected person.

Having bonded a little bit more with the women, that evening it was back out to join the *maz*, who were spending the night at and blessing the shelter known as the *bara*, which would be used in a week or so for Suri's initiation ceremony. A few girls came out too, and there was more whipping, the girls dancing round the *maz* and provoking them, the *maz* responding in turn with their ferocious strokes. Watching it again, I could see there was definitely a sexual element to the whole thing. The girls picked their favourites to be whipped by, there was the taunt and the stand-off, then an undeniable connection as they struck.

As before, the *maz* were cool and stand-offish with me. Sitting to one side watching them, I began to worry about being left out. Was this going to be the pattern of my experience with the Hamar, who seemed so much friendlier than the Nyangatom on the surface, but were proving so much harder to get to know? Eventually, as it grew dark, one of them gestured for Gallo and me to go over and join them. We sat in a loose circle under the criss-crossed leafy branches of the *bara* and finally started to bond, as I asked them all the questions I wanted answers to: about the whipping and the cattle-leaping and how their wives are chosen and whether they are faithful and so on.

The story seemed to be that the men's wives are picked for them by their fathers, but they aren't necessarily faithful to them. Sexual activity begins before the cattle-leap initiation, and might take place with both married and unmarried women. Meanwhile, men consider themselves superior to women, and have a right to beat their wives. (In fact, it has been suggested that this beating is actually some sort of perverse power play led by women. Beating Hamar females outside of wedlock is considered very bad in their culture, except, of course, the ritual whipping of those girls at the initiation ceremonies.) Once again, I was frustrated by the restrictions of translation. 'So do you feel powerful when you whip the girls? Do you feel like you want to hurt the girls?' I asked. And back came the unspecific translation from Gallo: 'Yes, they feel powerful.'

I slept badly under the stars. It was cold and uncomfortable sharing a single cowhide with four others. Doubtless exacerbated by the starchy food in my diet, my wind problem wasn't getting any better either. I had to get up several times in the night to release the painful pressure.

After coffee in the morning the *maz* slung their colourful shawls around themselves and loped off elegantly into the woods, to go who knew where and do who knew what.

Back in the village the slow build-up to Suri's big day was continuing. His sisters were starting on the beer-making process, mixing the ground sorghum flour with water and rolling it into big dumpling-like balls. These were boiled, left to dry for a few days, had honey added and were cooked again, two days before the big day. They were planning to make twenty-six jars of the stuff, and big jars at that.

It was Saturday again, market day, so I went into town with two of Suri's sisters, Duba and Kaira. They were going to sell the family's spare sorghum and buy some bits and pieces for Suri's ceremony, in particular the orange ochre to colour their hair, and *arak* – a much stronger alcohol than the sorghum beer – which they would drink before the whipping and give out to others during the day. With me I had the pot Ika had made. I'd promised her fifty *birr* if I couldn't sell it, so I was on the lookout for a gullible tourist.

As we walked I chatted to Kaira, whom I'd got to know quite well over the week. Sixteen or so, she had a pretty smile and a sweet, rather bashful air. The market was as busy and colourful as the previous week, though with a pot to sell and Kaira and Duba to chat to I felt considerably more connected. I had little luck with the tourists. The nearest I got to the fifty *birr* I had promised Ika was thirty *birr* from a German guy. I should have gone for it because an hour later I dropped it. (Ika got her fifty *birr*, but I never did tell her that her lovingly made pot had been reduced to a thousand pieces.)

Willow had meanwhile arranged for Jon and me to meet and talk to another young woman, Keri, an educated Hamar who had turned her back on the whipping rituals and now lived in town.

'There's a big difference between life in town and in the

village,' she told us. 'In the village, the girls grind with their hands and also get whipped. That's how they live; they have lots of physical work to do and a village girl will be given to her husband without her consent and at an early age. If your parents like a man, you will be given to him, even if you don't like him, even if he is too old for you. But because I live in town, I can choose what to do.

'If you go to live with your husband in the village, he'll have no proper respect for you. When he comes home, you have to take off his shoes and wash his feet. If he calls you and you don't come to him, you'll be beaten. If you don't go out and greet him and his friends when they come to your house, they will ask what you've been doing and you'll be beaten.'

She had been lucky, she said. She had once, long ago, been whipped at a ceremony, but since then her brothers had allowed her to go to school in town. Now she wanted to study hard and be a good example for other Hamar girls. She was engaged to a boy who had also promised to go to school. When she finished school, she might marry him, or she might marry someone else. She certainly wouldn't marry someone her family had chosen for her. As for letting herself be whipped, she wasn't going to allow it again.

'They look at me like I'm dirt, they think I'm a coward. But they don't think that it hurts.' In Keri's opinion, the whipping should stop. 'The government should ban it,' she said.

I left Keri impressed by her strength and independence of mind. In this society it must have taken a lot of courage to stand up against the prevailing cultural practices like that. Even Kaira disapproved of her stance. 'A woman like that is not a Hamar any more,' she told me. 'She's changed the way she thinks. She's no longer like us.'

As Duba and Kaira were on a day out we arranged that they and I would join the crew for lunch in a town café. Their eyes bulged as more and more of the little bits of fried meat the Ethiopians called *tibs* kept coming. Kaira had never tried a Coke before and her face was a picture as she tried to drink one. She just couldn't get used to the bubbles and fizz – and didn't seem to like the taste at all. But they were all set to carry on eating till they burst, so we called a halt after the fifth helping.

Back in the village, with both Alo and the chief's approval, it now seemed confirmed that I would be cattle-leaping with Suri on his big day. Even people I'd met in town had started calling me *okuli*. It was undoubtedly a real honour, to be allowed to participate in the most important day of Suri's life. I never felt as if I'd fully bonded with him as I had with the Nyangatom guys, but he seemed genuinely happy that I would be joining him, while his father Gofa told me that he was very excited that I'd be with him for the event. The next day we got together for some practice runs with two bullocks, a big black and white one with horns and a smaller brown one. They were held, side by side, by a small group of Suri's relatives and supporters. This was entirely for my sake, as they didn't normally go in for any practice.

Suri went first, taking a barefoot run-up, leaping up nimbly from the brown dirt, feet touching briefly on the first bullock's back, before springing on to land on the far side. No hands used, I noticed. Even though I'd done a fair amount of vaulting as a Marine PT instructor in the old days, getting up on these without using hands was going to be a challenge at my paltry five feet six inches.

Somehow I managed it! My first jump was a bit stumbly, but I reached the right height and flew off OK to make a safe landing on the other side. I could feel the cows' backs shifting under the soles of my feet, but they didn't seem to mind too much. Then it was the same jump in reverse. I contemplated using the brown bullock's first, but stuck with the big one. My third jump was undoubtedly the surest, even if by now I could hear the laughter of the surrounding Hamar women.

Gofa had been watching my attempts and gave us a little

speech for the cameras about how much harder it would be in two days' time, with the crowd all around. But he seemed confident that I would be able to do it. 'If he has the strength in his heart, he'll be fine.' The women, meanwhile, had explained that on the day I would have to do the jump naked. There was no getting out of that, it seemed.

Two nights to go! At Suri's house that evening the girls were getting ready for the nine-kilometre walk out to the cattle-herding area, where we would stay over and collect milk from the cows for the ceremony. A big crowd of girls and lads had gathered and they'd clearly been at the sorghum beer as there was a party atmosphere before we even set off; singing and much laughter when the girls tried to get me to attempt some song of theirs. No doubt the words were demeaning to me, as there were raucous cackles after everything I repeated. Finally we were off. We trekked in pitch darkness. How the girls kept such sure footing on these paths full of loose rocks and thorn bushes was a miracle. I was stumbling along terribly, even though I had them just ahead of me as my guide. We slept out at the cattle area, then first thing they were off in all directions to bring back the milk, which had been collected in big jar-like gourds over the past few days. I joined Kaira, who decided to show me how to drink straight from the teat. James was hovering around with the camera, so it made for a bit of amusing footage, as I kept missing the powerful – and erratic – stream with my mouth, and my face and neck were completely covered in milk.

Next up was blood-collection, which was done the same way as with the Suri and Nyangatom, with a blunt-head arrow shot from a little bow into the thick jugular vein on the neck. We watched as they speared cow after cow, a veritable production line, producing gourdfuls of dark red blood to be mixed with milk for the coming ceremony. Like the Nyangatom, they stirred up the liquid to remove the spaghetti-like coagulated stuff. A new twist here, though, was roasting the coagulated blood on a skewer on the fire, then mixing it with butter. It tasted fine, if a bit on the chewy side. Then I tried to swallow it. Half of it went right down my throat. The other half, attached by a tensile, rubbery length, remained in my mouth tickling my gag reflex and nearly making me vomit.

That night, back in Suri's hut, the girls were in a celebratory mood. There was laughter, screaming and pooping of tin horns until well into the night. The festivities were imminent. This particular programme hadn't been so easy for me. I preferred it when I got to know a few people and gently assimilated myself into their lives, until we were all going along comfortably together. This time, I'd spent time here and there with large groups of relative strangers, my paranoia telling me that they probably thought, 'Who is this twat wearing our clothes?' Tonight, at last, things had started to feel better. We shared the bitter beer and ate some flour dough and off-milk porridge mixture, which was nicer than it sounds. Eventually, I left them to it and took myself off to one side for a fantastic night's sleep.

I spent the morning of the initiation hanging out with Suri, watching him get his hair unbraided and brushed out into the traditional half-Afro, then shared a special pre-ceremony meal with him. Suri's relatives were arriving from all over. Meanwhile, Gofa, his charismatic father, was striding around being the hospitable host, making sure all the newcomers had a cowhide to sleep on, as the extended ceremony would last some days. 'I'm ready to feed them all,' he told us, with his warm, crooked smile, 'and give them all a drink.'

Things livened up at lunchtime as his sisters started getting ready for the arrival of the *maz*. The girls had been drinking *arak*, no doubt to anaesthetize themselves a bit, and were getting themselves worked up into a hectic anticipatory frenzy. James had told Willow to stick to them like glue, but this was easier

said than done. They just couldn't stay in one place, parading
down from the huts to the stream bed and back again, hooting
on their little horns, hopping and screaming. In the late afternoon, the word came round that the *maz* were in the area and
the girls went completely crazy. I hardly recognized Duba and
Kaira. They were like people possessed, up for the whipping
and nothing else. When the *maz* appeared, over the brow of
the hill, their calmness was in stark contrast to the women's
excitement. Now five or six girls gathered round each *maza*,
dancing and taunting, flicking their buttery hair, even head-
butting him on the chest to get him to whip them. It was even
harder to watch them go through it this time, knowing them
so much better. Poor Duba looked quite sick with pain, the
flesh of her back hanging off her.

After some time people started to head off across the valley,
a ten-minute walk to where the cattle were being lined up for
the big jump. I was somewhat nervous to say the least. Over
at the ceremony site, the girls were making things harder for
us by smearing dung on the bullocks' backs to make them more
slippery. In the meantime, I was prepared for my initiation.
Bands made from reeds were tied round my bare torso in the
shape of a cross: this is a symbol of power, which would protect
me from bad things I'd done in my past. Then I rubbed myself
with sand: this was to wash away the sins of my youth. Now
my white torso was smeared with brown cow dung: to give
me strength for my jump.

Then Suri and I got our kit off. The Hamar tradition was
that we must be naked at this point as if we were dead. We
were to die as children and be reborn as men. To further evoke
this transition, we now ducked through a little wooden gate
together, chasing after two calves, a gift from Gofa to Suri.
These represented the livestock he would be given when he
became an independent man. Symbolically, Suri was now leaving
his father's home.

We ran off together across the scrub. I was going rather

slowly because of the thorny ground, which – along with my white arse – caused no end of crowd amusement. We had to stay out of sight on the edge of the wood while the cattle were herded together. Then I had to choose a friend for life to help wash me, so I asked James to do the honours, after which we returned to walk among the cattle and pat their backs with closed fists. This was apparently to calm them down, though with all the surrounding hysteria and racket, I didn't think it would do much good.

Now the *maz* were lining up our mobile obstacle course: a row of eight cows and castrated males, representing the women and children of the tribe. The act of passing over them would make us men. The animals jostled together side by side, held in place by the *maz* by their tails and horns.

It was Suri's moment of glory – or humiliating failure. I watched as he took his run-up, then leapt easily up on to the back of the first cow. For a millisecond he hung there, before plunging on across the rest of the backs. Before I knew it, he had jumped down, turned, and was running back in the opposite direction for jump two. No faults this time either. Reserved and unassuming though he was, Suri was at peak fitness, and to my tense watching eyes it seemed as if he was just floating over the dung-slippery backs of the cows before sailing back down on to the ground. After his last jump a cheer went up and the tooting horns reached a crescendo. Down on the ground his reed bands were bitten off by one of the supervising *maza*, and he was whisked away.

It was my turn at last. My stomach was in freefall. There was no danger – I just feared the public humiliation of really screwing this up. This was the climax of our programme and there would be no second takes. Watched immediately by hundreds, and remotely by millions, I was naked and smeared with shit and about to try and leap over some cows. It was all a bit surreal.

Suddenly it was time to go. I took a deep breath and ran towards the blur of the crowd, eyes fixed on the first cow's back, a great big old beast, jostling back and forth. I leapt up and just made it, but with hardly any forward momentum left. For a moment I hung in limbo, then somehow, just, I managed a wobbly walk over the backs of the remaining animals to the end. Hell, that was a close thing. One down, three to go.

My second jump was an unmitigated disaster. In my defence, the other side was much more thorny and full of sharp stones, but also I think my approach was a bit lame. Either way, I somehow made it up on to the bull backs, then tripped and lost my balance and fell right on top of them. They scattered as I wrestled madly not to fall between them, managing to get away and back to the run-up area. Second attempt. I was running on pure adrenalin now. Was I about to cock it up again? There was no choice but to keep going, ignoring the excited shouts and screams and outright laughter of the onlookers. Somehow I managed it, though it was hardly elegant.

Second go from the original side, where the ground – thank God – was smoother and easier. With a bit of luck I was up and over. Now I had to try again from the stony far side. Once again I lost my footing and barely got up on the first animal. Only a friendly push on the bum from a nearby *maza* saved the day – and then, incredibly, I was there, leaping down off the last animal on to the ground to the cheers and screams and hooting of the crowd. Sheer relief flooded through me. It had been a bit messy, if not a bit of a cheat, but they all seemed to like it and I was hailed as having done it fine. Trips like mine were common, they kindly said.

After the ceremony, of course, the party. Back at Gofa's hut the sorghum beer flowed. At last, too, I felt accepted by everyone in the Hamar crowd. I was invited over to join their strange jumping-dance and now felt part of them enough to get involved. Two semicircles lined up to face each other. First the males came out and jumped together in a line, then went back to their side of the circle. Then it was the turn of the females. And on it went, with individual dance pairs breaking the line, pelvic thrusts to the fore, though no touching at this stage. As the sun went down over the horizon and the bodies of the dancers became beautiful clear silhouettes in the dusty air, I was thoroughly enjoying myself.

In my much-needed breathers between dances I had a chance to chat to some of the girls again. In reply to more questioning about gender relations, Duba said, 'We've seen your liberated girls who come from America and Europe. But we don't want to be like them. We don't want equality with our men.'

More than any other statement I'd yet heard during the making of the second series, that made me question my own views.

9. Murky Depths

The Dassanech of the Omo Valley, Ethiopia

It was our second day off between shoots and I was enjoying a bit of luxury in a tourist campsite in town, reading, watching videos, listening to my iPod and eating camp food. Two nights before it had been James's thirty-sixth birthday, and we'd seized on the occasion to have a party. After a fortnight drinking sour goat's milk, dried wheat flour, sorghum porridge and the like, the crew treats tasted pretty good. Their talented and thoroughly lovely chef, Haimanot, had rustled up a birthday cake, and we'd drunk fake bubbly, accompanied by such delicacies as Pringles, olives, shortbread, pesto Parmesan bread and more. Later the red wine and whisky had come out and we'd ended up at a bar in town, dancing madly. Our original researcher Jane Atkins having returned to the UK with our precious footage so far, we now had a new researcher in the shape of Renée Godfrey, an ex-swimming and surfing champion of national standard, a blonde free spirit who wore her heart on her sleeve. It was she who had brought out most of the treats we'd been gorging on.

After a pleasant day of rest getting over my hangover, I took stock of my physical condition. It wasn't good. Trekking in crap shoes had left me with bad sores on my left foot and right lower calf, which were taking their time to heal. Hardly surprising, really, because my worn-out body was fighting on a number of fronts. My guts were all over the shop, as indicated by constant rumbling and groaning, not to mention continuing terrible wind.

I was in better shape than Zablon though. He had come down with strong malarial symptoms. Like me, he'd had the illness many times, so knew the symptoms well. I started him on a course of medicine, but even so, this bout was going to slow down our move to the next location, so we all agreed that it was better to go in fully prepared and in good health. Quite apart from our regard for our friend's welfare, we also knew that the normally super-energetic Zablon was the linchpin for our arrival on any shoot.

We were headed now to the very end of the Omo River, where it flows through a dried delta into Lake Turkana, the largest closed-basin lake in the East African Rift. Two hundred and fifty kilometres long and fifty wide, it has a surface area of 7,500 square kilometres and runs from Ethiopia down into Kenya. In the delta area of its northern shores live the Dassanech, who came originally from the south-west of Ethiopia and Sudan, assimilating groups from other tribes as they travelled south. Traditionally cattle-herders like the Suri, Nyangatom and Hamar, the Dassanech ended up by absorbing groups of lake people who had lived for centuries by fishing and hunting for crocodile and hippo. In good times, the Dassanech lived from their cattle. In times of drought, they turned to the lake for sustenance. Those who had lost their cattle and lived from the lake were known as Dies, 'the poor', and were looked down upon, even though in hard times the cattle-herders relied on their fishing skills for survival.

To the surrounding tribal groups, the Dassanech are identified by a number of defining acts and rituals, one of which is female circumcision, performed on girls at the age of eight to twelve. A key preparation for this ritual is the *dimi* ceremony, celebrated by fathers whose eldest daughter is coming up to this age. People pack their homes up on to donkeys and travel to a temporary *dimi* village where cattle are slaughtered and there is feasting and dancing. The girls are blessed for fertility and future marriage by the *ara*, leaders of the most senior generation. Men and women dress in animal fur capes, and the daughters' fathers acquire the status of elders. We hadn't planned this, but it seemed from reports that the next *dimi* was due to start very soon, possibly even later that week, so it was crucial for us not to delay any more than necessary.

After another day in camp, Zablon had recovered enough for us to move, so Willow and Renée drove off to the muddy little town of Omorate to collect our new interpreters: a charming, good-looking guy called Ibrahim and a young man called Stephen whose reputation preceded him – apparently he had recently been expelled from his secondary school for drinking and breaking windows.

These two now accompanied Jon and me on the trek south, where Stephen's larger-than-life character soon became clear. Cocky, chatty and a bit of a lad, he was smoking pretty much non-stop, as well as chewing *chat*, the green, amphetamine-containing leaf that is used right across the Horn of Africa to bring a mild high. Ibrahim seemed equally bright and alert, but without the attitude, as he strode along with his Lucky Luke, bow-legged swagger.

The savannah we were crossing was bleak and bare and very thorny – the nasty little spikes were easily sharp enough to penetrate the useless canoe shoes I'd decided to wear. My original idea had been that if I wore flimsy shoes without cushioning, I would toughen up my soles a bit. Not to African standards, obviously, but enough to let me keep up better with the locals. One look at my battered feet showed how badly this plan had backfired. After a night crashed out at a roadside clinic where there was a water pump, I took a painkiller, something I do only rarely.

As we walked on in the morning light we passed people from a Dassanech village, hoofing it along the track on their thrice-daily trek for drinking water. They were as friendly and smiley as we usually find people to be, though clearly very poor, and with rotten yellow teeth (owing to impurities in the drinking water, apparently). By midday our destination village had appeared on the horizon. Across the windblown dried-mud terrain it looked like something from a *Star Wars* set, a series of makeshift dwellings patched together with reed mats and silvery oblongs of corrugated iron reflecting the bright sun. This was a very different scene from the well-built, permanent huts of the Hamar. Everyone seemed happy to see us, and there was much grinning and shaking of hands. It was baking hot by now, like standing in the open doorway of an oven, so we quickly dived through one of the narrow entrances into the cooler shade within.

The village chief was away, so in his absence we were introduced to a very charismatic lady called Abanesh, whose well-weathered features settled most often into a huge welcoming smile, generally accompanied by a wonderful gurgle of laughter. She had strings and strings of beads around her neck, mostly in orange and green, and bangles at her wrists and elbows, which jangled with her every gesture. She wore a brown headband through her braided hair and canned-drink ring pulls as earrings. She exuded character from every pore. As we sat chilling in her hut and drinking coffee, I knew instinctively she would become a big part of my stay here.

'Peace to the country you come from. May God grant you what you're looking for,' was the translation of her welcoming remarks. To the younger women seated on her left, she nodded sagely.

'These are real men,' she told them. 'They came here on foot. They carried bags on their backs. And now they're exhausted.'

Just for now I wasn't to understand this aside, but it was instantly clear that, the bigger picture of gender dynamics notwithstanding, the women ran the show round here. To the right of the doorway sat a couple of blokes who were clearly the worse for drink, swaying and lolling and making little sense; while to the left sat Abanesh and the other ladies, bright-eyed, sober, and very much on the ball.

I remarked on this to camera, which was fine until Stephen translated my comments without me knowing. It was a blunder which could have been disastrous. I could tell the men were trying their hardest to muster some sort of retort. But their protestations were flimsy and only lasted half a minute before they were henpecked back into silence. Luckily it turned out later that my comments weren't considered rude and were seen by both sides as a simple observation reflecting an all-too-real truth.

James had now arrived with Willow and Renée in one of the vehicles, so we headed back to the newly set-up crew camp, under a tree on a dry river bed a kilometre away. Perhaps it was mild heat exhaustion, or maybe bad water, but I felt dreadful and was soon throwing up. Essentially I felt fine, but I couldn't hold down any fluids at all, despite taking anti-emetics and doing my best to drink bottled water and rehydration salts. It was potentially quite a dangerous situation, so I was half serious and half taking the piss when I asked Stephen to drive to the border and get me some weed from the contraband smugglers he'd told me about at some length. I've seen marijuana oil do wonders to stop vomiting when modern anti-emetics haven't worked, and felt as if I needed to stop my depletion of body fluids before I had to put myself on a drip. This was no recreational request. The ensuing debate was comical. According to BBC regulations, the only way I could take illicit drugs was if it was a filmed part of a local ceremony. My imminent death wasn't reason enough! Willow came up with a herbal remedy. At last, I began to feel better.

We had just made two films about cattle-herders and James was looking for something different for this final Omo episode, so the obvious choice was going to be the Dies fishermen down on the lake. James's plan was for me to accompany them on one of their distinctive crocodile hunts, before following the preparations for and celebration of the *dimi* festival in the village. So, after a day flat on my back recovering from my dehydration, we drove the four kilometres or so down to Lake Turkana's green, reed-fringed shore. What a sight – a wide expanse of water after all this parched-dry land. Further along its edge we found a Dies fishing camp, which despite the lovely location was even more basic than Abanesh's village, nothing more than a row of shelters made of flimsy mozzie nets and blankets strung between sticks. There were a few fishermen fixing nets and laying out fish to dry in the sun. The place was littered with bones and scales and the occasional skeleton of a fish-head. Some of these heads were massive, an indication of what lay in the depths of the lake, and one of them had its gaping jaw open so widely that a Labrador-sized dog could easily have walked through it. Later we came across a number of hippo ivory tusks decaying on the ground. Many of the kids had large crocodile teeth as necklaces.

I was introduced to Orkotch and Bario, two crocodile fishermen Zablon had arranged for us to meet. Wearing a red Manchester United football shirt above his tartan wrap, Orkotch was at work repairing a 2·5-metre harpoon. Bario was a much older guy, with a jokey manner and a wily smile. We waded out through the reedy shallows to their dugout canoes, which were treacherously narrow. I found it almost impossible to sit in them facing front to back, so tried twisting sideways, which was hardly comfortable. As we wobbled along over the smooth water, poled by a standing Orkotch, Stephen, who was in my boat too, kept complaining about my lack of balance. I was surprised, because I didn't think it was *that* bad. It soon transpired that it was in fact *he* who had never been in a canoe before and was upsetting our equilibrium.

On our return to the village, we came upon a fish flapping around in a net, which Stephen decided to appropriate for our supper, despite the fact that it all too obviously belonged to a young boy who was tending his nets a few metres away. I questioned his actions but he assured me this was all fine – he'd spoken to the kid. As he was the local, who knew the language, who was I to disagree? Only when I heard the boy crying as we left did I realize our new interpreter was rapidly turning into a liability.

Orkotch and Bario gave me an on-land lesson in how to catch crocodiles with a harpoon. The sharp, barbed metal hook is quite short and it's to this that the rope is tied. The harpoon is then inserted into a sawn-off oryx horn, which is in turn attached, as a tubular head, to the long pole. When the harpoon strikes the prey, the barbed head detaches from its horn holder, and the rope is allowed to feed out, with the thrashing croc at one end and the canoe at the other. When the croc has tired itself out, it's dragged closer and the beast is finished off with a spear.

I asked the obvious question about the largest croc they'd ever caught and was rewarded with the usual fisherman's answer. It was huge, they told me, longer than the canoe we were standing by – which would make it over 7·5 metres long! Its teeth, they added, holding out their hands, were as big as *this*. Even if they were exaggerating, the lake was famous for its massive crocs and the nocturnal hunt, which we hoped would be one of the high points of our film, was going to be seriously exciting, not to say scary – especially from within a small dugout canoe.

Later that night in camp we discovered that, contrary to what we'd been told before, the *dimi* ceremony was not happening this week after all, so croc hunting was now at the top of James's agenda. The following afternoon we headed back down to the lake and Orkotch and Bario's camp. Before we went out too far on the lake, we'd decided to organize a back-up safety boat for the crew, but it had failed to turn up, so we spent the time instead with me practising my boating skills – joke time for the camera, not to mention for Orkotch and his friends.

The canoe was very long and banana-shaped, the pole long and heavy, and even without Stephen on board my balance was somewhat suspect. With the help of some dodgily translated instructions, and with Stephen adding his own style of commentary – 'Do it like this, do it like that!' – I finally got under way. Just keeping the thing in a straight line was hard enough, and essential, because there was only one narrow channel out through the reeds to the deep water of the lake. The boat's shape gave it a permanent drift to starboard, and the bow only had to touch one of the reed-tufts to send the nose glancing off to one side. Advice on what I was doing wrong was being shouted at me by all and sundry, including James and Jon, so I just carried on with a grin on my face. Only after I'd fallen in a couple of times did I finally begin to get the hang of it. The sun was setting now, turning the sky orange and the distant lake purple. It was all incredibly serene and beautiful.

The old boy Bario had told us that he was the best hunter in the area and had a fleet of boats, which his sons were going to bring over that evening. He was a good, strong and entertaining character and he invited me to stay with him in his hut, but just before I agreed we discovered he'd been fibbing all along – about everything. No boats turned up because he had no boats. Or, as it happened, sons. He probably didn't have a hut for me to stay in either. He was a master waffler and although I enjoyed his company, James thought he was probably too unreliable for me to live with. So we headed back to camp to accept the wonderful Abanesh's offer instead.

'You'll find all you want,' she said, 'by living in a hut like this. You'll find all you need here. You're welcome to stay with me.'

'What a very generous and kind offer,' I replied, shaking her hand.

That evening we were off on our first croc hunt. Our back-up safety boat had finally arrived, a fishing boat with a crew of three. Initially it was hard to see how it could follow the canoes into the reedy shallows where we'd most likely find the crocs; but it turned out to be ideal, solid and steady, with a very shallow draught.

We set off at dusk, in two canoes, with the sunset still a yellow-pink glow beyond the silhouetted reeds. The moon was just a skinny sliver, lying flat on its back. By the shore, the lake was windless and the water still. Apart from the canoes and the safety boat following, the only sound was of croaking frogs and the incessant mosquitoes whining in our ears.

'Before we go out on our first hunt,' I asked Orkotch, 'is there anything I should know?'

'Nobody talks,' he explained. 'We signal with our hands. We don't speak to each other. We just point. You won't do anything when the crocodile approaches us. We'll harpoon it. We'll fight it. And you just watch.'

These were their words, in their language, which I only found out later from the detailed translations of the filmed footage. 'They say that you do nothing. You just stay and see how they hunt,' was Stephen's version of this.

'If the crocodile is too close,' Orkotch added, 'it'll try to bite the canoe, and then dive underwater. If the crocodile does bite the boat, the boat will be crushed. Only God can protect us from this.'

'Only God,' said Stephen, 'can protect us from these kinds of dangers.' It was lucky I didn't realize at the time how lame his translations were.

Orkotch and his team paddled us expertly down the long narrow channel and on to the open waters of the lake. There was quite a swell out here, and the water was choppier, slapping against the canoe's side. I was in one canoe with two hunters and there were another two hunters in the second. Behind, invisible in the darkness, the safety boat trailed us. If and when we got a croc, the plan was that I would radio them in to film the kill. Otherwise I was on my own with the Bruce-cam.

We made good speed towards the northern end of the lake. Once we were in among the tall reeds again the wind dropped and the mosquitoes became intolerable. I decided to bring out some repellent and hand it round. There was a bit of confusion as the guys kept inverting the bottle so that the spray pump didn't work, but we got there in the end. Now we were poling slowly and very quietly, scanning the beds with torches, which they held in their mouths. Suddenly we saw what we were looking for: a pair of orange eyes shining back through the darkness. They were over thirty centimetres apart, so this was a biggie. My heart was in my mouth, but the guys whispered among themselves and decided to let it go. It wouldn't be safe to try to bring it in with just two boats, I found out later. I would have probably agreed with this assessment. Our canoe was only centimetres from the water. My elbows dragged the surface. If anything kicked off I was definitely at teeth height.

We poled around for an hour or so, but after our first encounter that was it. Nothing else doing tonight. It was too windy, they said. We headed back across the lake in the dark, an extraordinary feat of navigation as, even with Orion shining brightly above us, one set of rushes looked identical to another. But the guys knew their territory and soon we were poling up the channel towards home. We went in some way, and then they jumped out. I blithely followed suit, assuming they knew these shallows were free of crocs. Then, just as I'd turned to look for the crew boat, everyone jumped back in and poled off. I wasn't expecting that. Maybe it was too shallow for all of us and I'd inadvertently volunteered to be the wader, now I was stranded at least 500 metres from the bank with the safety boat nowhere to be seen. I splashed along behind the canoes, rationalizing an otherwise simmering fear by telling myself that these guys must know what they were doing. Then, halfway home, my naked foot landed firmly on something scaly that wriggled then splashed out of the way. My heart skipped a beat.

'Hey!' I yelled by way of adrenalin release, and then quickly calmed myself. There was laughter from the bank. Soon enough, thank God, I was there too, climbing at speed out of the water. I was reminded all too powerfully of the time when I'd been crossing the Awash River in the Afar region of Ethiopia, which was full of big crocs. My colleague's translation of what the locals had told us was that it was safe to swim across. It was only when I was halfway over, pushing my floating camera case ahead of me in the water, that I sorted out the translation properly in my head. What they had in fact said was: 'It will be fine only if you go with the camels. They are too big for the crocodiles and together you won't be attacked.'

A few minutes later the second canoe and the safety boat arrived back and, lo and behold, they'd caught a little croc, though whether it was the one I'd just stepped on wasn't clear. It was only a metre long, tiny against the whopping 2·5 metre harpoon. They finished it off in front of us with four or five blows to the back of the head with the spear.

We jumped into Zablon's vehicle and took the crocodile back to the village where it was chopped up and put straight into the pot at two in the morning. Hungry, we ate it there and then. The flesh was white and sticky, more like pork than fish. I liked it a lot. There was no attempt to skin it, so, like the hippo ivory, it suggested there was no trade in animal parts in the area.

With a pleasantly full belly I crashed for the night in Abanesh's pitch-black little hut. Perhaps it was all the excitement of the hunt, my full stomach, or the softer straw mat that I'd been given to lie on, but I slept like a baby, even though I woke a couple of times to find one of Abanesh's daughters crawling all over me, limbs entwined with mine, her rather fishy breath very close to my face. I tried rolling away from her, allowing her the benefit of the doubt and hoping that her closeness was just because the hut was overcrowded or she was having an excitable dream. But when I surfaced in the morning and looked around, the hut was almost empty. My new night companion had been the youngest, unmarried girl, I was fairly sure – she was fifteen tops. Abanesh had obviously heard the girl because she quizzed me about it over our breakfast of unleavened bread and soya porridge. We were communicating entirely in sign language and I was fully under the spotlight. I'd done nothing but to deny the girl's advances would be like admitting guilt, so I nodded and agreed that something had happened, but laughed it off with a 'Don't worry, I wasn't interested' look, at which the wonderful old lady let out a quick squeal at the poor adolescent before laughing heartily and defusing the whole situation. Phew! Honesty had paid off for me, at least, and as I caught the girl's eye, she gave me a sly, twinkly flash of a grin before putting on a straight face for the matriarch. Luckily nothing more was said and the situation never arose again.

Mid-morning Willow and Jon appeared from camp with Stephen and we had a long chat with Abanesh and her equally cool friend Bota, who was the local healer, about everything from the myths of the tribe to the controversial topic of female circumcision. There was little need for translation as the women explained this process with all-too-graphic gestures. The top of the finger represented the clitoris, held by the other hand to show just the tip, then there was a slicing action to show the first part of the removal, followed by a scoop and so forth. The girls who are being mutilated in this way are often no more than eight years old. After the event they have their knees tied together to encourage healing. In my travels I'd become aware of the incidence of infection and death from this act, as well as the human and female rights arguments, but as a new guest in her house, I didn't feel it was appropriate to probe Abanesh just yet. It made me squirm to watch just the mime of this custom, but Abanesh and her friend were unwavering advocates. It was Dassanech culture, they said. 'No one will ever stop this. It's the most important tradition for us. The huts we live in are not important. I could live in a tree, or a house, like other Ethiopians, but changing our culture about this is impossible.'

Later they did a separate interview with Willow, as they were unwilling to go into too much detail with a man. 'If a woman with a clitoris gives birth,' they told her, 'she, her child and everyone will die. Her clitoris will come up to her head. It'll come out of her nose, and then back into her head. It'll kill her; she'll die. Her father will die, her mother will die. That is why we cannot stop circumcising girls.' Not only was Bota the local healer, but she was also one of the women who would be directly involved in the circumcision of the young girls at the *dimi*.

Newcomers were now starting to arrive for the ceremony. Donkeys clustered round the makeshift huts, laden down with building material. We watched from the shade as one lone woman slowly constructed her house, banging tentpole-like sticks into the hard ground with a big stone, then adding the various components. The family's possessions, meanwhile, were scattered on the ground for all to see. Putting up the house was, like so many other things in this culture, the responsibility of the female, and even as this woman toiled in the heat, her husband was sitting under a tree somewhere and would return at the end of the day expecting the house to be completed. I decided to give her a hand, even though I knew we would be off hunting before long. She was grateful and my efforts provided amusement for the other women watching. As always it felt good to be doing something constructive rather than having to act the privileged white man, something it was impossible not to do over in crew camp, surrounded by vehicles, hi-tech equipment, bottled water, good food, and everything else that distinguished us from the locals. Desert dwellers are not shy of asking, and it's a tradition out here that people should give when they can. We, by contrast, were waiting until the very end of our stay before offering gifts, as we knew from experience that to give out stuff too early could create an imbalance in the community as well as problems for the shoot. I hated the whole business of sitting in luxury, drinking water, eating well, and denying our hangers-on even the most basic gifts like empty water bottles. But the disparity was inescapable on this type of shoot. One of the advantages of staying in the village was that I was temporarily away from that awkward divide.

As the sun sank in the sky we headed back to the lake for a second croc hunt. Dusk saw us poling out into the reeds. After half an hour there was a loud whisper of 'B-e-e-er-uce' and Orkotch pointed at a pair of glowing orange eyes away to the left. But as we approached they sank into the black depths and were gone. We stayed out for most of the night but returned empty-handed.

At James's request I crashed in the crew camp. We didn't want to disturb Abanesh in the early hours again (especially as we'd caught nothing), because she was always so welcoming that she would have woken everyone up to fuss over me.

The next evening it was too windy and choppy out on the lake to go hunting, so I joined the crew for dinner in the camp: pesto mash, accompanied by sushi-style slivers of ginger, washed down with white wine; we scoffed them all down in seconds. In this second series I was definitely letting slip my previously strict rule about not enjoying crew luxuries; I ate so much I could hardly move, and back at Abanesh's I couldn't sleep because I was so stuffed. As a result I was awake at dawn to hear the familiar crackling of twigs outside as the fires were started, lit from a single flame carried round the village by a woman from the 'fire-starting clan'.

Later there was more talk of the approaching *dimi*, now, it seemed, scheduled for the coming weekend. So when the crew arrived we filmed one of the fathers who would become an elder at the ceremony. He had three daughters, the oldest of whom, Lochye, was due to be circumcised. She was too young, I thought, watching her giggling at the attention of the cameras, to understand fully what was going to happen to her. Meanwhile, Abanesh titillated us with descriptions of the festival, days of dance and song, with everyone dressed up in clothes so smart – as she put it – you would think they were Europeans. She herself had a suit of ostrich feathers, leopard skins and giraffe-tail elbow wands. (For a second I wondered if the last tourists through had been from Milan!)

That evening we were off to try to catch crocs again, this time taking sleeping gear so that we could stay out and continue in the morning if necessary. But when we got out on the water at dusk we had to turn round and come back. The wind was up again and the waves on the open lake were too high. James was visibly annoyed, having been reassured earlier by the guys that all was going to be fine. It was an all-too-modern culture clash, I thought. On the one hand our BBC deadlines; on the other the timeless Dies. Eventually the wind dropped and we were able to go. We ventured into the tall reeds at the north of the lake, where we saw a pair of telltale eyes in the water. Even from 300 metres away they looked huge, so I thought we'd spotted a whopper.

As we got close, the harpooner stood up – very late, it seemed to me – chucked the harpoon and missed, so it just stuck there in the mud, like Excalibur. Undaunted, the guys swept the scene with the torch beam and to my utter amazement the foolish croc re-emerged, barely ten metres away. A quick regroup and turn, a better throw and we had it. With the harpoon buried in the croc's flesh, we backed off into the reeds while the other crew came in to help. This convinced me it must be a giant. But there was little splashing and I soon saw it was quite small. The second harpoon was plunged in for good measure. By this time the crew boat had arrived, the lights were on, and Jon was filming the final dispatch on the bigger camera.

Our blood was up now. It had been an exciting scene, but the croc was only a tiddler and everyone wanted more. So we set off again through the reeds. It wasn't long before we saw another one, motionless in the still water, and then, after a magnificent throw from Orkotch, we'd pulled it into the boat. With two crocs caught we turned for home, but the canoe was leaking badly and filling up with water. Up the front, Orkotch was sitting on my camera box and in the back another of the guys called Ngiriey was standing, so they ignored my comments at first. Eventually they saw fit to bail, but it was too late and the boat tilted right over and nearly capsized. Ngiriey went overboard head first. Dressed in his best shirt, he wasn't amused, especially as Orkotch and I were sniggering like schoolgirls.

The hunt was over. We drove back with Zablon to camp and in the morning I gave Abanesh the smaller of the two crocs, which she roasted right away on the fire. Boiled croc had been nice enough, but roast croc was something else, delicious with a slightly smoky flavour, even tastier than pork. Abanesh had an oddly intimate habit of popping morsels of food into my mouth with her fingers, as if we were young lovers. It was surely a local custom, so I felt ashamed at finding it a bit of an invasion of my notion of personal space. Belly full, she was her usual feisty self. 'God decides everything,' she told me. 'If he decides you'll kill a big one, then you'll kill a big one. If he decides you'll be eaten, then you'll be eaten.' Thanks, Abanesh.

Life is tough in this scorched and barren landscape. Later that day I joined the kids collecting water. It was a good thirty-minute walk away from the village in flip-flops, carrying a 23-litre plastic can.

'So how old are you?' I asked one of them.

'I am ten years old,' came the reply, in English.

'And how old are you?' I asked another.

'Ten years old.'

They were all ten, it seemed, even the tiniest of them. They laughed at my feigned confusion.

Whatever age they really were, these kids were amazingly hardy. With the continuing drought throughout Dassanech lands, they were making this journey to get basic water three times a day. We arrived at the dry river bed to find a series of large holes, in which women from all over were struggling to fill up their water cans. My little posse walked past several crowded ones to find a well where we could climb down and scoop up some very murky liquid from the tiniest of puddles at the bottom. But even with the little cups we were using, the hole wasn't refilling as fast as we were extracting. We had to visit two more before we had enough.

By the time we set off home it was overcast. I was relieved. Trekking back in direct sunlight would have been hell, and I would probably have had to drink half of my can just to stay hydrated. Then the clouds grew darker, a sudden wind got up, swirling the dust up from the dry ground, and there were brilliant forks of lightning on the black horizon, approaching fast. In a moment of rare paranoia I switched off my radio mic, in case the lightning found the one electrical receiver for miles. There was everything a storm should have except rain. We slogged on through the swirling dust, the jerrycan balanced on my head dripping water on my face, the wetness picking up clinging sand, which I couldn't sweep off; I needed both my hands to try to keep the heavy wobbling can steady. How the young girls and boys beside me carried theirs, vertically, with no hands, God alone knows. Every now and then, as if to confirm my inadequacy, they put in a little run, still with no hands. As we reached the village, the sun was setting through the storm – a spectacular display of colour. That night I was kept awake by the sound of singing and dancing. It had been the rain clan, Abanesh told me in the morning, praying unsuccessfully for rain.

I sat with her while she elaborated on the Dassanech's clan system. There are eight groups, she told me, and everyone, herder or fisherman, is a member of one of them. Galbur, the largest, is the water and crocodile clan; these people have the power over (unsurprisingly) water and crocodiles, and are responsible for any glandular discomforts in the society. Fargano, the next biggest, is the snake and fire clan. Members of this group have power over snakes and diseases; they are responsible for dealing with snakebites and also for lighting fires, using sticks known as *miede*. It was one of these I'd seen the other morning, going round the village like an old-fashioned lamplighter. Next up are the Turnyerim, or circumcision clan; they are always first in line during the ceremony and they dig the hole where circumcision blood is ritually discarded. They are also, for some reason, responsible for cattle raids. Then there are the Edhe, with power over the wind, responsible for eye infections; the Turat, who are healers, responsible for burns caused by fire, who spit on scalded flesh to cure it; the Illi, the scorpion and spider clan, with powers to cure bites from these insects; the Murulle, the magic clan, responsible for sorcery and also removing discomfort caused by muscle ache; and finally the Tieme, the smallest clan, responsible for the correct working of the pancreas. Strict rules forbid people to dance with or marry others in the same clan.

Abanesh herself was one of the Turat, the healing clan, while her son was one of the Galbur. His prayers would keep me safe, she told me, while I was out hunting. 'Before you go,' she said, 'this will be said: "My father's lake, my father's fish."' This, accompanied by a hiss–spit, would protect me. 'After this blessing, nothing will happen to you.'

I certainly hoped so as we headed out on to the lake that evening one last time. Although we'd caught a few crocs, none had been worthy of a really good TV sequence. I knew any catch would provide some much-needed food, and I hated myself for it, but in a way, short of sleep, sun-dazed, quietly longing for home, I was swept up with the same obsessive desire to shoot a decent climax for our film; modern desensitized audiences required big drama.

And for our excursion tonight the guys had cut a trail through the reeds to a new hunting area, so we were hoping for a good result. The moon was bright; we waited for it to set before we departed, then poled out in the pitch darkness over the silent, gently rippling water, eyes peeled. After only ten minutes in the new area we had one in our sights. The glowing orange eyes were far apart. This was no juvenile.

Orkotch was at the front with the harpoon while Ngiriey stood steering at the back. I was the only one sitting, just centimetres above the water, the closest thing to the croc itself. Against the torchlight, I saw Orkotch's arm raised, then the harpoon was thrown and the water erupted. Judging from the wild thrashing and splashing, this was a much bigger beast. I did my best to keep the Bruce-cam and its infra-red light trained on the action, while Ngiriey at the rear poled us backwards at speed towards the reeds, the boat rocking madly from side to side. It was all I could do to help keep it upright.

Capsizing now didn't bear thinking about. The croc was wounded, angry and thrashing wildly.

Once jammed into the reeds we were thankfully much more

stable, and Orkotch could start to tug at the harpoon with the rope. The crew boat had closed in now, the lights were on and Jon was filming with the main camera. With seemingly relative ease the croc was dragged towards the reeds. Now one of the guys stabbed down sharply with the spear, into the neck. A couple more blows subdued it. Bizarrely, the croc went down far quicker than some of the smaller ones we'd struggled with on previous nights.

So there it was, lifeless in the water: an adult crocodile. Only then did I notice that our metal spear was completely bent over from the death blows, like a plastic joke spear. We set about dragging him on board, laughing with nervous relief. We'd done it – everyone was happy, crew and Dies alike.

Back on land a hole was cut in the crocodile's gullet and a rope fed through. It was a heavy old beast to pull over the ground, but there would be plenty of meat to eat, enough for the whole village. We dragged it to the vehicles, hoisted it up, then strapped it to a roof and drove off to the crew camp to show Zablon. There were celebratory fizzy drinks all round and lots of back-slapping, and then as the dawn approached we carried it into the village on our shoulders. Abanesh was there to welcome us, and one by one the community turned out to see what we'd brought in until a large crowd had gathered. On the ground the animal was swiftly cut up. The huge tail vanished into one of our hunters' huts, while pots appeared from every corner to collect offal, feet and slabs of meat from further up the carcass. There was no shortage and everyone was visibly delighted.

It was mid-December, we'd been on the road for three months, and were feeling it. The thought of a soft bed and some time to recover from the tribulations of being in the bush were all too powerful. Zablon, meanwhile, was racing around as energetically as always, trying to find out when exactly the much-heralded *dimi* would take place. Initially we had rushed down here thinking it was going to be on our first weekend. Now it wasn't clear when it would occur. The Dassanech were in no rush. Day by day, people were still arriving. The ceremony would happen when it would happen.

That evening James and Zablon came back into the village with me. The hope had been for me to interview Abanesh about circumcision, but there would be no chance of that. The place was noisy with new arrivals, many of them drunk on *arak*. Worse still, Stephen, our troublesome schoolboy interpreter, had gone on a major piss-up and had ended up abusing everyone and everything around him. As we arrived he was standing, drunk, at the centre of a mob who were on the brink of kicking ten barrels of crap out of him. Whether he was in the right or the wrong, we couldn't allow that to happen. So Zablon dived into the crowd and, after protracted and heated words, managed to drag him out. This was serious. Although a local himself, Stephen was inextricably linked to us and any bad behaviour on his part only reflected poorly on us.

Back at camp we sat around in silence, contemplating the options for the end of the shoot. Even without Stephen's unhelpful intervention, the *dimi* was, at the very best estimate, many days away.

After a good night's sleep things seemed clearer. One final discussion over breakfast, then James took the decision not to wait for the *dimi*. What with the crocodile hunts and the warmth of my reception from the wonderful Abanesh, we had enough material to make a film. So we would have one more day of filming and then be off: dust-storm shots when the wind was up in the morning; a couple of great final interviews with Abanesh; then another with Lochye, the little girl who was about to be circumcised.

Abanesh knew now that we weren't staying for the *dimi*, so a bit of dancing was arranged to wish me farewell. After that, I slept out under the brilliant stars – at least until 4 a.m., when cold drove me back into the hut.

The following morning, after an hour or so of payments and gift-giving, it was time to say goodbye. I was genuinely sad to be parting from this warm-hearted woman. 'I can't say how much you've meant to me,' I told her. 'I can't express it. You have just done everything for my stay here. You've smoothed the way, you've fed me, housed me, and more than anything, you've informed me and entertained me. Abanesh, you're a million dollars.'

She smiled and nodded along to the translation Ibrahim gave to my words. 'It's all right, it's all right,' she repeated. Then: 'I think he's saying he won't forget me.' Then: '*Yamari, yamari* – I hear it, I hear it. No problem, have a safe journey. May God be with you.'

Abanesh was undoubtedly one of the most amazing women I'd ever met – a strong village leader as well as a generous and gentle host who'd taught me much. Not least, she'd reinforced my views about remaining positive and cheerful in the face of harsh times.

As we drove northwards towards Addis, I thought about her staunch views about female circumcision. Despite all the positive aspects to my recent experiences, there were one or two highly challenging areas. My Sanema-inspired conviction that I should never judge another culture had been fully tested on this three-month journey. With the Nyangatom there had been Challis's zest for war; with the Hamar, Duba's rejection of female equality; and now Abanesh's firm belief about something that seemed so barbaric from the perspective of my culture.

What to think? Well, maybe it *was* OK to admit not liking something without actually going so far as to judge it; agree to disagree without hatred or superiority.

I must admit that I did hope that one day the young girls of the Omo Valley would be able to maintain the same pride in their culture that Abanesh shared, while not having to generally feel inferior to their menfolk or undergo ritual whipping or circumcision in order to be seen as one of their community. I knew that it wasn't my role at that time to voice those opinions – unwanted external pressure is not the best way to invite change; indeed it can often have the reverse effect. To my mind, real change can only come from within, and I thought that brave Hamar girl Keri was a shining beacon of hope for the future.

10. A Sour Taste?

The Matis of Amazonia, Brazil

It was the start of the third series and I was travelling upstream into the Amazonian jungle in a little boat, which came complete with a thatched roof. Just behind us on this beautiful, wide, silvery expanse of water was a stores boat, laden down with food and fuel, and behind that a speedboat that we were using as a filming platform, idling along at its lowest possible rev, then speeding up to nip round and get different camera angles.

As we chugged on up the river, the sound of our little two-stroke engine echoing against the wall of jungle trees was uncannily similar to a troupe of babbling monkeys. I had plenty of time to read about the remote tribal group we were visiting. Called the Matis, they had remained isolated from the outside world until the 1970s. Although their first official contact had been entirely peaceful – an exploratory visit by Brazil's National Foundation for Indians (FUNAI) – it had brought disaster in its wake, as they had subsequently mixed with loggers and miners working in the area and had contracted a number of

Western diseases. Within a few years epidemics had wiped out almost a third of their population, leaving fewer than a hundred alive. To rebuild their community they had had to adjust their long-established taboos about how close a kin they could marry and procreate with; as a result of these extreme measures their numbers had increased and things had begun to improve. Then in 1996 their land had been designated as part of the huge Vale do Javari National Park, over twice the size of Belgium, from which all commercial operations were banned. Now outsiders were only allowed in with special permits, which were hard to obtain and carried strict vaccination requirements.

After three long days on the river, we reached the edge of this National Park, and stopped off at the riverside FUNAI post to get our paperwork and vaccination certificates checked. Everything was in order and we were allocated two armed guards, who were partly for our protection and partly, it was soon clear, to prevent us from stopping to film another indigenous group who lived near the edge of the park, the Korubo. Unlike the Matis, they remain almost entirely uncontacted. They are known locally as *caceteiros* ('head bashers'), as the story goes that they have in the past lured passing boats to their banks, then invited the boatmen on shore, clubbed them to death and taken their goods. Now, as we pushed on against the stream, we could see a few of these people on the shady banks. On two separate occasions they were making distinct beckoning gestures. Whether the tales we'd heard were true or not I didn't know, but I was glad that any temptation to film or talk to them was stopped by our stern-faced guards.

Two days later we finally pulled up at the village of Aurelio, one of only two existing Matis communities. Under the tall trees stood a crowd of villagers in brightly coloured T-shirts, waving. At least I thought that's what they were doing, as I waved back cheerfully. But as the boat came closer to the high muddy banks, I realized they were busily slapping off sandflies. This didn't bode well. My arms and legs were already covered in tiny red dots from these ubiquitous insects (known locally as *pium*), which have a painless bite but soon leave an itchy red dot of blood. I had dosed myself up on antihistamine to reduce my maddening desire to scratch.

I called out the Matis greetings I'd rehearsed: '*Braa*', which means 'OK' or 'Everything's fine', and '*Awutsi mibu pia?*' which is a kind of 'How are you?', literally meaning, 'What have you eaten?' It was good to hear the same phrase in reply, followed by a string of other words which could have been another form of greeting or possibly a long list of someone's lunch menu.

I stepped off the prow and across the wooden gangplank that had been placed between us and the two-metre-high riverbank.

The coloured T-shirts were a sign of change and trade, but as I got closer to the Matis I could see that their faces showed more traditional decoration, with pale tattooed lines running in parallel on forehead and cheeks, and whisker-like sticks prickling out from the base of the nose (they've historically been called 'Jaguar People' by many outsiders). A couple of men had crescent-shaped bones through their septa. Most had big ear plugs, two-centimetres wide. One man had two conical shells in the ends of hollow tubes which went though his earlobes; they looked like two sink plungers hanging from his stretched ears. As I shook hands all round there were plenty of smiles. Ivano, our Portuguese-speaking Brazilian fixer, and Philippe, our Matis-speaking French anthropologist, translated our greetings back and forth.

The village was set back in a wide clearing some hundred metres or so from the river. It looked perfect for our film. There were large wooden huts with V-shaped thatched roofs, set up a metre off the ground on stilts. Among them stood banana groves in various stages of growth, and the odd love palm reaching for the sky. Spider monkeys loped around, one or two actually piggy-backed on a child's shoulder. At the village's centre was a magnificent longhouse, like a huge thatched wedge of cheese, its roof running right to the ground. The door that took you into its gloomy interior was barely a quarter of its total height.

The chief of Aurelio, Chema, was all smiles. He wanted to talk about our filming intentions immediately, but it was last light now and we were all exhausted after our long journey. So Wayne Derrick, our director, managed to postpone this discussion till the following morning. We set about moving our gear into two huts that had just been cleared ready for us: myself and the crew in one; support team and kitchen in the other.

This was Wayne's first *Tribe* project, but I'd worked with him the previous summer on *Blizzard: Race to the Pole*, a six-part BBC2 series about Scott of the Antarctic. A laid-back American, he had made many films about indigenous peoples over the years. Alongside Wayne, Philippe and Ivano, we had my old friend Willow Murton as researcher, together with Matt Fletcher, who had been out on a preliminary recce of Aurelio some months before. We got ourselves settled in, had a little supper, then crashed out. I fell asleep to the sound of rain on the thatch and Domingo, our FUNAI patrol man, doing some shamanizing on a sick child, singing gently to him in his native Marubo language.

It was lucky Wayne had kept our negotiations till we were fresh. Despite Chema's friendly aspect, this meeting wasn't nearly as easy as I'd anticipated. To start with, the people of Aurelio didn't want us to do any filming at all until their terms had been settled. Then, when I explained that we didn't have a list of items we wanted to film, we just wanted to watch and record life as it was, it didn't meet with the familiar warm reception.

It was all very well us wanting to film, they told us, but they wanted a school, a clinic, even an airstrip in return. In particular they wanted medicines for hepatitis and anti-snake venom. This was all very worrying because our filming terms and gift payments had been agreed upon down to the finest detail during Matt's recce. This was a complete change of mind and we had relatively few extra goods to offer anyway, let alone anything else with which to meet these extraordinary demands.

Their main objection seemed to be that we were offering an unfair exchange: we – the *turistas* – would make a film of their lives, which would last for ever and make us rich; while they in return were only going to get items such as solar panels, an outboard motor and fuel, which would run out after a few years. And if the motor broke down, who would fix it? The Matis were not trained as mechanics. Meanwhile, they argued, the photos and film of their spirits went on and on.

Many of the protesting voices were young. When outsiders had arrived before, they said (the Matis have been filmed many times), the elders had let them film without giving money. Now the younger people knew better. 'We're learning,' said one, 'and teaching the elders.' The younger people had heard that these films were sold for a lot of money in the world outside and if they were going to hand over 'their spirits' they wanted a share of that. Despite the fact that these new negotiations were potentially disastrous to us, the overt protective love and respect of these youngsters for their parents was a touching thing to see.

Their other key point was that they didn't want to be filmed 'in the old ways', as some crews had demanded: by removing the clothes they now wore and performing rituals that they had stopped doing years ago. On this point I was quick and clear with my answer. The whole philosophy of our programme was to film things as they are, not pretending that it was fifty years ago. I told them that if they let us record this meeting now, for example, we would include some of it in the film to prove that we were being honourable and telling their story sincerely. At this point they let Wayne go and get his camera.

We were on the same side, I reiterated. Regardless of their other filming experiences, we didn't want to hide the truth and make them take their T-shirts off; we wanted to film them as they are. And, I added, we wanted to tell the story of what they had been like before first contact, and what they wanted now. Our gift to them would be to help inform the world about their situation and their needs. I also wanted, I explained, to show the similarities between them and us, not highlight the exotic differences. I also felt confident that our payment was fair.

There was a lot more emotional talk about the school and the clinic, even a further demand for shotguns. But in the end, as they realized that in fact we were both wanting the same thing, the mood changed. Chema's furrowed brow was replaced with a smile.

'If this is true,' came the translation, 'then I welcome you.'

I caught Wayne's eye as we both simultaneously let out a huge sigh of relief.

With all the tribal communities I'd spent time with to date, I'd always stayed with the chief. But Chema didn't think it would be a good idea for me to live with him and his family in his hut and I never probed as to why. Instead he asked me where I'd like to stay and I suggested that he find a volunteer. Almost instantly a young-looking elder called Tumi offered to put me up.

So in the morning I moved into my new home. It was a recently built hut in the new style with a thatched roof and walls made from bamboo slats, full of arrows, darts, long blow-pipes and other fine examples of local craftwork. The hammocks were incredibly intricate in design. The fine latticework was an almost elastic weave of fibrous, rolled tree-bark string, which must have taken years to make – a definite upgrade from the previous South American design I'd slept in with the Sanema. Tumi and his wife Tupa were going to sleep in the same little room as me, in hammocks one above the other. On the other side of the partition in the hut slept their two daughters and two sons: Tume was a girl of about thirteen, Pousa a boy of ten, Txana a girl of about eight and Tumi junior a boy of about four. He reminded me of little Batana, the full-on child of my Darhad hosts in Mongolia. Even though we didn't share a language, he was cheeky and boisterous and full of questions.

Tumi senior was exactly the same age as me, thirty-six (though Willow quickly remarked that I looked forty-six while he looked twenty-six), and could remember first contact when he'd been a small child. 'I will never forget that,' he told me. Most of his family had died of the illnesses that had been introduced at that time to the community; he himself had been too ill to bury his dead parents. After that catastrophe, he had grown up with all the traditions from the old days but with constantly expanding horizons opening to him. He saw himself as a 'modern' person now, but it was instantly obvious to me that he was in fact the most traditional of his peers. He wore the obligatory T-shirt and shorts and lived in his newly made hut, but was the only man of his age who still knew how to make a blowpipe and knew the old songs.

Once I'd moved in, Tumi offered to take me out with his family to collect peach palm fruits from the forest. We walked a little way from the village to a clearing where these fruit trees stood together. Tumi then shinned up one of the trunks, taking a long, hooked pole to wrench bunches of fruit from adjacent palms. As these came crashing down noisily into the under-growth they were collected by me and his daughters in a basket. After an enjoyable morning of foraging in this way, Tumi took me down to the longhouse for lunch. This was a great social gathering, with the men sitting in an oblong in the middle of the space, while the women from each family prepared separate pots of food in different sections. Children ran around on the dirt floor while furry black monkeys climbed up and down the tall wooden poles and crossbars that held up the roof.

When each woman had cooked her husband his lunch, it was placed in front of him in a pot – but was then immediately shared round with the other men by him. Orange, fibrous peach palm soup and boiled manioc tubers seemed to be the staples, with bits of meat thrown in here and there. I was on my own now, without Philippe or Wayne, and didn't know the protocol for asking for food. Instead, I came in for a right old ribbing. Everything I said was immediately repeated round the group, to great laughter. One guy had been about to show me the stinging lotion they drip into each other's eyes as a ritual preparation for hunting, and I'd said, 'Wait, wait,' gesturing that I'd do it when the cameras turned up later. 'Wai, wai' came right back at me, over and over, until it was almost my new nickname.

After lunch Philippe was summoned from the crew hut, and we watched one of the Matis go through the eye-drop ritual. A small amount of sap was squeezed from a wrapped leaf palm into one open eye, then the other. As his face scrunched up in agony, he sang out a chant. He was repeating the names of fast animals, Philippe said, wishing himself to be like them:

'Humming bird's going, humming bird's going,
Quick ant's going, quick ant's going,
Fast bird's going, fast bird's going,
Deer's going, deer's going ...'

Inevitably I was asked again if I'd like to do it. Having seen how painful it was, my quick answer was no. I'd only just arrived, I said. In any case, thinking televisually, I wanted to build to such great scenes. But this was hardly an excuse I could use here. They wanted me to do it now, they repeated. Otherwise tomorrow, on the hunt, they'd be waiting too much for me to catch up. The eye drops made you faster, stopped you being lazy.

I had no answer to that so, with the cameras rolling, I sat down and took it. My right eye was first and that got a good dribble of juice. It was blindingly painful, and felt like an eye drop of Tabasco. My left eye was now wincing so much as reaction to the first stab of pain that it didn't get quite as much. It still stung like hell. The translation for me not to rub my eyes as it would only make them worse predictably came much too late.

I was then told that I'd accomplished the first of the four Matis pre-hunting rituals, which were, Chema explained: eye drops, whipping, frog poison and the *poces* leaf. Great! Can't wait! I thought.

It turned out that I needn't have bothered with the eye drops. There was no early shake to go hunting after all. Instead I spent the morning helping Tumi and his family with their daily tasks: chopping wood, washing bowls and collecting water. It was good to be working hard, and, as always, a great way to bond.

Around lunchtime I was summoned to the longhouse by Tumi's young son Pousa and invited to take my place at the southern end of the oblong of hungry Matis men. Food was shared out of individual pots and bowls as before. But when the soup went round I was yet again conspicuously left out. Why? Did they think I was still eating and drinking with the crew? Finally, after everyone had their bowls full, I was handed a mug of the stuff. This was a welcome relief, as my peach palm fruit and plantain were all very dry. But was my separate mug to distinguish me as a guest, or were they understandably para-noid about contracting a disease from me? I didn't feel it was something I could ask just yet.

After lunch Tumi took me down the path through the jungle towards the river, where I found a dozen or so men getting dressed up: in decorated headbands, with thin leather straps around their naked torsos and skirts made of green palm fronds at their waists. Besides that they were smearing themselves all over with the crimson flesh of a seed pod that looked just like a rambutan fruit.

They were preparing for a dance, it seemed, and they soon had my shirt off and were making me up like them, daubing the red *urucum* all over my white skin. As an outsider, I was given zigzag lines on my headband, not the spots of the Matis.

Philippe arrived and explained that this is a preparation for the peccary (wild boar) dance, a pre-hunt ritual which supposedly attracts their prey towards the village.

Once we were all ready we set off in a conga-style line, honking like hogs in a very evocative style. Some guys cracked pig jawbones together, and every now and then we all had a little squawking fit. We ducked to enter the gloom of the longhouse, then danced round and round the perimeter, keeping to the sides, sending the monkeys scurrying up into the eaves high above. An old woman chanted a song about killing a peccary, while keeping a beady eye on us.

Finally everyone ran back out into the sunshine and down to the village waterhole to wash off the red dye and cover themselves in clay. We replaced our palm-leaf skirts with waist straps made of tree bark and used big dollops of clay with protruding grassy tufts as our nose- and mouthpieces, whistling and squawking into them like some Second World War RAF pilot might hold his leather microphone. This was the capybara dance, in imitation of the giant jungle rodent of that name.

In the evening there were more dances, involving simulations of all kinds of jungle animals and birds. Unsurprisingly I became the brunt of most of the jokes. On a couple of occasions I was willingly 'killed', only to resurrect myself to great laughter. Then I was made to walk into a trap. After my loud – and, I hoped, charismatic – demise I was duly gutted and quartered by a gleeful bunch of trappers. It was brilliant fun.

The next morning we were at last off hunting. I barely had time to get my stuff together before Tumi was hurrying me down to the dugout canoe. We headed off downriver, outboard chugging, with about a dozen people on board, including a couple of boys and a woman. I counted six dogs, eight shotguns, two blowpipes and three sets of bow and arrows.

Our journey was longer than I'd expected, about an hour, and then we started dropping off small groups of two or three on the muddy bank. With just four of us left, we tied up the boat, climbed up into the jungle and were off. We were looking up through the tall tree trunks at the bright light of the high canopy. Almost immediately Tumi saw a small monkey and brought it down with one shot from his blowpipe. It was fantastic watching his skill with this seemingly unwieldy, 3·5-metre-long weapon. The poisoned darts are taken out of a small bamboo quiver, a groove is cut on the spot with a piranha jaw near the end to ensure the poison breaks off in the prey's body, then clay (carried in a monkey's jaw) is used to weight the front end, and a central stopper made from a cotton-like lint is spun with nimble fingers around the dart's shaft. This seals it tightly in the pipe until a big lungful of breath forces it out at speed, ensuring a deadly shot with a range of forty metres or more.

The rest of the day was manic. Tumi set a rapid pace and I was running almost constantly to keep up. But being alone without a cameraman meant that I could be fast and flexible. After an hour or so Tumi spotted peccary tracks and gave the blowpipe to Pousa and took up the shotgun. The peccaries' loud cries made them sound very close. White-lipped peccaries' can congregate in large herds and are sometimes aggressive, so I was becoming quite excited, spotting a tree stump refuge in case we were suddenly set upon by a pack of angry tusked animals. Then Tumi came back to get the blowpipe. Not for the boar, surely? A mimed conversation with Pousa confirmed my suspicion. The noise wasn't boar but howler monkey. I nipped through the undergrowth after him with my Bruce-cam and was just in time to get a great shot of the quarry, a reddish-brown howler, its snubby black nose almost silhouetted against the bright light from the canopy above. Tumi took aim, fired, and hit his target squarely in its chest. The monkey was now semi-paralysed with the arrow's poison, but still clinging to a branch until the neurotoxin took its effect, when it released its grip and fell to earth. A quick parcel was made out of a fern and Pousa got the load.

The day went on and on. At one time the dogs chased a lone collared peccary into one of its refuge lairs. I arrived as the hunters were frantically blocking off the various exit holes with sticks. Suddenly, with a great theatrical roar, the boar leapt out of a hole by my feet, ran almost between my legs and was off. It was all so quick that nobody fired a shot. The chase was back on again, the dogs right behind it, and us hunters behind them. This time when we cornered it, the beast was visible at the end of its hole, eyes shining with trapped fear. The barrel of a gun was nosed in and a shot fired.

Finally the hunt was over. After hours of running to keep up I was exhausted, but they accepted my offer of carrying the huge pig home. I had no idea how far we were from the river; but as we paced on, it dawned on me that it was going to be a long trek.

As when carrying wood with the Sanema, the pressure on my head made my left eardrum feel like it was going to explode. Worst of all was the fact that after only a few days in this heat and humidity, I was still completely unacclimatized: badly dehydrated and lacking strength. I felt I might faint at any moment, but didn't want to let on to my companions as to my weakness. The jungle was full of obstacles: particularly fallen logs, which I had to get on my knees to crawl under or scramble over, dragging the heavy carcass which kept getting snared in the undergrowth. The path seemed endless. It was reminiscent of my Commando training, yomping across Scottish bogs weighed down with heavy kit. I couldn't even get my Bruce-cam out to record my agony, as it was now malfunctioning because of the damp. The whole thing had become a personal struggle simply to try to keep credibility with my fellow hunters.

After a few hours we finally reached the river. I sat, shaking with exhaustion, as the boat headed slowly home against the current. As the sun went down it started to pour with rain and my problem of being way too hot rapidly became one of being too cold. Everyone was shivering in the gathering dark. It had been a tough day.

But that evening, with some palm beer inside me, I was in high spirits in Tumi's little hut, regaling the assembled company with the story of the boar charging out between my legs. I was glad that I hadn't let the side down during the hunt, although I was sure my struggle had been obvious, but then Tumi suddenly remarked that hunting with me was like going out with his brother and I hadn't held anyone up once. I don't think I'd ever received such a compliment during the whole making of *Tribe*. I played it cool but inside I was glowing.

The next day was altogether gentler. I still hadn't quite worked out the eating protocol at longhouse breakfast, so as ever missed out on the meaty soup that was being shared round. After a morning with Tumi foraging for fruit upriver, back in the longhouse for lunch, I decided not to stand on ceremony any longer with the communal food, but just help myself. When I did, they all grunted and nodded as if I'd done exactly the right thing. I felt a bit silly I hadn't got stuck in earlier. As usual, I'd been treading on eggshells unnecessarily.

In the afternoon Tumi called me to drink the juice of the sacred sour vine that they call *tachik*. They grate the outside of the vine on a hard stick with a monkey's molar teeth acting as the grinding edge. The tiny shavings are then squeezed into a bowl and a small amount of dirty fluid is extracted. When you drink it, Philippe explained, you have to swill it round your mouth before swallowing. The effect is quite disgusting, furring up your mouth with the acrid bitterness. But, as with the eye drops, this is supposed to improve your hunting ability, as sourness is all important. Normally, the Matis belief goes, men are sour and women are sweet; and everyone needs to be made sour to hunt effectively. White people are supposed to be especially sweet, so I dutifully drank three bowls of the bloody stuff.

'Anyone for tennis?' could have been our call the next

morning, as we got aboard the boat again for a fishing trip, all carrying racquet-sized and -shaped nets. It was back down the river to the hunting grounds of our previous day out, then a short trek into the jungle where a clearing was made. While the men went off to collect the poisonous root they use to asphyxiate the fish, the women stayed behind to cook lunch: manioc and a jungle fowl that had just been shot.

I decided to stay with the women and take the opportunity of asking them a bit about their lives. They began by showing me how they'd lit a fire in the past: with sticks. It was hard work making the flame, they said, and it hurt your hands. Now they had outsiders' matches and they preferred them.

They talked about the good side of life in the days before first contact. They weren't dangerously sick then, they said. If you had a headache, the shamans sucked the illness out of your head. If there was something wrong with your liver they could cure that too. Then the outsiders – the *nawas* – came; and their smell made the Matis sick. The older people were cold and shivering, and then they died. Most of these women were too young to remember it in great detail themselves, but it was clear, as the story came out in snatches from each of them, that the group memory was strong. Their grandfathers and grandmothers, aunts and uncles had all disappeared. Others scattered deep into the forest and washed themselves with sand, trying to remove the disease-bearing smell of the outsiders, but that hadn't helped. None of them got any better. The terrible smell of death in their villages was overpowering.

In pre-contact days, they continued, the Matis settlements had all been far more mobile; moving around the forest to different hunting grounds. Now, like the Sanema, they preferred being by the river as it was easier to get into town. Only the elders still went out hunting; the younger men stayed in the village and played football, something they'd learnt from outsiders. Nearly every Matis had been to Atalia, a town we'd passed through on our way up, where Brazilian girls in tight jeans rode around on motorbikes and the disco in the centre of town played happy house at full blast. Many had been further afield, to São Paulo, Brasilia, even Rio de Janeiro. All Matis families were fully aware of what the outside world looked like, but not necessarily confident of how to live there. So they went to town to sell their handicrafts: necklaces, hammocks and blowpipes. They got money to buy clothes. And beer, which made you fat, they said, laughing. But they liked Atalia to visit.

Before, they told me – loosening up now – the children had had many fathers. 'Now,' the women giggled, 'we don't go having sex with other men. These days the husbands get jealous.'

'He would be a good husband, this one,' said another of the women, smiling as she pointed at me. 'But our ancestors told us never to marry a foreigner. They told us to marry our own people.'

As Chema had informed me, the Matis have four key rituals to make them good hunters. I had already done the first, the agonizing eye drops. The next day it was time for the second – whipping. A short way downriver from the village Tumi, Philippe, Wayne and I disembarked and went looking for a rattan-type plant, from which the central stems were pulled. Pulled, not cut, as it is important that you should sweat while collecting them. After an hour or so we had quite a collection of long stems and sat down to whittle out their ends into a more flexible whip.

As we went on with this, I asked them why whipping was important. Tumi explained that if you are whipped by an elder the tiny thorns on the surface of the whip will pass on *sho* – their word for a human being's essential vitality. If you lose your *sho* you die. (I found *sho* a difficult concept but, as ever, having the brilliant Philippe at hand offered me a rapid insight into this complex culture.) Like the eye drops, the whipping also helps you get rid of laziness, as well as meaning that you can walk in the jungle without being scared. 'Even if you are shaking,' came

Philippe's translation, 'the jaguar won't attack. Being whipped gives you courage.'

Back at the village people had started to queue up for the whipping; if their hunting skills hadn't been up to scratch recently this would put them right. I knew I was going to have to do this sooner or later, so I drank a couple of bowls of bitter *tachik*, then stripped off my shirt and put my hands up on the special whipping post. I had no idea what to expect, but it wasn't so bad; though the whip brought a sharp sting, the pain didn't linger unduly, even as I was left with three impressive crimson stripes.

Meanwhile a more sinister form of whipping was going on in the longhouse. Two 'forest spirits' – or *miriwin* – had turned up, supposedly from the depths of the jungle. These were men whose bodies had been blackened with soot and thickly covered with vegetation like the dancers of the Babongo. Their faces were covered with evocative red clay masks and they carried the same long whips, with which they struck out at children who were being dragged forward by their parents for punishment. A couple of strokes round arms or legs and the kids ran off outside screaming: whether more from the pain or just the fear of the terrifying jungle spirit wasn't clear. Tumi explained to me that Matis parents have no corporal punishment at all but disobedient children are threatened with the *miriwin* as a form of deterrent – or an actual punishment if the parent feels it's deserved.

Before first contact, the *miriwin* had symbolized the forest spirits of the dark jungle all around this little gathering of humans.

Then, one day, the Matis had come across other strange beings too. Chema the chief remembered the first time he had encountered the *nawas*. He had been a small boy at the time. Their radio had been the first thing he'd heard.

'It sounded like a monkey,' he said, with that gentle smile. 'Yak, yak, yak.'

The family possessions

The kids collected water
three times every day

The one that didn't get away

Abanesh. I will never forget this woman

The peccary dance

The capybara dance

Tupa painting little Tumi

No one told me the
dye would last two
weeks. I looked rather
silly at Heathrow

Kencho loved his beer

The houses were beautifully and intricately designed

Penjo and his nephews in his amazing tent

'I like your island'

The heavyweight boxing
champ of Oceania

The Anutans of Polynesia, Solomon Islands

A real community day

Trying to keep up with Reuben

Then another time, when he was looking for the *tachik* vine by the Rio Branco, he saw them. The *nawas* were in the forest cutting rubber trees. White men. When he saw a shirt for the first time it looked like a necklace of teeth. 'But when I came closer I saw that it was not. It was a white shirt with a black stripe across the middle.

'We knew about these *nawas*, because our elders had told us about them, but we wanted to see them, despite the fact that we were afraid. And we got our first knife when they were carrying wood to the river and left their camp unguarded. After that we'd hide in the jungle and sneak into the camp to get things when nobody was there.'

The knives were a wonderful new thing, and very useful; they thought it was a special hardwood. But Chema and his companions were still frightened of the outsiders. Then the Matis elders had told them they weren't dangerous, and could in fact be very good for them. And when the *nawas* came to visit, it seemed they were right. They gave them gifts: steel pots, knives, machetes and hunting dogs for the first time.

But then the outsiders had revealed a darker, more dangerous side. Chema's wife, Kana, joined in, telling us what had happened to her namesake, an older woman, around this time of first contact. This other Kana's husband had been shot in the neck by rubber tappers, and she and her friend Showa were kidnapped and taken to their camp. By the time they had finally escaped Kana had long hair and Showa had a baby, which she'd had to leave behind in the escape. Showa had brought back conjunctivitis with her, which had spread to everyone in the village: brothers, sisters, cousins, everyone.

Two more rituals to go, and then we would do one final day's hunting and see whether my performance had improved. In the meantime Tumi was going to teach me how to use the blowpipe. It was a bit heavier than I'd expected, but beautiful in both feel and balance. Tumi took me down to the river and

I had my first real go with it, aiming at our chosen target, a fork high up in the tree. Provided they did the difficult job of preparing the dart, and I was firing vertically, I found the pipe to be incredibly accurate and I could hit our target two times out of three.

Later I sat and watched Tumi as he and a couple of others put the poison tip on the darts, which are the stems of palm fronds hardened in a fire. The last couple of centimetres of the dart is rolled against a piece of wood which has been dipped in a bowl of the black poison.

'If I were to lick that,' I asked Tumi, 'what would it do to me?'

'If it gets into a cut, it will poison the blood and you will die. We keep it well away from our skin. No one aims at people with these. Children must not touch them.'

The poison itself is made from a vine, which is grated like the *tachik*, then poured into a leaf cone, so that water can be filtered through it. This toxic liquid is then reduced over a fire until it is a dark paste. This has to be done slowly, often for days, accompanied by sacred chanting. And the process must not be seen by others, for that will reduce the poison's strength. Even photographing the poison was kept to a minimum.

The next day came my third pre-hunt ritual: the frog poison. When you take it, Philippe explained, you vomit and empty your bowels so that you feel light and cleansed, ready for action.

An old lady in a bright blue top was on hand to do the honours. Her name was Tupa; I'd seen her around the village but hadn't yet talked to her. Like so many of her age, her parents had both died after first contact. She had a thin-lipped, impassive face, just right for the treatment she had to administer. This poison had been collected, Tumi explained, by stalking the particular type of frog very slowly at night, following its call. The collector slips twigs under both front and hind legs so that it grips both. They then raise the twigs and the frog continues to grip tight, fearful of falling. The poison is scraped off the sides of the frog under its stretched-out arms and smeared into the cleft of a crescent-shaped leaf stem, which is carefully wrapped and brought back to the village.

As well as the poison, Tupa had a length of a hard malleable stick, bent double in a tight U. This was burnt until the ends were glowing, at which point she stabbed hard with it at my right bicep. Then she pulled off the burnt skin and applied the poison to the visibly bleeding capillaries. I felt a very mild tingling sensation – then nothing.

I sat waiting, while half the village watched. I felt a little woozy and light-headed but nothing more than that. Gradually I started to feel more ill. I retired to a little outhouse that had been prepared for me and sat on a log seat. I was now feeling nauseous and shivery, but not yet ready to actively vomit. Tupa meanwhile was watching me with an expert eye. She smeared more poison on the wound. There was still nothing doing except that I now felt as if I were seconds away from death and my head was about to explode. One of the young guys complimented me by saying I must have a strong constitution as usually the vomiting was instantaneous, although I wished I didn't because I'd have preferred it all to be over. After half an hour Tupa came over and made two more burn marks, this time on my flank. She gestured in the direction of my left bicep, but then, sly old vixen, jabbed sideways into my naked waistline. I was caught by surprise and let out a little yelp, which amused the crowd. More poison was applied – but I still wasn't vomiting, though my head was throbbing like a drum. Another twenty minutes later she applied more poison to my flank – and then finally I was sick. Violently. Several times, until I was dry retching. Then I felt my bowels move.

Now she seemed happy and in just one minute washed all the poison off all four of the tiny wounds. I wouldn't feel sick any more, Philippe said. Like I believed that! I felt as if I was at death's door. I got to my feet and stumbled off into the jungle, all set for a day of misery. But returning from emptying my bowels I suddenly felt the whole malaise lift right off me. I felt not just OK again, but brilliant – light and easy, as predicted. Had we been off hunting there and then I would have danced along.

I had now taken on some of the spirit of the frog. This would stay with me for a month or so, while the frog itself would go and tell all the other animals in the jungle to come close to me, which would make my hunting easy.

But there was no hunt the next morning, so my testing of the rituals would have to wait. Instead we went to chat to two more elders who could remember first contact and life before it. Having experienced a first contact myself in the jungles of New Guinea, to hear about this from their point of view was fascinating to me, quite apart from being deeply moving. Both these elders had the same name – Bina – and appropriately their memories were an overlap of repetition, one Bina echoing the words of the other.

Like Chema, they both remembered walking round the jungle before the arrival of the *nawas*. From a hiding place they had seen the white people fetching water. Then people from FUNAI had come to meet them. After this contact, the Matis elders invited all of their people from all the scattered villages and settlements to live together in the same place. 'We explained to them,' said the older Bina, 'that we had made a contact with the white people and it would be better if we stuck together.' So they settled in the same village and planted corn. Then there was a big meeting with FUNAI when they were given dogs and machetes. But afterwards they had all got sore throats. Some of them had a fever too.

'My cousin died,' said the first Bina. 'And after he died, his brother died also.'

'And then another one died,' said the second Bina.

'After that a lot of people died.'

Between them they listed the names of all those they could remember who had died; it was long.

'I was very skinny then,' said the first Bina, 'very, very skinny.'

'White people came again,' added his friend, 'and they wanted to give us injections.'

'I was so skinny I nearly died.'

'We buried them all.'

'We didn't bury them far away. We did it close by.'

'We didn't bury them properly, because there were so many.'

'We didn't have the strength.'

Now a new generation had grown up, who wore clothes and copied the outsiders, the white people. Before they didn't dance like the white people, now they did; their sons knew all about it. Neither Bina wanted to leave the village and go to the city. If you went there you got ill. There was nowhere to plant manioc, no peccaries, no fish – it was better to stay in the jungle.

'You have to pay for everything there. What are you going to pay for things with?'

'I don't have anything to pay for things with in the city.'

I returned to Tumi's house to find a hilarious body-painting session under way. The paint was the juice of the genipapo tree, and the patterns they were painting on each other ranged from the skin of a frog to a Brazilian football shirt.

Tumi offered to paint a jaguar pattern on me, and all too soon I was covered with little black spots, with two swirling solid lines down my back.

I was summoned again to the longhouse: as I'd guessed, for my fourth and final pre-hunt ritual – the *poces* leaf, a broad green leaf which they slapped lightly on the skin of my face and torso. It was like a stinging nettle and made me tingle all over; quite irritating trying to resist the urge to scratch, but not as bad as the eye drops or the frog poison.

I spent the rest of the day practising with my blowpipe; the next day would be our final hunt. Wayne was going to accompany me this time, and hopefully record a suitable climax for our film.

We left the village around one in the morning and crammed into a full dugout canoe with outboard for a long journey upriver to a special hunting ground, reserved for occasions where they want to guarantee game. At first light we had breakfast on board the boat, then kept going for another hour or two. This time I had my own blowpipe with me, complete with a quiver of poisoned darts.

First found in the thick jungle was a troupe of spider monkeys. Rather frustratingly, Tumi asked Wayne and me not to go in and film as these animals are notoriously alert. Three of the six monkeys they brought down had offspring of various ages. These beautiful, almost human-looking creatures had fallen from the treetops with their mothers and continued to cling to their cooling carcasses, their huge affecting eyes darting hither and thither in their tiny black heads, screaming pitifully as they tried to make sense of what had happened.

But for the Matis it was just another day's hunting. The very youngest baby was killed, while the other two were taken back to the village to become pets. Meanwhile the dead mothers had their ulna, radius and humerus bones unceremoniously broken by a foot placed on the shoulder followed by a sharp tug upwards. Their hands were tied together as they were bundled into carrying parcels, their babies still clinging to their dead mothers' corpses.

Next we came across a hunting sign: three palm fronds with leaves all tied into separate vertical tubes. This meant that the other group had spotted some woolly monkeys. They had Damu, one of the village's best hunters, with them and one of our team predicted he would shoot at least ten. I decided it was time to leave Wayne and the camera behind and get up front with the action.

I ran ahead and watched in awe as the famous Damu crept to within firing range of the middle of the troupe and silently administered his deadly craft. While he prepared and loaded each dart he never once looked down at his busy hands, but kept a trained eye on his prey in the treetops. Then he lifted the pipe to his mouth and fired at a target maybe forty-plus metres away. I counted eleven silent darts before he stopped. Over the next ten minutes eight monkeys crashed to the ground. It was an unbelievable display of hunting prowess, like nothing I'd ever seen before.

Near me a woolly monkey sat in a tree. Tumi gestured that I should get it while he crept off to bring down some others. It was static and not very high and I was convinced that it had already been shot. After a few attempts I hit it and it fell. I was sure I was finishing someone else's catch off, but everyone congratulated me as if I'd shot it myself. I picked it up and carried it by its tail, my blowpipe in my other hand. We'd got eleven woolly monkeys to add to our six spiders, three baby spiders, three jungle fowl and one peccary shot elsewhere. It was going to be a tough load to carry home. I ended up with three dead primates and a live baby over my shoulders – but as we were close to the river, it was nothing like as bad as the last time.

That evening, as we sat in the longhouse eating some of our cooked meat, I began the process of saying farewell.

'I know I'll never be a hunter,' I told them. 'But to spend a little time being with you and watching has been an amazing experience for me. I want to thank you all. Being here has been such fun and you've been such great hosts and great company.'

'We will also miss you,' came their generous reply. 'We'll think about you a lot. People who are no good, we don't miss or think about. But we will think about you.'

On my last day I had a final chat with Tumi and Chema. They spoke to me as they had never done before. It was as if they wanted to send me off with a message. They tried to articulate what it was like living with the mind of an older Matis. They said that the new-found outside world had brought both good and bad. Since they were young their universe had expanded with every year that passed. They knew that they'd gained some things but undoubtedly lost much too. Chema told me that before they'd known the outside world they were probably happier. This was quite a statement. Ignorance really had been a kind of bliss for them. But now they knew what was out there. How could he alone stop the tide of change? Their youths wanted outside goods, but didn't know how to get them. If they went into town they could not compete with the townsfolk. They were often cheated and abused by them. They felt that the outside world owed them something for the death of their loved ones to disease, which was why they had asked for all those things on our arrival. It was a kind of desperation. And they were worried about the future.

As I headed back downriver I thought deeply about these powerful words. Sadly I knew that, heart-wrenching as it all was, these Matis were in fact relatively lucky. With government-protected lands and an organization like FUNAI looking after their interests, they were better off than most other indigenous peoples around the world. I had heard plenty of horror stories during my stay, but how many more were out there, not yet told by other tribal groups, who'd lost their land to outsiders, their loved ones to disease, and their freedom to slavery and marginalization?

11. Beyond the Pass

The Layap People of the Himalayas, Bhutan

It was early May 2006 and we were in the mountain kingdom of Bhutan, high in the Himalayas, hoping to reach one of the most remote tribes we'd yet visited, the Lunap people of Lunana. Their scattered villages lie on the far side of a series of dramatic passes, 5,000 metres in altitude, right up against the border with Tibet and blocked off for over half the year by snow. Arriving as we were at the start of summer, our plan was to trek first to the village of Laya, at an altitude of 4,000 metres, acclimatize there for a few days, then attempt the crossing to Lunana, taking supplies for ourselves and gifts of food for the Lunaps on a train of yaks, the horned, black-haired beasts who understand this dangerous terrain far better than any man. I was excited. I much prefer trekking than arriving by vehicle, and this time, it seemed, there was going to be plenty of that.

We had flown into Thimphu, the capital of Bhutan, set in a mountain valley and full of wonderfully characterful buildings, with coloured balustrades and guttering and dragon emblems painted on their whitewashed walls. Many of the people on the streets wore national dress: brightly coloured checked or striped coats like dressing gowns with huge white cuffs; below that, black shoes and knee-length black socks. I discovered later that it is the law for anyone who holds a governmental appointment to wear national dress. (My imagination ran riot for a second imagining what London would look like with such a strict ruling.)

Our chief fixer and guide, Chimmi Dorjee, had met us at the airport. He had a kind and thoughtful face under his distinctive black Stetson, set off by a little black moustache and half-beard. He spoke excellent English, a result of long service as an officer in the Indian army. The pass over to Lunana was still closed, he told us, because of heavy recent snow. But he was very optimistic that by the time we got to Laya, we would be able to get through.

On our side, there was a brand new crew for this trip. Researcher Matt Dyas was a former youth tennis hopeful who had done amazing preparatory work for this programme. Renée Godfrey had proved her worth behind the scenes on the second half of our long Omo journey the previous autumn – another great athlete. I was working with director Gavin Searle for the first time; charismatic and highly intelligent, a touch left-field, he was full of great ideas. He and I had already had some discussions about Bhutan's national religion, Buddhism, a subject I knew only superficially and wanted to explore. Gavin was keen to make this a programme about a spiritual journey. I liked his thought processes but was a little worried that his demands for profound, philosophical pieces to camera were going to be beyond my capability.

We left Thimphu crammed into a minibus and were soon on steep single-track roads climbing high into the mountains. The quite frequent traffic in the opposite direction would wait till the last possible moment before swerving out of our way. As the road was often bordered by a sheer precipice, it amazed me that there weren't more wrecks down below in the valleys. The views were incredible: towering peaks all around, trails of misty cloud floating between them, dramatic waterfalls, then we'd suddenly turn a corner to see a monastery temple perched on a mountainside.

We overnighted in a little roadside hotel. An early start the next day saw the road become narrower, then downgraded to a stone track, then finally it petered out entirely. Waiting for us at this point was a train of thirty-two mules and horses attended by Chimmi's team of about ten helpers, raring to go. Most of them spoke a bit of English, so as we loaded up the animals I was able to start getting to know them.

By lunchtime we were on our way. The onward track wasn't flat, but not nearly as steep as I'd expected. The animals were clearly used to their job, but with a habit of suddenly stopping and needing to be chivvied on. At one point one poor mule nearly managed to slip off the edge of a wire suspension bridge we were crossing, and had to be pulled back by the guys to prevent it from tumbling to a horrid fate way down in the valley beneath us. There were plenty of leeches on the trail, too, and Renée got a bad case of leech paranoia, having to stop and check her ankles every few minutes or so.

At one point we came to a grassy opening where a row of coloured and embroidered marquees had been set up, with bunting strung between them. The Queen of Bhutan was due to visit the next day, apparently. The men who were putting the final touches to her welcome insisted on inviting us all in for tea, so we had an unexpected break of *chai* and biscuits served on silver trays.

We camped that night by some hot springs, soothing the first day's aches and pains in three big tubs of sulphurous therapeutic mineral water, which flowed straight out of the ground at a perfect bath-hot temperature. After a further day's trekking, on muddy paths through beautiful woodland, full of red birch, larch and flowering rhododendron, we finally came in sight of Laya in the early evening, a collection of long dark wooden houses with white windows and roofs at a low angle, nestling together on the hillside across the valley. There were about 700 in the village, Chimmi told me. The first people we ran into were a bunch of schoolgirls, grinning under their famously distinctive hats, cones of woven straw with a single stick, often decorated, rising from the centre.

'You like Laya?' one asked and I laughed.

'I like it so far,' I replied.

We dumped our gear and set up a base in a little wooden house that Chimmi had found for us at the edge of the village, belonging to a quiet and hospitable chap called Asher (meaning 'Uncle') Kinley. I'd enjoyed the long trek, but it was great to be snugly in a building again, drying out and warming myself by the upstairs wood-burning stove.

We weren't at all sure how long we were planning to stay. If the pass to Lunana was open we'd be on our way shortly. But the next morning Chimmi brought us bad news. The consensus among the locals was that we shouldn't even think about making the crossing for two weeks. The weather was not as it should be this year, and the passes were still deep with snow. A group of teachers and a doctor from Lunana, who knew the route well, had been stuck in Laya all winter and even they hadn't tried to get home yet.

We decided that we might as well make the most of whatever time we had in Laya by filming with a family straight away. So Chimmi introduced us to a man call Kencho, who was a *gongchen*, or local spiritual leader. He lived with his wife Amom and her twelve children, of whom six were his and six his older brother's. Laya was one of the very few places in the world where they still practise polyandry – where one woman has two or more husbands. Kencho had originally shared Amom with his brother, but he had recently died, leaving Kencho and Amom alone together. Chimmi felt it was OK for me to ask about this.

'So how does it work when two or three brothers marry one woman?'

Kencho smiled. He knew that polyandry wasn't considered normal by outsiders; he had his answer ready. 'There is no jealousy,' he replied. 'There is a mutual agreement between brothers. One day she can be with me, one day with another brother, but the eldest gets to choose.'

'And what if there are three of you?'

'If we are all there together we take it in turns.'

We sat cross-legged on the floor of his living room, which contained a big pile of folded rugs and ten sacks of rice (a display of wealth in this remote community where food is at a premium). Kencho knew the mountain passes well, so we thought we'd quiz him about our chances of getting to Lunana.

'If we get a week's worth of sunny weather,' Chimmi asked, 'what are our chances of making it?'

'Warm weather will melt the fresh snow, but it won't penetrate down to the icy base layers,' Kencho told us. There were two such layers below the surface, and these would be the problem, as the sharpness of the ice could easily cut a yak's hoof. He himself had tried the crossing last year with some soldiers from the Bhutanese army, but they had had a near disaster just trying to get over the first pass, let alone the highest, most treacherous one, Ganglakarchung.

We were in a Buddhist country and one of the central messages of that fascinating religion-cum-philosophy is that suffering comes from attachment to worldly objects and desires.

As we were now clearly stuck in Laya for the time being, perhaps we could turn our delay into a virtue, Gavin thought, and learn more about the dangers of desire and what it might be like trying to live without it.

At any rate, I should make the most of Kencho. He had been trained as a monk and could explain at least the basics of the Tibetan variety of Buddhism they followed up here, mixed as it seemed to be with ancient animist beliefs. He sat me down and made a big circle on a red cloth with white grains of rice.

'This is the Wheel of Existence,' he told me.

Into the circle he now laid six little piles of rice.

'Here are the different realms. If you do good deeds in life you'll be born in heaven as a god, a demigod or on earth as a human. If you do bad deeds you'll be born as an animal, a demon or a hungry ghost.'

I learnt more about my future fate that afternoon when the village astrologer paid a visit to Kinley's house. He sat on the far side of a table in his red robes, as the smoke from a joss stick trailed heavenwards. Having looked me thoroughly in the face, he wanted to know exactly when I was born: year, month, day, hour. As I gave him each bit of information he chanted it back as he leafed through the pages of his thick astrological book.

'1969 ... 1969 ... 1969 ... What month were you born?'

'March.'

'March ... March ... March ... What day were you born?'

'Monday the seventeenth.'

'Monday ... Monday ... Monday ... What time were you born?'

'Eleven a.m. GMT.' I wasn't sure whether to convert this to local time or not. I let it go.

I was an earth bird (a rooster), it turned out. 'He has a lot of envy,' the astrologer said, 'and in order to try and outdo everybody he tries to do one better all the time.'

Well, that was certainly something to think about! Between now and the age of seventy, he went on, I was going to experience ill health seven times. At the age of fifty-two, I would need to be very careful because that was a bad year for my health. In my previous lives I'd been a monk, then an evil spirit.

'Because he was a monk and then went to the other end of the scale to become an evil spirit, he now finds it difficult to articulate his emotions,' he added.

In my next life I was going to be a monkey; then, after that, a chicken, unless I undertook extensive rites and prayers and made 10,000 ritual statues, in which case I could offset all this negative karma and secure my next coming as a human born into a very religious family. A life swinging through the trees began to seem quite appealing.

Chimmi's question was more down to earth, and potentially disastrous for the making of the film: were we going to get across the pass to Lunana?

'There is a path,' the astrologer replied, 'but I see no clear way through. If you insist on going your journey will be very hard.' But then: 'Once you make it to your destination everything is good and things will happen the way you want.'

I was relieved that this was his answer. Had he said we weren't going to make it, it would have been ethically incorrect to expect Chimmi and his helpers to take the chance. Whatever I might have thought privately, up here the astrologer's word was gospel.

We continued to record the daily life of Laya. If we didn't make it through the pass, this would be our film. Luckily for us, the next day was an important one in the house where I was still staying with the crew – the holding of the annual ritual rites ceremony, when the place is blessed and cleared of bad spirits for the whole following year. So Kencho got me dressed up in traditional Laya gear: a lovely high-cut black jacket with coloured sleeves rolled back and gold-embroidered lapels. Over this, my heavy woven wrap – or *zom* – was held in place by an unbuckled strap wound very tight around my waist several times. The boots were the best of all: high cut, made from fine woollen cloth with intricately designed buttons and hide soles. Truly beautiful, if somewhat tight and cold. I was glad it was a hot day, or else my feet would have instantly frozen with so little insulation.

The day that followed was extraordinary: a mass of chanting and talking and drinking and praying, with Kencho at the centre of a group of traditionally dressed local *gongchens* and musicians, including his strapping oldest son Pianki, also a *gongchen*. In this role Kencho became a completely different person, leading the chanting and clanging two heavy gongs, which he clashed horizontally to left and right as others drummed in the background.

In the room next to all this music and prayer sat the astrologer. He was surrounded by tubs of flour dough and knobs of hard yellow yak butter, making effigies and models for the ceremony. People brought him in grass turfs, and on these he laid out three-dimensional scenes. The centrepiece included effigies of the house and its owner, Asher Kinley, who was predicted to have a very bad year coming up. Next to his statue-like model, moulded from butter, was placed a net of woven coloured cottons, to catch bad spirits. Each colour symbolized an element and they all had to be in the right order: blue for water, white for iron, yellow for earth, red for fire and green for trees. Various other symbolic items were placed on the turf: little cards with drawings on them representing previously held sacrifices of yaks, horses and mules; then grain and other foodstuffs to tempt the spirits. The statues are called *tormas*; and when the whole arrangement was finished, they were placed in front of the house-altar in the festival room with the musicians. Other *tormas* on green turf bases were decorated similarly and added. Butter candles were lit. More food and drink – including alcohol – was added, as prayers were said, chants were chanted, and the tempo in the room got more and more frenzied, attracting all the bad spirits for miles around, who would then gorge on the food and get drunk on the booze in these little effigy worlds. At the climax, the turfs were taken quickly from the room to specific points outside the house where they were instantly set upon by waiting dogs and crows and eaten, the idea being that the bad spirits were eaten with them. It was rather sad to see these painstakingly made *tormas* just lying there with no more use. I saw a couple being kicked aside, and one nonchalantly stepped on by a passer-by; their job was done.

Around two in the afternoon the time had come for a woman called Neyjum to be possessed by a benevolent spirit and talk in tongues. With her were two other women, and all were laden down with beautiful pendants and amulets. Kencho began this part of the ceremony outside, pouring holy water on the three women's heads and faces and tipping it in their mouths. Back inside the house, the family sat to one side: Kinley, mother and baby. Then Neyjum came in, with the two other women. She had her eyes closed and was stumbling about a fair bit, breathing noisily and mumbling through clenched teeth, picking up objects from around the room according to the whim of the spirit. She picked up a glass and drank a bit of the local wine, *chang*, giving some to one of the others in the room. Then she was spitting out liquid on the lino floor and speaking coherently.

Chemmi was beside me explaining much of this, but at the time, I didn't understand it fully. Reading back the translations later, it became clear exactly how Neyjum had been welcoming gods and spirits to the room.

'I feel the three gods are on their way. Yeshey Wangchuk Tandin is here. Come here and sit, Yeshey, at the head of the line. Now Ashi Thuji Chem is here. It's good to see you too.' She was speaking to the gods as she might to old friends, then offering them drink and food. After that she stopped being herself and let the gods speak through her; they were quite demanding, criticizing Kinley for the quality of the drink they were being offered.

'We've finished with this drink, now we want a better one. Get the good stuff out. If you don't treat me right I'm going to make your life hell. Come on, Kinley, pull your finger out, bring us the good stuff.'

Kinley was duly apologetic. 'Stay calm, it's on its way. I'm sorry. Please accept my humble apology.'

It was a bizarre atmosphere. At the centre was Neyjum,

alternating between being herself and an angrily demanding spirit or deity. All the others in the room sat watching, but not in silence; they were laughing and chatting and on one occasion mocking the spirits that Neyjum had conjured up.

'Neyjum, we don't know that spirit,' one man said, laughing.

'Don't worry, you will know it,' Neyjum replied, her voice now changing into the spirit's. 'Because I will come after you.' Then she was Neyjum again. 'The spirit has come from a dead man who is no stranger to you.'

This stopped the mockery short. 'Please don't let the spirit come after us,' said the man. His tone had changed completely and there was fear in his voice.

Later, in private, the crew discussed what we'd seen. Renée, interestingly, believed it all fully; she thought the words were coming from real spirits who had possessed Neyjum. I feel that it's a great privilege to see such things but I am cursed with a desire to rationalize everything to the last degree. Of course, provided the locals believed it, then it was true to them anyway – but what was physically happening? If they weren't actual spirits, had Neyjum been speaking from her own subconscious or a greater collective consciousness, and if the latter, why did it only ever seem to deal with current local issues?

In the morning, the pass was still looking treacherous, so we decided to make a side trip and take part in another of the activities that kept this remote village sustainable: the collecting of a rare fungus called *Cordyceps sinensis*, a prized ingredient in traditional Chinese medicine. The fungus, which the locals know as *yigatsi gimbo*, is parasitic and actually grows out of the head of a caterpillar, killing it as it does so.

It was a great trek up from Laya to the remote pastures where this bizarre caterpillar–fungus combination can be found. We followed the Mochu River most of the way, huge wispy clouds drifting past us as ever. Renée had gut problems, so she was staying behind in the village. With me were Gavin, Matt, and Kencho's son, Pianki, along with Chimmi and his Puffa-jacketed team of cooks and helpers.

After a day of following the river, we camped overnight by a cave, then trekked straight on up the hill, passing a picturesque yak herder's hut on the way. This was occupied by a toothless old lady who, if she'd been cast as a Shakespearian witch, would have been slated for her over-the-top make-up! She and her daughter invited us in for some salted yak butter tea and were very friendly and welcoming. Finally we reached the high pastures Pianki recommended. It was a beautiful place, a stunning high valley with a waterfall to one side. Ahead of us were the towering upper slopes of a mountain, swathed in shifting cloud all day – we never once glimpsed its peak.

We got down and dirty on the cold ground looking for our bizarre booty. Pianki had told us encouragingly that it was like trying to find a needle among all the grasses. The caterpillar itself is a burrower and only the tip of the fungus protrudes through the soil. Pianki got one first and called us over for a look. When excavated, the caterpillar itself was tiny, and the shoot of fungus growing out of its head was no more than five centimetres long.

We all had a good look and then went back to our own efforts. The cloud had come in and it was now hailing tiny balls and the ground was damp and freezing, so just searching for ten minutes was miserable enough.

Eventually, after much scrabbling around and a couple of false alarms, I found one. The tiny centimetre-long stem was almost invisible at first, but once excavated it revealed a good-sized caterpillar. Gavin had talked about the *Cordyceps* collection in terms of a gold rush for the locals, so I asked Pianki how much this little stem would be worth.

'Eight rupees.'

'Eight rupees!' I laughed in amazement. That was about ten pence! Yet in a few months, the locals could secure three times their annual wage by collecting *Cordyceps* rather than yak herding.

On our way back to Laya the next morning, we came across a group of *yigatsi gimbo* hunters working through another pasture. One of them, Dawa, spoke English and had also been to Lunana. If we made it over there, he said, there should be no problem finding a family to live with, but getting hold of food would be really difficult. At the end of the winter it would be in short supply for them, let alone for any visitors. The Lunaps were a strong-willed, independent-minded people and wouldn't necessarily welcome a group who arrived without their own supplies; ideally, we should have enough surplus for gifts.

I asked him about the trek over. He wasn't encouraging.

'There are big boulders, falling rocks, landslides and narrow passes,' he said. 'It's a real risk for you, the porters and the animals. A landslide could kill your animals and then you'll have to pay for them and even you will be washed away by the rocks. These are the dangers. If it's a dry day, it's OK, so long as there's no snow on the pass. If there's no snow you have a good chance of making it. But if you get to Ganglakarchung and it snows overnight and you get stuck there, you might not be able to get down.'

It was hardly what any of us wanted to hear.

Back in Laya two days later it seemed as if our chances were as good as they were ever going to be. The weather was a little warmer and Chimmi thought the snow was starting to melt. Renée seemed recovered from her stomach trouble. We had already been in the village for over ten days, with a week's travelling before that. It was time to give it a go.

Everyone had told us how treacherous the first day would be, but it didn't feel so bad at all. Despite the occasional landslide the path up from the village was in good condition, and our surroundings were once again stunning. The woodlands were full of rhododendron and interspersed with grassy glades, carpeted with alpine flowers – white, violet, deep purple. Below us down the valley roared the turquoise river. I was enjoying being out alone at the front with my thoughts. Back home, ever since the screening of the first series of *Tribe*, my life had just got faster and faster and though I was aware of how lucky I was, I'd got to the point where I felt I had no time for myself. Then I had started complaining about this awful situation to my friends, who were understandably unsympathetic. Because no one would listen, I'd say it even more and I had started to become a moaner. Now, up here in the mountains was the first time I'd been alone and unrushed in years and I suddenly had a moment of clarity. Thinking about the wonderful Kencho and his *joie de vivre*, looking at the Buddhist philosophy of tackling all things in the head, I realized that all I had to do was flick that internal switch back to my old usual positive, 'glass-half-full' self and things would go back to normal. I made a vow there and then on the mountain never to moan about how busy my life was again. Looking back now, this was one of the greater moments of my recent adult life.

In the afternoon we were out of the tree line and a more stunted alpine shrub took over. The clouds still hid the highest peaks, but the views across and down were spectacular. I decided to stay at the back with the crew, which was slow, but more sociable. We arrived at our camp and a little yak herders' summer settlement called Rodophu just as the rain swept in. But Chimmi's team were all pros, our tents and chairs were up in no time and tea and biscuits were not far behind. That BBC luxury again. We sat round a blazing fire and warmed up. Ahead of us the next day's path wound up through the rocky, boggy valley.

The going was slow the next morning. Renée was up at the front, while the rest of us stayed together just behind her to avoid kicking rocks on to each other. I was feeling remarkably fit and strong, ready for anything, but I could see poor Renée was struggling, having missed the acclimatization trip to collect the *Cordyceps*. When we stopped for lunch she hardly ate anything. Whether it was gut problems or altitude sickness, or a combination of both, she just wasn't well, so Matt was designated to take her back down again to base camp at Rodophu.

The rest of us headed on up the first pass, the yaks ahead of us. What magnificent animals they were, I thought, weighed down with our packs and boxes full of food and equipment, adorned with a myriad tinkling bells and tassels, grunting and snorting as they crunched through the snow. But then, suddenly, their mood changed. On a slope covered with patchy old ice there was a revolt, with yaks turning and galloping off with their loads in every direction. Only the skill of the yak herders got them back on track and up, eventually, to the very top of this first pass – the Tsimola; 4,700 metres. We added to the collection of colourful, tattered prayer flags flapping in the breeze. Although the visibility was terrible, we all felt confident. After this we had the big pass – the Ganglakarchung – and once we were over that the going would be easier and we should make it to Lunana.

But barely thirty metres after our stop we turned a corner to see a mêlée of yaks and herders in a right muddle. The snow was too deep, the head herder told us. We wouldn't be able to go on. I couldn't believe it, didn't want to believe it, so he demonstrated with one of the yaks, leading him down the little slope until his legs sunk right in.

He was able to pull this one back out, he said, but there was a danger with the others that they would get stuck. Yaks were powerful and wilful animals. 'If the herders then try and pull them out,' Chimmi translated, 'the yaks could kick them to death.' He had had deaths before on his treks and he didn't want to risk anything, certainly not with us. We decided it would be best to head back to base camp and take stock.

Back at Rodophu there were four new trekkers on their way over to Lunana. They were the teachers who had been waiting for weeks in Laya. They were going to give it a go first thing. Without any yaks to slow them, they would try to cross in one quick sprint in the hope that they didn't get caught out in a storm in the high passes.

What about us? It was all looking a bit bleak until Gavin and I, chatting it through, came up with an idea: if the snow was too deep for the yaks, perhaps we could solve the problem by cutting a path for them. We shared this plan with Chimmi in the morning and he thought it might work. So we spent the day in Rodophu sorting stores and charging batteries, and early the following morning Chimmi's team left to start hacking a track through the snow.

Renée still wasn't feeling well, so it was decided she would return to Laya and head home to the UK. I really felt for her as she set off down the valley. She was a national-standard athlete and surfing champion and had never been defeated physically by anything before. I would also miss our fun chats, not to mention having female company. Now it was just the boys.

After our fond farewell, the remainder of us headed up to the top of the pass to see how Chimmi's trailblazers were doing. They'd done a great job, cutting and scooping to excavate a wide path for the yaks. I joined in; the day was much warmer. By mid-morning the following day we were back at the point where the yaks had foundered the last time in the deep snow. The path was clear and our plan had worked. We were over the first pass again, yaks in train. Climbing up into the second pass we had another yak revolt, but Chimmi's guys were having none of it. They ran after them, shouted, cajoled and pushed. The lead bull was now completely ignoring the pre-laid path and making his own way up the very steepest incline, through what seemed like impossibly deep snow. But he knew what he was doing. He'd made it. The others followed dutifully in his path.

That hiccup out of the way, we pushed on. We were now at about 5,000 metres, but everyone was acclimatized and it was a relatively easy stroll. The big mountains around us occasionally showed their faces through the clouds, but never once their peaks. It was an awesome place, high and lonely. As the day went on we could hear the incessant roar of avalanches, one after another – an impressive sound, and a reminder of the dangers all around us.

Mid–afternoon we made camp. I didn't join the herders unloading the yaks for the night. They were big, impetuous animals, clearly hard to control. Quite apart from not having the skills, I seemed to make them nervous. Packs and baskets were being dropped all over the place.

It was now day seven of our attempt to get through. The yaks remained in camp while we went out to clear a path for them through the rest of the Ganglakarchung. It was very steep and for the first time I really felt the altitude, becoming increasingly breathless as I hacked at the ice with my machete. It was a bright, clear morning and we could see Mount Chomo Lhari in the distance, poking through a surrounding collar of high cloud. This is one of the highest peaks in Bhutan, right on the border with Tibet.

That evening we all had a big discussion in the tent about the way forward. We had come so far, but if things screwed up again, what would we do? There were lots of potential options. One was clearly to forget the yaks and just carry everything ourselves. That was fine by me; I much prefer to be self-sufficient and love having my own gear on me. But in this instance that wasn't going to be the answer. Yes, I could easily have got over the pass myself with a guide. No one doubted that, it was just that there was no point doing it if it wasn't going to be filmed. And we couldn't film without our equipment, which needed the yaks to carry it. More to the point was that in order to stay on the other side for the time needed to make a film, we had to take enough food for everyone. Lunana had been shut off for six months. To arrive without supplies and expect to live off the locals was not just ethically wrong; from all the reports we'd had, without food they might not even let us stay. No, frustrating as it was for me to be so close to our tantalizing destination, I agreed that we needed the yaks. In the end I cut short the endless circulating discussion by making a decision. We would try one shot at it with the yaks the next morning and if they didn't make it we'd turn around and come back. We'd already pushed people excessively hard and changed our minds endlessly. I could tell that the desire to get there was now coming fully from the crew and me. I told the guys there would be no reneging on this promise. One go and that was it.

Day eight. I woke filled with anticipation. A cold night had turned our thawed path to slippery ice again. Gavin and I watched the first slope as the yaks began their ascent. Amazingly they managed it. Then, as they vanished round a corner on to a steeper part of the pass, and we were just starting to believe that we might do it, I heard a loud shout. Three yaks were charging hell for leather back down the slope.

So that was it. No Lunana. I'd given my word: no messing Chimmi's guys around any longer. Our desire to make this film had pushed these lovely people very hard. I sat down on the slope and did a couple of pieces to camera about how my desire had been thwarted, so was experiencing the suffering that the Buddha talks about at first hand. This had been Gavin's idea of the previous night and it gave us a let-out for our failure.

'What would the Buddha say of me now?' I said to camera. 'Well, frankly he would be laughing at me, wouldn't he, because I'm feeling suffering. I'm feeling pain and anguish and that has come about because of my blind desire to get to Lunana.'

It took us the whole of the rest of the day to get back down to Rodophu. The snow was slushy in the continuous rain and there were many rivers to cross. My feet were wet and cold. We'd been over this same route six times in our attempt to get through and ultimately we had failed. But I no longer minded. I was now looking on the bright side with my renewed positivity, and as a result felt genuinely happy and relaxed.

Without Lunana, we realized it was going to be a challenge to make the programme: Laya would now be the focus of the film, but we would not conceal our failed attempt to get to Lunana. It had happened so it would be part of the film; stories of failure can be just as interesting as tales of triumph. The problem was that we simply didn't have enough footage for nearly sixty minutes of TV about Laya, so we needed to return there to do some 'pick-ups' (shots missed first time round). I didn't envy Gavin's job in the edit suite though. Before heading back to Laya we decided to make a virtue of the area we were in. Pianki had a base he used when he was up here at Rodophu looking after his yaks, so Gavin asked him if I could stay with him for a short while and Pianki agreed.

His place was like a tiny stone crofter's cottage, maybe three metres by six, stacked with rice and blankets at one end, with the usual cooking utensils on display above the central fireplace.

A single solar-powered light hanging from the ceiling lit the room. Outside there were a number of wooden outhouses with blue tarpaulin roofs.

The *yigatsi gimbo* season had now started in earnest, so there were plenty of harvesters up from Laya, camping nearby. Besides the guys, there were two young women, both called Zam. One of them had a little boy called Sangachind; the other was unmarried, very pretty, and a terrible flirt.

The next morning I went out with them, collecting and chopping firewood. I was fine with the altitude when just walking, but as soon as I started in on any serious physical exertion, I was knackered. Luckily the girls had some gentler work for me too, picking flowers from a lilac rhododendron bush. These they threaded on sticks and put in their hair. They sang as they worked and it was a lovely moment, high in the hills with the sun shining.

As we ate a lunch of the usual chilli soup with rice, I took the opportunity to ask the girls a bit more about the Laya custom of polyandry. What were the good and the bad things about having two husbands?

'The good things,' said the first Zam, 'are that one husband can stay with the yaks and one can stay in the village and look after the family.'

And the bad things?

'One problem,' said the second Zam, 'can be that the two guys might get jealous of each other. If they envy each other they might start drinking and fighting.'

'Would you rather have one or two husbands?'

'I'd prefer to have one husband.'

'But if you're asked to marry two, then would you?'

'If we're told to, then yes,' they said together, smiling as they agreed.

'Could you refuse to marry two?'

'No, we can't refuse.'

After lunch the two Zams went back down to Laya and I spent the afternoon gathering the bracken-like branches of the local conifer they call *bom*. This we laid down on the floor of Pianki's little house – a brand new green springy carpet for us to sleep on. Later, we went together up the incredibly steep slopes to round up the yaks and bring them back down to the lower pastures – a truly tough daily activity.

The next day we took the cameras to visit an old boy called Penjo, who lived in a traditional yak herder's tent fifty metres from Pianki's stone hut. This tent was amazing, made from woven yak hair, dark from the outside, but beautifully lit on the inside, owing to its many large perforations.

The size of the holes made me wonder how on earth it could be waterproof, yet when it rained later that day it proved its worth: it was perfectly dry inside. Another advantage of the big weave was that smoke dissipated through it easily. The tent came in two halves and could be carried on a single yak when dry; separated and carried on two yaks when heavy and wet. I considered trying to procure one as a very cool festival tent. Inside, Penjo had all he needed, mod cons included: solar battery charger and everlasting bulb, pots and mugs, bags of rice and yak-hair cushions.

Penjo lived in Laya, but spent three months of the year up

here at Rodophu. Many things had changed, he told Chimmi and me, since he'd been a young man. Many people had sold their yaks and moved to the town to start businesses. Others, like him, thought that the yak had an important place in the culture of Bhutan, so they stayed in the country looking after them. To him, yak herding was still everything: the cheese, the wool, the meat, everything depended on the yaks.

That evening we finally tasted the *yigatsi gimbo*. Penjo broke them into small pieces, fried them in butter and added some of the whisky I'd given him as a present. There was plenty for everyone and they tasted fine: a bit like prawns, if you could distinguish anything through the overpowering flavour of the whisky – he'd ended up pouring in about half a bottle.

Gavin, Matt, Pianki and the others got up to go to bed and I was left with the wonderful old man. I had no idea what to say to him and the silence was tangible. He cooked me up a massive dinner of dried yak entrails, chilli and rice, which I couldn't finish, the meat was so undercooked and chewy. Fortunately, neither could he, so we had a little laugh about that.

In the morning I woke fresher than I'd felt since we'd arrived. I'd slept like a baby, the aches and pains from all the hill climbing had all but gone, and I experienced a strange sensation of well-being. I had no doubt that this was down to the magical properties of the strange caterpillar fungus I'd ingested. I did a little goodbye session on camera with Penjo, then left him with a load of gifts: a new torch, a fleece jacket, some laminated pictures of the Dalai Lama, some blocks of tea, and some cash. He was delighted.

Back in Laya, the crew returned to stay with Kinley and I moved into Kencho's house for a short while. The annual village festival was coming up, so we decided we should stay on for a little longer and film that. Kencho, it emerged, was more than just the village *gongchen*: he was the spiritual leader for all the nearby villages, a far more important figure than I'd realized. There were only seven in the district who could perform the grand Buddhist rituals; there were thirteen different ones a year and they were all done by Kencho.

This was his spiritual guidance: 'Live for the moment, Bruce. You might die today or tomorrow, or you might live for a hundred years. Enjoy your drink and food, sing, dance, make relations with girls.'

This was hardly fire and brimstone and it struck a chord with me. I loved being with Kencho. When he wasn't leading the spiritual ceremonies, he was almost buffoon-like in his effervescent silliness, but it reminded me how cynical, how 'cool' and 'controlled' I'd become in my adult life at home. These days, I found it hard to make a fool of myself in such a carefree way. I envied him this freedom. I had so much to learn up here in these hills.

The annual festival was huge fun, like a more elaborate version of the annual ritual ceremony, only in the whole village, not just in Kencho's house. There were more *tormas*, surrounded by more goodies to entice the spirits. The grandest of all was an effigy in butter of the whole village, which at a climactic moment of the day was thrown into a fire. Prayer flags fluttered in the breeze, and there was an archery competition, and a lively, chanting procession through the village up to the *zong*, or temple.

'Desire, competitiveness, anger and ignorance,' Kencho counselled, when we were back in his house the day after the festival, 'they are the worst. If you give in to anger, you'll always end up fighting. If you are competitive, then you'll always be trying to outdo everybody. You should avoid this because if you become obsessed by what others have, then that feeling of envy will destroy you. If you can overcome these terrible afflictions, then you're on your way to enlightenment.'

We left the next morning, back down the long road to Thimphu. Kencho was so unwilling to say goodbye that he wanted to join me on the trek for a bit. I told him not to come but he was insistent. I thanked him dearly for all that he'd taught me and explained that more than anyone I'd met in a long time he'd changed me as a human being. It was no lie.

12. Paradise Found?

The Anutans of Polynesia, Solomon Islands

At dawn on our fourth day at sea we finally saw the island – a tiny speck on the horizon in the golden early morning light. Anuta – truly one of the most remote communities in the world. From where we were, cutting across the huge undulating blue wastes of the south Pacific, there was nothing else in sight. It had been a twelve-day journey just getting this far – Singapore, Brisbane, the Solomon Islands capital of Honiara, then a final flight to Lata in Santa Cruz to board this yacht – but at that moment it felt like it had all been worth it. With me on the *Margherita* I had a veteran *Tribe* crew: director James Smith, cameraman Tim Butt, and researcher Renée Godfrey, back to peak fitness again after our last trip to Bhutan.

It took us three more hours to get close enough to land. We were purposely taking our time, to allow the islanders to see us early. Visits from outsiders are extremely rare here, limited to a passing supply ship every six months or so and the occasional curious yacht. Our *Tribe* researcher Matt Fletcher, who had done an initial recce of Anuta earlier in the year, had left the islanders with an arrival time of July/August. But there had been no way for us to confirm. The radio they had been given by the Solomon Islands government had broken some years before.

Our skipper Peter anchored the yacht well away from the surf line and we waited and watched. On a strip of white beach little brown dots of people were launching some kind of boat through the swirling surf – a tiny dugout canoe with stabilizing outrigger, we saw, as it came closer. Suddenly it was beside us and the camera was pointing right at me. It was my moment and I hadn't given a second's thought to what I was going to say.

'Hello,' I managed to the two burly guys in the boat. 'You had a nice day? Welcome.' What was I thinking – welcome! – who was welcoming who here? Luckily, they barely noticed, and Joseph and Caulton were soon scrambling on board the *Margherita* for a cup of tea. They both had excellent English, and it rapidly emerged that Joseph was extremely organized and had already got every aspect of our stay worked out. He had, he told us later, thought of little else for months.

There was just enough room for three of us in the tiny outrigger. Tim, meanwhile, boarded the *Margherita*'s inflatable boat, to film us as I went ashore. It was a wonderful feeling, being canoed in through the crystal-clear turquoise water, towards the white sand and swaying fronds of coconut palms behind, lining the beach's edge. There was a big rock at one end and I could make out about thirty people, most of them women, sheltering in its shade.

As we reached the shore Joseph jumped out and Caulton used the steering oar to keep us nose to land, skilfully catching a wave so that we surfed right up on to the beach.

The kids were waiting in a group, so I had a great welcome, shaking hands and asking names and ages. The Solomons were once a British colony, and there was plenty of English spoken here, even by the children.

It was perhaps lucky I couldn't understand what they were saying in their own language:

'Don't stand too close to him, he may spit on you.'

'He is really sweaty.'

'We don't know how to speak English, all we can say is la la la.'

'He is asking you your age, tell him how old you are.'

Once I'd shaken every hand on the beach, about fifty in total, and we were all safely landed, Joseph was keen for us to go off straightaway to meet the island chiefs. We cut through a village of little huts covered with a thick thatch of dried palm leaves, then on past rows of neat little vegetable gardens, flowers growing on the borderline between the cultivated plots. Within a few hundred metres the sea was visible on the other side. The island really is that small: about forty hectares in total. We were now in Anuta's second village, St John, and once again I was taken round to meet the inhabitants, shaking hands with each and every one. Then I was led off to meet the chief, Pu Koroatu, in his beachside hut, where Joseph explained that I had to observe a traditional protocol.

I entered on hands and knees, making sure to keep my head lower than the chief's. He sat cross-legged across the hut from me in a brown and white striped sports shirt, smiling from behind a thick white beard, the hair on the top of his head bushy and white. I had to crawl towards him and place my nose on his knee or shin, at which point he put his hand under my chin and lifted my face up. Now I had to put my nose next to his. Our lips almost touching, we both simultaneously drew in a deep nasal breath. This was the *pikita* – or Polynesian nose kiss. What an amazing greeting: a show of reverence and a mutual exchange in one action. Almost as if I were breathing in his pure essence. It was very intimate. Then I had to do the same with the chief number two, an even older man, whose ribs were all too visible under the saggy skin of his torso; his smile was soft and gappy, and he had hardly a tooth left in his mouth. Of the four clans on the island these old men were the heads of the two most powerful ones.

I introduced myself in my usual way, saying how happy I was to be on the island, explaining that I was hoping to join in with the daily life and rituals. For the first time ever, this was in English, without any translation; the two chiefs nodded along, clearly able to understand. Then I gave them some token gifts: a pipe and some tobacco each, which they seemed more than happy with. Joseph then indicated that it was time to leave. I had to crawl out backwards, making sure to keep my head lower than theirs.

Joseph was firmly in control of proceedings. Now we went back to the village by the beach, St James, to meet the burly head of the church, Father Nomleas. We did the *pikita* again, then a handshake, and I gave him a Bible with waterproof pages, which James had found at home in the UK. After that it was back to St John to be shown the little hut where the crew would be staying – and me too for the first couple of days. We hadn't even finished ferrying our gear up from the shore before we were told we had to break for a welcoming meal: fresh fish, accompanied by the island staples – the boiled root vegetables taro and manioc, all cooked with coconut or banana in different ways. The soup, made from taro and coconut milk, was exquisite.

At 5 p.m. we heard the clear, foghorn-like note of a conch shell, summoning us all to church. The Anutans have been devout Christians since Anglican missionaries converted them ninety years before (though some traditional beliefs remain).

The service was a wonderful mixture of Melanesian, English and pidgin, with loud and raucous hymn singing and responses. Women stood to one side of the little church, men to the other. At the end of the service we newcomers were asked to go up front and introduce ourselves with a few words.

It had been a very long day and I could hardly keep my eyes open. After the service I fell asleep on the floor of our hut, only to be woken up for yet more food. What a welcome we'd had! It didn't look as if I would starve on this episode of *Tribe*.

I was woken at 5 a.m. with a call from Joseph: 'Bruce, Bruce.' My new friend wanted to show me the male toilet area, which was considerate of him. It was down the beach, beyond the big rock. Once in the designated stretch, you basically dug a shallow hole with your foot anywhere between the high and low water mark. The strong currents made sure that all waste was taken straight out to sea and away from the beach. The female site was on the opposite end of the beach, out of sight. That was it for sanitation on this island. Any people gardening or foraging for shellfish in the vicinity would discreetly make themselves scarce as they saw you approach.

The next day Joseph attended the chiefs' council – or *maru* – and came back to tell us that all was well; we would be formally welcomed with a feast in two days' time. Until then we were told to take it easy. Both chiefs had asked whether we'd brought any betel with us, the nut which is chewed across Asia to give a stimulating high, staining your teeth orange-brown in the process. Luckily we had, so we took them a good supply. Afterwards, I began to explore the island and make friends with the numerous children, watching them play with their wonderful home-made model outriggers in the still water of low tide. Meanwhile, James and the crew were trying to find someone to be my on-screen interpreter and guide. Our first choice, Caulton, seemed ideal: tall and good-looking, with a ready smile – but he was the schoolteacher and too busy, he said. So Joseph recommended a young single guy called Manusay who was keen to help. We invited him to dinner and after a nervous and quiet start he opened up and spoke in perfect English – so we signed him up.

My formal welcome day began with an early Communion in the St James church. Father Nomleas officiated and at the end of the service said a few nice words about us to the assembled congregation. After a quick rest back at our hut I was summoned to the sandy clearing beside the church to be traditionally dressed as the ceremonial guest of honour. I was wrapped in an off-white cloth made from the pounded inner bark of the paper mulberry tree (called tapa cloth), which was quite stiff and card-like but not nearly as rough on the skin as it looked. One of the women smeared me with a strong-smelling, bright orange paste made from ground turmeric and one of the men put a garland of white flowers round my head. Then Joseph took me off on a tour of the island, in the company of what seemed like the entire Anutan population.

As we walked up to the highest point of the island I could see how cultivated it all was. From a distance Anuta had looked quite unkempt and jungly, but on the ground I soon realized how every inch of soil was being used to grow food. As we climbed, the coconut palms and banana groves gave way to little fields of manioc and taro. It was relatively steep in places, with some huge boulders strewn around. Joseph kept asking me what I thought of his island, so I replied that I'd tell him when we reached the top. There were two summits, the lower having the best view. From here you could see nearly the whole of Anuta, girdled by its white ring of surf. Beyond, the ocean stretched featureless in every direction. We really were in the midst of endless sea. It wasn't hard to tell Joseph how much I liked his home.

Back down in St James, we were told that our yacht had snapped its anchor chain in the rising, gusty wind, so had set sail for a safer port on the island of Tikopia, 110 kilometres away and our nearest inhabited neighbour. Rather him than me, I thought, as I watched the *Margherita*'s outline dwindling at speed towards the stormy horizon. Now we had no outside influence left, and somehow it felt better that way.

It was time for our welcome feast. First the crew were smeared with turmeric and dressed up too in tapa cloths and garlands of white flowers. Then we sat down on reed mats in the sandy patch between our hut and the little St James church. Steaming food wrapped in banana-leaf bundles surrounded us. Beyond sat little family groups. There were twenty-four families on the island and all of them were present. I was asked to give a speech, which was hard against the noise of the wind in the thrashing palm trees above us. I had lots I wanted to say, but refrained from waffling on because most people couldn't hear me anyway. Joseph asked if I could show and explain the gifts we had brought with us, as agreed during Matt's recce. So, despite feeling a little self-congratulatory, I described some of the larger items we'd brought: such as the HF radio and solar cells, drums of fuel for their outboard engines, and the contributions we were going to offer to their schooling fund. The gifts of actual cash would be saved until the end, I told them. But everything would be split, Joseph explained, between the families. Sharing whatever came in to the island was an article of faith here, a way of expressing what the islanders call *aropa* – your love and compassion for your fellow human beings.

I sat near Father Nomleas, which proved to be a good move, as he'd caught a bluefin tuna the day before and was now eating the meaty head. After the lunch he made a very short speech in the local language, which ended with everyone shouting back: '*Howai! Howai! Howai!*' ('Thank you! Thank you! Thank you!'). Then we had some dancing, accompanied by a knocking beat, stick on hollow log. Men, women and children joined in singing, strolling backwards and forwards in rhythm to each crescendoing song. Some dances were very simple, but one or two had complex kick and clap moves, which I had great fun trying to keep up with.

Joseph had now told me it was time to move into an island hut. But before I did so Caulton the schoolteacher wanted me to visit his father, Paul, who had a bad foot. We set off towards St James with both med kits just in case. By God, did we need them! As soon as I entered Paul's house I could tell this was no minor cut. I could smell the wound from metres away and flies were buzzing everywhere. It was really bad. He'd stepped on a fish bone which hadn't been properly removed. The wound had gone septic and his foot had swollen up hugely. I said a few words of comfort then got straight on the sat phone to a doctor mate in the UK, who gave me a prognosis from my reported examination. As I'd expected, it didn't sound good.

I prepared some sterile cleaning gear and sorted out some injectable anaesthetic, a scalpel and syringes, to investigate the wound fully in case I could find the source of infection. But the foot was too swollen to search inside without causing more harm so I did my best to just clean it, remove dead tissue and drain any obvious lesions. Paul was an absolute stalwart and didn't flinch once, though I could see from his taut, pale face that he was in agony. Then I told Martha, his wife, who sat beside him batting away the flies with a palm-leaf fan, to soak the foot in warmed boiled saline solution for half an hour a day and elevate it after reapplying the dressing. I dressed it myself as best I could and left them with a week-long course of two types of strong antibiotics and proper daily dressings, rather than the pus-soaked cloths they'd been using. It was the best I could do. There was no clinic or other medical know-how on the island, despite offers from the Solomon Islands government. Hardly surprisingly, this issue was a source of considerable dissent, as I was to discover later.

My host in my new home was Hudson, the gentlest man I'd ever met, who'd been to school in Honiara so had excellent English, if somewhat softly spoken. Under the thatched dried-palm roof, his house was magnificent: very solidly constructed, with criss-crossed palm trunks lashed to poles sunk deep in the ground. All Anutan houses are built to survive the numerous South Pacific storms, he told me, including the notorious Hurricane Zoë, which had devastated neighbouring Tikopia in

2002. Hudson had grown up in this place and his mother still lived with him, along with his pregnant wife, his brother and a little boy whose father had gone missing on a recent fishing trip. The child had an Anutan name, but was known to all around as Mel Gibson, despite there not being a TV set on the island. Manusay and I sat down with Hudson for a lunch of chicken and taro while the women ate separately. Normally, I discovered, they would have eaten together; but I was getting special treatment because I was a guest. So when the meal was over I explained that I wanted to be treated as one of them; and after that we all ate together. The meal was rounded off with a good pipe smoke, which everyone – men and women – took part in.

I spent the next day or so tagging along with Hudson and his family as they went about their lives. That afternoon we went to the household cooking spot in an open-sided hut not far from the village. I helped make balls from taro and manioc mixed with baked coconut. Then we planted a few taro plants in their family plot, and ended the day with a swim in the sea. Bliss. The following morning we went to weed another family plot up on the volcanic hill. We'd hardly been working ten minutes before Hudson called for a break. Out came his pipe and some cigarettes and also some delicious sugar cane. When we finally went back to work he managed another ten minutes before calling it a day. He was adamant that I was not to work too hard, despite my protestations.

That afternoon, I finally got to do something constructive: setting up the new, solar-powered two-way radio that we'd brought with us to replace the old broken one. Joseph skilfully shinned up a couple of coconut trees to fix the horizontal dipole antenna.

'Tikopia on the radio,' he later called into the receiver, 'how do you read me, over?'

But although we could hear the neighbouring island, they couldn't hear us. It was frustrating, as everyone was hoping for news of Mel Gibson's father and the lost fishermen. We would try again when the solar batteries were fully recharged, in the hope that we could get through properly.

After the call of the conch shell to summon the village to worship came the makeshift church bell in St James, an old metal diving cylinder whose sonorous clang announced the start of the service. Hudson wasn't a fanatical churchgoer, generally only going once a day, so I did as he did, missing some of the services that were taking place right next to his house. It was weird how guilty I felt about this – a hangover from my Christian upbringing, no doubt.

I was happier getting stuck in to the more practical activities, such as the communal fish drive, which happened monthly on high tides around the full moon – now shining bright at night in the stormy sky. The first job was to repair the stone wall they had built across the lagoon, against which they would drive the fish. With everyone helping, diving down to replace rocks knocked off by the tidal currents, this was quickly accomplished. I was working with Manusay and Hudson, and after half an hour's reconstruction work we joined the long row of beaters, whose job was to block the fish's exit to sea and push them towards the small bottleneck at the base of the wall, through which was the killing zone. They did this by slapping the surface of the water with sticks, while obstructing all exits, and eventually the fish were bunched up in the small pond-like section, at which point the spears came out. These had a rubber tube attached to one end, which was pulled back and stretched like elastic, then released so the spear went zinging down with extra power through the water. The larger fish glistened a lovely light blue as they swam back and forth and were picked off one by one. The last few smaller ones were caught by boys who dived into the pool and swam alongside them in order to spear them. The final catch was divided into twenty-four, one for each of the island families. *Aropa* in action.

*

Joseph's original idea was that I spend each night with a different family, as is traditional for visitors. However, although we hated interfering with the island's plans for me, James pointed out that if I had a new family every day, the programme would be impossible for our audience to follow. So I asked whether it might be OK for me not to move every day, but perhaps every week instead, so as to have a level of continuity for the film. I felt awful asking this, as I knew how excited everyone was at the prospect of having me to stay. It was such a big decision that Joseph felt that a meeting of the chiefs' council would be needed to ratify it. In the end they agreed, but with one concession. All the crew, including myself, would have to dine with a different family each night, so that everyone would get a chance to host us.

So that evening we kicked off with Derek's family, the biggest on the island, which consisted of fourteen members, spread over eight different households. The meal went so well that they asked if I would live with them in my second week. They were expert fishermen, something I wanted to learn to contrast with Hudson's farming. So we happily agreed.

Before I left Hudson's he was keen to show me another island tradition, the burying of grated foodstuffs in pits, where it ferments slowly into a starchy paste, known as *maa*, which can be dug up and eaten as emergency food after a cyclone or drought. Hudson's family were all on hand to help as we collected graters, pots and huge, double-handed oval wooden bowls and headed up the hill towards the family manioc plantation. First off, Hudson and I had to find the waxy leaves that the manioc would be wrapped in, which were covered in tiny but aggressive ants – the only poisonous creatures on the whole island. Then, our hands now peppered with crimson bites, we had to pull up the manioc tubers from the ground, which looked easy enough but turned out to be impossible until you'd mastered the special rhythmic tugging technique.

The field was full of plants, but only those of a certain age were pulled up. Replanting was easy. Hudson cut the stem just above the tuber, stuck that back in the hole made by the pulled plant and pressed down the surrounding earth, leaving the offcuts as mulch. Next came the grating, using a wonderful old tool, which looked like a long paddle with a metal grate at the flat end and a sturdy handle to hold it steady against a tree. We filled six of the big wooden bowls. The waxy leaves were then laid in the *maa* pit in bunches of three. Finally, in the late afternoon, we were ready to lay on the grated manioc. More green leaves were placed on top, then covered in older, wetter leaves from the pit, to make a seal. These – stinking as they did of rotting compost – were then held down with stones to help make a good seal.

Dinner that night was with Caulton the schoolteacher, who struck me as part of a new generation on the island. Like Manusay, he was still single. He was not planning to marry a girl from the island. 'I don't like them,' he told me, 'because they all smoke.' He himself was a teetotal, non-smoking Christian who never even chewed betel nut, as evidenced by his perfect white teeth and slim, powerful physique. He was quite outspoken, too, about the power struggles and politics of the island. He was frustrated that the chiefs' council – the *maru* – were, in his words, so fearful of losing the spiritual power they held from faith healing that they still banned a medical clinic which might undermine this. Consequently his father's life hung in the balance. He was especially angry because the elders, he said, were quite happy to call for Western medicine from the supply ship when they got ill.

A farewell breakfast marked the end of my stay at Hudson's house. Hudson gave me a gift of a *sura* – or sarong – and offered me the biggest bunch of bananas I'd ever seen to take with me to my new house. I declined because I couldn't even lift them, let alone eat them, but said I would share one with him whenever I came to visit. Hudson then announced that he and his family had been talking the previous night and they had a request to make.

'Yes,' I asked, a bit nervously, 'what is it?'

'Would it be OK', he replied, 'if we became friends?'

What a question! I replied that as far as I was concerned we were of course friends already. At which the whole family broke into broad smiles. I was so deeply touched by this question that once again the full impact of how amazing my life and job really are struck home.

I was moving in with Derek and the biggest family on the island. Of the four clans, this was apparently the lowest in the island pecking order. But to me they were just a big, boisterous, friendly group. Big in every way: Derek was a vast man, a monster of muscle and sinew, without an ounce of spare fat – and his family took after him. He had a very gentle manner, yet I could tell he'd been at one time a bit of a lad. He told me that night that he'd fought during the recent unrest in the Solomon Islands, and that he was the undefeated heavyweight military boxing champion of Oceania. Then he told me that he'd actually seen me on TV, when he was in Honiara. I laughed. That was another first for the series.

The next day, despite the continuing poor weather, I went fishing with Derek, out beyond the reef on the open sea. To get through the impressive surf we waited for the right moment then lifted and shoved the canoe into the waves, jumped aboard and paddled like crazy. A couple of guys at the back kept pushing, then clambered on when we were at waist height. My paddle was huge and very heavy; I could hardly get my fingers round the handle. No wonder these guys were so powerfully built. Once we were away from the shore a couple of the crew members got up to unfurl the sail, winching it up the mast with a single pulley. The wind picked us up and we were off, racing over the waves. James, Tim and Joseph, who were following us in the *Margherita*'s inflatable boat, were left far behind, despite their outboard motor. I had a moment of romantic glee as I realized that I was out in the south Pacific with Anutan sailors in the kind of traditional craft that had been used to colonize these tiny specs of land thousands of years ago.

They told me in some detail how they read the waves and can feel the presence of land or reefs from various key signs: clouds on the horizon; changing colour of the sea; birdlife; currents; and the shape of the waves. The way they played the wind was remarkable, untying and retying knots and unfurling the sail accordingly. We cut through the waves at a terrific speed and I just sat there in awe, tingling with excitement.

Some way from the island we reached some outer reefs and lowered sail. Two of Derek's guys jumped out and checked the fish stocks in the water. We moved location a couple of times and then the fishing began. I lowered a line over the edge with some squid bait and instantly caught a fish. Nothing big, but it was a result – fifteen centimetres of bright pink reef fish. Pulling it into the boat I managed to get it caught by the dorsal barbs on its back, before one of the guys killed it with a wooden cudgel, unhooked it and threw it in the back of the canoe.

Derek and the others, meanwhile, had jumped right out into the open swell. They had their lines with them, which they lowered from their positions floating on the surface. I was happy enough watching, but then Derek beckoned for me to join them. Damn! I knew that was going to happen.

The stormy swell was not insignificant, and holding and lowering the line with my hands meant that, with my lesser experience and ability, I needed to use my legs to tread water fast. Looking around, everyone else seemed motionless and calm, but my frantic legs were working overtime and getting tangled in my line. The waves were huge and I was swishing about all over the place, getting far too many mouthfuls of salt water for comfort. Then, suddenly, I hooked a shark. Well, it certainly felt like a shark, jerking me hard to one side. My crappy local goggles without a seal were full of water and one eyepiece was slightly dislodged, so I couldn't even see under the surface what kind of monster I'd hooked. Whatever it was, it was swimming strongly in the opposite direction to the canoes, pulling me with it. I was tugging and tugging, trying to swim, finding myself dragged underwater, getting to a point where I could hardly muster any more energy. Thankfully, after one final tug it broke free. I resurfaced and swam hurriedly back towards the boat, trying to maintain my composure. As I began hauling in my line it gradually dawned on me that I'd probably just snared my hook on a rock and the swell had made it feel like a struggle. Idiot.

That was it for me in the water for that day. With no hook or sinker I was on paddling duty. The wind was against us, and it needed four of us paddling hard just to keep the boat near the bobbing fishermen. They truly were experts. Most had their spare reels tied on a rope belt around their waists, which were by now lined with a string of mostly bright pink fish. It was amazing to watch them at work, using their hands to fish, kill and string their belts while effortlessly treading water and barely breathing, it seemed.

Us paddlers were freezing by the time the fishermen returned to the boats. Up went the sail and we skimmed back over the sea to the island, where we rode the surf into shore before jumping out and dragging the canoe up the sand.

My day wasn't over yet. It is apparently a custom that every Anutan has a ceremony after their first day's boat fishing, which will normally be when they are about fifteen. For me it was now. It was pouring with rain, and cold with it, but the crew members took me straight over to Derek's house, washed me in warm water, massaged my aching limbs, painted me with bright orange turmeric (which smelt lovely mixed with coconut oil), put me in a tapa cloth and sarong, and gave me a huge feast of fish and taro. After which there was a further celebration, first in St John's church, then at Father Nomleas's house, with singing, speeches, Bible readings, and even more to eat. What a day!

The following morning it was the island's Thanksgiving Day, a time when the women traditionally process the turmeric. This is a ritual that takes place down on the beach, and I was going to be allowed to join in. The women were all sitting round a huge green mat made from woven palm leaves, which was full of the little muddy-red turmeric roots, held up round the sides against the women's knees. We were sitting just far enough up above the surf to catch one wave in twenty which gently rinsed the mud away. All the women had both hands in the mix, rubbing the roots against each other in the swirling seawater to get them clean, singing loudly as they did so. One woman in particular, Izzy, was making all the others cry with laughter with her song lines and jokes. Every time I caught someone's eye they would burst into hysterics, which was very contagious. All the while, the island kids played around us in the surf. The curved bases of huge palm fronds were the perfect thing for boogie boarding, and the smaller children in particular were brilliant at riding the waves right into the shore.

Later the men joined the women to pound and grind the washed roots. Once mashed up, the turmeric is twisted in a special grass to extract the brilliant orange juice. Some will be used to flavour food, but most will be mixed with coconut oil and used in rituals and ceremonies.

Derek took me fishing again the next morning. He prepped a reel for me and took me down to the beach. This was a trip without a canoe, so we swam out together through the swirling surf of the passage through the reef. Even out in the open sea, the current was quite strong, and though I'd now learnt to calm down my kicking feet I was still fighting to keep up with the expert Derek. After an hour of bobbing around, catching nothing, I decided to head back and Derek kindly came with me.

The gentle giant then headed back out to sea for more fishing. He returned some time later with two live turtles under his arm. He had seen one, followed it and lowered a dry hook, then yanked it up as the turtle swam over it. Catching it somewhere on the body, he'd then wrestled with it in the water. How he'd managed to then catch the second one with the first wriggling under his arm was a mystery to me.

Now he prepared them for cooking. The first one he butchered alive, cutting round the soft underbelly with a sharp knife, while remarkably the turtle never flinched. I asked whether he would ever kill it first to avoid unnecessary suffering and he told me that they never did. But then, when he got to work on the second one, undoubtedly out of respect for me, he cut the turtle's throat before continuing. But this was not a very effective way to kill such a reptile, which can swim underwater for ages without breathing. Sure enough, this time when he came to his gutting procedure, the turtle went mad and flapped around like a maniac. Once again I was reminded that to interfere in longstanding local custom, no matter how innocent or well meant, is rarely a simple matter.

That night I woke to find a rat running right by my head. Cats had been introduced to the island to keep their numbers down, but they had failed with this brute. It was the second time he had woken me. A couple of nights previously he had crawled right across my face, so that I could feel his tiny claws on my cheek and lip.

The next day was beautiful: calm and sunny and seemingly the perfect day to take the canoes out fishing again. But when I asked Derek what his plan was he reminded me that it was Sunday, a day of total and enforced rest on this little Christian island, so we weren't going anywhere.

Church was a two-hour marathon of songs and a mighty sermon from Father Nomleas. The rest of the day we followed island precept and just chilled. I caught up with my diary and made some calls on the satellite phone. It was today that I heard the sad news about Locho of the Nyangatom being killed. Looking round at my new Anutan friends, I could hardly imagine two more contrasting places to be.

We had Sunday lunch with the number-one chief, Pu Koroatu, after which I interviewed him on camera.

'As chief,' he told me, 'I must ensure everyone lives in peace and harmony.

'The people must stay together as one. They must love each other. I think that since I was young, of all the chiefs I have seen I am the best at keeping this island under rule. Now the people of Anuta are experiencing the changes I have made.'

I asked him about influences from the outside world. 'New things come to the island,' he replied, 'but they don't last. Things come that try and spoil our traditions. I am aware of things that are against our religious beliefs. Also there are food problems: when we buy food with money it's against our tradition. It's not right to sell food here.'

He was referring to an incident I'd heard about from Joseph. As cash is needed for batteries and fishing gear and the like, it is much in demand on Anuta. But islanders have limited access to hard currency: if they don't have a relative working and earning on one of the other islands, about the only things they can actually sell are shark fins to the occasional passing trade vessel. So some entrepreneurial families had started selling food to others if they were in need. But that was the problem. They were in need and *aropa* should be the answer for that. Sharing and giving. The incident had caused an uproar and had split the island in two. The council of elders eventually decided against any cash for food, but it seemed that many others were not happy and wanted to modernize.

The chief was against change of another kind too. New instruments, such as the ukulele and guitar, are also against their old traditions, he told me. They had created useless ways of living.

'The lives of the young should be free of trouble,' he went on, 'they should stick to the old rules, remain virginal.' But the young today didn't want that. 'Things were going from bad to worse,' he said.

There were 250 people living on this tiny island, less than half a square kilometre in total. That number was double what it had been twenty years ago and external changes and new rulings were inevitably taking place. There were certainly undercurrents of tension within the community about a number of different issues. In our short stay we were getting a glimpse of all this and it was fascinating, like watching the world in miniature.

I had breakfasted a couple of mornings on cooked seabird, which tasted a bit like pigeon. The following evening Derek's brother Reuben took me up to the cliff top to show me how they are caught. We rushed up the hill after church to try to get there before sunset, when the birds came flying back to their roosts. We reached the optimal spot, a field by the cliff's edge, to find two or three other hunters already crouching in the gently swaying cassava fields. I took the lightest net and crouched down, waiting.

The guys all had brilliantly realistic birdcall imitations to lure in their prey. My efforts were hopeless, both with the birdcalls and the swipes of my net. One bird I tried to follow with a complete 360-degree turn and got my feet so twisted up that I nearly stumbled over the cliff's edge, which would have been a sixty-metre drop down to the rocks beneath.

Eventually, more by luck than skill, I managed to catch one; even better, keep it in the shallow net and land it. I was so overzealous at the twisting and turning of my net as I pulled it in – the technique I'd been shown to stop the bird escaping – that it took Joseph five minutes to untangle it. The birds are not killed immediately. They have the ends of their longest flight feathers tied to those of another bird. Then, held by the knot, both birds dangle down together. Their calls of distress will, paradoxically, lure others into range. We all carried on as darkness fell. It was a hilarious sight, like some Monty Python butterfly-catcher sketch, with everyone swiping their nets wildly in all directions while uttering the ridiculous-sounding bird-calls.

The *Margherita* had reappeared, back from its safe haven in Tikopia. We had three more days, skipper Peter reckoned, before bad weather set in again, and he wanted to be away before that. I knew my time on the lovely island was coming to an end and wanted to make the most of it.

So the next day Derek took me fishing one last time in the outrigger. There was a good breeze and once the sail was up we were racing away from the island. We were hoping to catch shark, marlin, sailfish or tuna, all of which take the same bait. We headed for a different reef this time, and put out three more lines, including one for me. One of the guys, Cecil, got a bite, and for a few moments there was excitement as the line went taut, but whatever was down there hadn't quite got hooked. When we hauled the line in, the bait had some impressive teeth marks, but we had no shark. It was a pity because it would have been a great sight to see these strong men tackling such a big fish with just their hands then getting it aboard our tiny little boat. Derek told me that he and two of his brothers once spent seven hours bringing aboard a five-metre marlin.

Back on the island we discovered we'd been pipped to the post by Father Nomleas, who'd also been out fishing and caught a ninety-kilogram shark. The fins were sliced off and placed in the sun to be dried out for sale. Not that it's a vast sum of money, in our terms: a three-month collection of shark fins will fetch SI$500 in Honiara, which is around £40 in the UK. Globally this devastating trade ends up mostly in China, where the fins are a delicacy, used to make soup.

★

On the day of our farewell feast it was pouring with rain. I made a visit to Caulton's father, Paul, to say goodbye and make a final assessment of his foot. I had been popping in to see him most days and the antibiotics and daily salt baths had been visibly improving things. Most of the dead tissue had disappeared, leaving four vast cavities in his foot. But when I put it in the daily saltwater bath I could still press out some pus. I could only hope that with continued elevation, antiseptic and dressing it would recover completely. The official supply ship was due in a few days and we'd alerted them to the situation by satellite phone and they had promised to send a medical team with supplies.

Meanwhile James and Joseph had contacted all the islands within the Santa Cruz group and spoken to Tikopia again, but there was no news of the missing fishermen. The chances were that they were lost on the vast ocean and that little Mel Gibson would grow up with an adopted father.

Our farewell feast was delayed and delayed until there was a gap in the rain, which eventually came in the early afternoon. Each family had erected their own tarpaulin cover, under which they sat with their food on woven palm mats. James kicked things off by making a thank-you speech to everyone. He then invited the family heads to come up one by one and collect envelopes of cash, the centrepiece of our gift payment to the islanders for allowing us to film them, as arranged on the original recce. Every family we spoke to said that they would use the majority of the money for school fees.

As we had done at the welcome feast, we sat with each family in turn to join in their meal. There was pretty much every combination of recipe I'd encountered during the whole trip: fish and shellfish of every kind, cooked seabird, taro and manioc of course, all the different forms of *maa*, and coconut and banana, all wrapped in leaves and fresh and delicious. Luckily Father Nomleas, acting as community spokesman, joined our little group and orchestrated the move between families, otherwise it would have been hard to extract ourselves from some of the groups whom we'd got to know so well. None of the families touched their food until we'd joined them, and even then most of the individuals sat one row behind while we tucked in with the heads.

I was truly sorry to be going. But, as Peter had told James, if we missed the window of good weather we could be stranded on the island for some time, complicating our onward journey. Finally we were packed and ready. It was time for the leaving ceremony, which proved to be one of the most extraordinary hours of my life. I was dressed up by my latest host family in a tapa cloth and grass skirt, with a big cloth bow tied round my head.

Then, down on the beach, I was told I'd be joining in with the display of island dancing. I was given a special carved wooden paddle and put on the edge of the line-up, where I did my best to keep up, trying to copy Reuben's movement with the paddle. This proved impossible, as his grass skirt, wrist and armbands almost completely obscured my view of what his hands were doing. After six sets it was all over and we got down on the sand for the traditional goodbye session.

Everyone sat in a huge circle and I was asked to sit in the middle. A song started and almost immediately people were wailing and singing in the local language:

'We are very sorry
You are leaving
And going away from us.
We will miss you.
You have been a good friend,
We will miss you very much.
Please remember us.
We are very sorry you are leaving us,
Going back to where you come from . . .'

An ex-Marine, brought up in an old-fashioned English way, I'm not really one to let myself go in tears too often. But after catching a glimpse of Hudson, Joseph and the huge and totally masculine Derek blubbing away, I decided to release myself to the moment. It was incredibly powerful, letting myself weep with the sad singing all around and all eyes on me. When the songs had ended every islander in turn came up and gave me a big hug and a snotty-nosed *pikita*. There was no need for words. I just nodded, gave each shoulder a squeeze, and mumbled thanks. And to think I'd been worried about remembering everyone's name!

Then, all too soon, we were on the outrigger and away over the water to the gap in the reef, the *Margherita* and the rest of the world waiting beyond. Under the surface, paradise, Anuta, like anywhere else, had its problems. How would they resolve the ongoing discussions about the clinic, let alone the other tempting technologies of the wider world, which can only be bought with cash? Nothing would be easy, but as long as they hang on to their guiding philosophy of sharing and looking after each other – of *aropa* – they will remain an enviable society, and one with much to teach the rest of us.

13. Freedom on the Ice

The Nenets of the Yamal Peninsula, Russia

My departure for the Siberian winter to live with the Nenet reindeer herders came straight after a gloriously sunny month off at my home in Ibiza – it wasn't a trip I'd been looking forward to. Back in Cardiff, the *Tribe* production team had started wading through the masses of red tape and logistical conundrums as much as nine months previously, when our clothing sizes had been sent to our prospective families for them to start making our reindeer-skin clothing.

The journey out was long and difficult. With no porters to help, we'd lugged our thirty-odd boxes of camera gear and warm clothing through numerous crowded airports, where each load and unload would take hours. Our final urban resting place was the little town of Yarsale, a collection of heavily insulated modern buildings surrounded in every direction by snow. Inside our little hotel it was beautifully warm, but outside it was bitter, an average of -25°C in the day and much chillier at night. Even with all our modern clothing, lingering for more than a few minutes was painfully cold.

In these very tricky conditions, we were lucky to have an amazing fixer, a German social anthropologist called Florian Stammler, who was fluent in Russian as well as being able to speak the local Nenet language. Besides having a wealth of knowledge about his study subjects, he was also highly practical: he'd managed to get us Secret Service passes, enabling us to largely bypass the heavy bureaucracy that is still a big feature of Russian life. He'd also recruited a great translator, Roza Laptander, a young Nenet woman who spoke that language in addition to Russian and English. She had watched the Darhad Mongolia film five times, Florian told me, so she could better understand my accent. Dedication indeed.

Now we were on the very last leg of our journey, flying from Yarsale by helicopter across the snow to join the Eighth Brigade of reindeer herders – my hosts for the next month. This militaristic title dates back to Soviet attempts to settle these people, which were countered as they sorted themselves into units and agreed to give some of their herd in to the state collective every year. On board with us was our host, Alexander Serotetta, who had been waiting for us in town since the last time the brigade had passed through, four months ago, just to show us the way to his brigade.

After 150 kilometres of undifferentiated white flatness we suddenly spotted a migration beneath us. It was unreal, like nothing I'd ever seen before. Hundreds of sledges in motion, in separate articulated caravans of about ten apiece, with a team of two reindeer pulling each sledge and four at the front of each caravan, a long snake of human and animal activity outlined against the snow for miles.

As it happened, this was the Fourth Brigade, not the Eighth. All the brigades were converging on Yarsale for the annual sorting of the herd, after which the older deer would be slaughtered in the town's abattoir, and the carcasses sold on to provide the herders' income. As they got nearer to their destination, they were moving closer to each other, their routes like the spokes of a wheel. We touched down briefly while Alexander took directions, then we were off again. Ten minutes later the Eighth Brigade appeared below us. Our hosts had made camp as prearranged for our arrival date. Beyond the massed herd of reindeer was a string of tepee-like tents, grey-brown cones frosted with icing-sugar whiteness, each with a central puff of grey smoke winding up into the sky – *chooms*, as the Nenets call them. Sprinkled all around like toys were the numerous sledges of the brigade.

I jumped out of the chopper with Alexander and strode towards the waiting group. They were all wearing *malitsas*, the local clothing made from reindeer pelts which totally wrap the head and hands, leaving just a small circular space for eyes and smiles to peep out. I was ready with my first words of Nenet:

'*Andorva, andorva, andorva. Man Bruce.*' (Hello, hello, hello. I'm Bruce.)

After we'd unloaded our gear from the helicopter, Alexander invited us to take shelter inside one of the *chooms*. The tents were covered in a double thickness of reindeer fur, with a little door flap at one side. Inside, a planked central floor was skirted with a sort of reed matting made from woven sticks, which in turn was overlaid with felt carpet. On top of that, providing another layer of insulation, were strewn reindeer skins. At the centre of the room was a metal stove, with its chimney running up to the apex of the tepee. Laundry hung drying from the pine poles that made up the base structure of the tent.

Normally filming my first entry into the place where I planned to stay would have been straightforward. But not in this cold. Producer/director Wayne Derrick was having problems with his batteries, the light was very low, and every time someone new came in through the tiny triangular door the temperature dropped, which was hardly popular with the gathered group inside. Poor Florian was getting quite agitated as we struggled to document my arrival in the *choom*.

Luckily, though, the family itself seemed happy enough with all our palaver, and once we'd got the sequence we needed we were soon sitting with a cup of tea – or *chai* – accompanied by hunks of rock-hard bread. As each brigade only visits town once or twice a year, these had been dried in the sun three months before to preserve them, Alexander's wife Tatiana explained. Then the vodka came out and Alexander and his brother Sergei, who was the overall leader – or brigadier – raised their glasses in a toast.

'Let us drink to your first day,' came Roza's translation from the Russian. 'By working together, hopefully we can find a common language. I don't think we'll have any problems,' Alexander added, 'but you should know that conditions will be tough for you.'

The toasts were followed promptly with more food. While waiting for the thick fibrous reindeer stew to cook we all tucked into frozen slabs of raw meat. Using a pocket-knife, chunks were hacked off and dipped in a hot and pungent horseradish sauce. The texture of the meat was amazing; it literally melted in your mouth without any need to chew at all.

In the cosy warmth of the *choom*, the toasts continued. It was only mid-afternoon, but outside it was already getting dark. Up here in the Arctic Circle, the winter days were only a few hours long.

The layout of the *choom* was interesting, as it was effectively split into two halves, each housing a separate family. In this case, as Alexander and Sergei were brothers, they shared goods and food. But this was not always so, and two completely independent families would often share a *choom*. Another difference from my usual filming trips was that this time the crew were living alongside me, albeit staying on Sergei's side of the divide. Besides Wayne, we had researchers Matt Dyas, who'd also been with me in Bhutan, and Willow Murton, veteran of many a *Tribe* shoot.

We sat drinking and talking, with lots of chat between the two sides of the tent. I explained to Alexander about our plans for the film. At first, he seemed reluctant to get involved at all, fearing an official reprisal if he made any negative political statements. This wasn't the first time they'd had a film crew stay, and they hadn't been impressed by their previous experience, when a Russian team had made a set-up documentary about the Nenets, using actors who pretended to live as the Nenets had done a hundred years ago. Luckily, after further explanations, Alexander finally agreed to be involved provided we only told the truth about their life as it is today.

Alexander was a very interesting man. He had been to university, become a national standard sportsman in the cross-country skiing championships, and been involved in the opening ceremony at the Moscow Olympics (where he'd met Seb Coe, Steve Ovett and Daley Thompson). He had travelled extensively, but didn't like hot places and in the end had chosen to return to the traditional migrating life for himself and his family. He had worked for a long time as a teacher in big cities, but stopped, he told me, when his salary had started to get 'embarrassingly low' compared to that of his brother who was still herding. Over the other side of the *choom*, Matt and Willow were having a whale of a time with the brigadier's family. Sergei's grandson Danil was first to bed on their side; on ours it was Alexander's 78-year-old mother.

The *choom* that night was sleeping eight Nenets, three TV crew, translators Roza and Florian, and myself. It was quite a squeeze. The difference in temperature between my feet near the stove and my head near the edge of the tent was probably 20°C, making getting comfortable quite interesting. On one side I had Florian, stiff as a corpse; on the other, producer/director Wayne, kicking me in his sleep. I fell asleep with a warm glow, partly because of the vodka, but more because I was now genuinely excited about the coming month.

We woke that first morning on the frozen steppe at 5 a.m., long before the sun was due to show its face. I was busting for the loo, but there was no question of running outside just yet. First I had to warm my clothes. Having been left at the inside edge of the tent, my modern arctic boots had frozen solid and took half an hour to defrost.

Stepping outside the *choom* was truly breathtaking. At this high latitude the motion of the sun at this time of year is painstakingly slow. It gently breaks the horizon, does a tiny arc, then dips beneath again. The resulting red, purple and orange sunrises last so long that they seem to drift into the equally spectacular sunsets, with hours of glorious grey-blue twilight before and after. Every morning the herd of reindeer were corralled into a makeshift pen just beyond the perimeter of the camp, a mass of jostling antlers, their breath and body steam rising slowly in the frozen air, intensifying the orange. There were perhaps 1,500 here, but this wasn't the whole of the Eighth Brigade's herd. These were just the semi-domestic ones they used to pull their sledges. Four times this number were grazing out some way across the snow.

We were staying put in camp today, but Nenet men were still in among the herd choosing animals to pull whichever sledges might be needed for the day's chores. On migration days enough animals were collected to pull every single sledge. The reindeer were owned by the different *chooms* and were marked accordingly with special ear cuts. The herders were picking animals which hadn't been used the previous day and were therefore rested. My job was to stand holding the rope that marked the edge of the corral, going 'Wa-aay!' at any reindeer that tried to escape. The beasts crowded together, facing out, their impressive antlers inches from my eyes. They were more scared of me than I was of them, but I could easily imagine the mayhem if they'd got overly spooked. Every now and then one made a bid for freedom, either trying to hurdle over or duck under the rope. These would be recaptured using long ropes of reindeer skin called *tenziang*. Once the necessary sledges were all sorted out with deer we stopped for a well-earned *chai* break inside the *choom*.

The crew spent the rest of the day attending to their equipment. At this temperature, batteries lasted minutes rather than hours and handling the cold metal equipment, even with gloves, was treacherous. Quite how Wayne managed to film at all was beyond me. The difference between the cold dry exterior and inside the warm humid *choom* was so extreme that all cogs and lenses would freeze up instantly if not properly acclimatized for an hour or so in an airtight container.

Meanwhile I was getting to know people and having some interesting chats. During one food break I talked with Florian and Tatiana about overgrazing and state control. Russian environmental laws, they told me, are strict, and there is now regulation about how many reindeer are allowed on the Yamal Peninsula. The Nenets, understandably, are reluctant to cull their animals to meet these quotas. They feel they are best placed themselves to decide what is too dense an animal population and what isn't. What right did some environmentalist from Moscow have, Tatiana argued, to tell her how many reindeer she could graze on this land when they had never even been here?

In the evening, Sergei, the brigadier, returned with the other men, having found and collected a hundred of his reindeer from the Second Brigade. As the brigades converged, it became easier for stray deer to mix with other herds; they needed to be collected and returned to the right herd. Before we left in the morning, the men from the Second Brigade were going to come over to us to claim *their* missing deer.

We were up at five again for a breakfast of tea, jam and dried bread. We were on the move today, so the eight *chooms* of the brigade had to be taken down and painstakingly packed up. It was hard for me to join in because it was instantly obvious that each procedure followed an intricate routine that I wasn't privy to. If I thought that I could simply learn one or two skills to get me by, I was kidding myself, as every knot and loading order was different with every sledge. This get-out-of-work card might have been fine in other circumstances, except that here, as soon as I stopped moving, I could feel my core body temperature plummet. Many of the tasks I did manage to copy and learn required dexterity of ungloved fingers and mine were already frozen, even in mitts. I stood watching all the Nenet men and women getting on with their chores with their bare hands and realized I was physiologically unable to be of equal help. It was a frustrating feeling of uselessness.

As the magnificent *choom* came down, it exposed its entire contents, the planking floor and mass of furs and rugs on top. It took minutes to collapse and after an hour or so most of the sledges were packed and ready. Meanwhile, the 1,500-strong herd of sledge-pulling reindeer had been edged across the snow towards our camp. Still jittery, despite this routine being regular, they ran round and round the camp with little dogs yapping at their heels. In their path stood men who, by recognizing each animal's face and antlers, knew exactly which one needed to be lassoed. Often more than one person would skilfully lasso the same reindeer from a charging group of many closely bunched beasts – an amazing skill. Once caught, each would be carried off to be harnessed to one of the twenty or so sledges that pulled each *choom*'s possessions.

The remainder of the herd were corralled towards a make-shift half-circle fence, while the women and I closed the other side of the circle with a waist-high rope. Just holding this turned my hands to ice-blocks after a few minutes. The herders forged their way into this mass to find their allotted transport animals, remaining alert to the eye-level antlers of these timid but jumpy beasts. Meanwhile others were harnessing and packing the 380 sledges which made up our brigade train.

After a few hours we were ready to go. I was astonished by just how laborious it all seemed – and to think that they did this nearly every other day of their lives, whatever the weather. Just before departure everyone sat around and had a little picnic, drinking hot tea from flasks with snacks of raw fish, sweets and Wagon-Wheel-like chocolate biscuits. I couldn't sit. It was just too cold. So I stamped around on my frozen feet.

Finally we were off! I joined Sergei on his sledge at the head of the whole caravan. As we skimmed over the snow behind the reindeer it felt like a dream. All the preparatory hustle and bustle was over and I sat watching these splendid animals pulling hard in front of me, heading straight towards the huge low yellow sun, which flickered between their magnificent frosted antlers.

There was no sign of other life in any direction. The only sound was the panting and hoof tread of the reindeer behind us, and the crunch and glide of the sledges on the snow. Sergei held a long pole with which he prodded each reindeer in turn to urge them forward. A long rein to the animal on the far left controlled the steering. Just behind us two reindeer were attached to the back of our sledge, and they in turn were pulling Wayne and Roza on the sledge behind us, and so on back for about six to ten sledges. That was our immediate train. There must have been, in total, about forty of these trains. Looking back, the line stretched over the low white undulations behind into the far distance, to what looked like a forest in the snow, but in fact was the rear reindeer herd. It was incredibly beautiful and romantic; I'd never experienced anything remotely like it in my life. I said on camera that if Sergei had been my girlfriend I would have proposed there and then. (I meant the sentiment, but I'm not sure where it came from because I didn't even have a girlfriend at that time.).

Every now and then Sergei pulled up his reindeer with the rein and the whole train stopped for a few minutes' break. After four hours or so, he got off the sledge, strolled across the snow and placed a long pole vertically in the ground. This was where we would camp. I was elated as my feet were now very painful with cold. The other sledges from our *choom* drew up alongside in a neat curve. Everyone jumped off and got to work untethering the deer, which immediately started digging through the snow with their hooves and feeding on the lichen beneath. Meanwhile the sledges with the packed-up *choom* were unloaded and piece by piece our little dwelling was put up with all its contents.

Much of the unpacking of the *choom* contents was theoretically a woman's sacred task, I discovered later; but I was unaware of this then and Tatiana seemed happy for me to get stuck in helping. It was great to get moving again and feel, as I worked, a little warmth creeping back into my frozen extremities. With the floor laid down, and the stove and carpeting and bundles of furs laid on top, Sergei and I held aloft the central two poles of our *choom*, which were joined by a loop of rope. Then everyone ran round putting in the rest of the poles through the loop. Though each one looked pretty much the same to me, Florian explained that they were all slightly different lengths. Each had a certain key place in the order of erection. Now, finally, the coverings were added, made from stitched-together reindeer skins: two huge inner halves and two thick outer ones, with a tiny perspex window either side of the little triangular door skilfully aligned.

It was another couple of hours before the *chooms* were up. Once we were all safely inside ours Sergei gave us our orders. We weren't moving for two days. That suited me. I needed to get sorted out with some warmer gear or I would freeze up completely on the next leg of the journey.

So the next morning, while the rest of the women went off to collect firewood, Tatiana tried me out with the local *malitsa* which we'd ordered months before – and what an amazing item of clothing that turned out to be. The boots come in two parts. The inners have fur on the inside and came up almost to my groin, while the outers have fur on the outside and are even longer. Both have ties, which are attached to a felt waist belt to keep the boots up. Over this the coat is like a fat hooded poncho with arms, with another, outside belt around the midriff. The cuffs have a built-in fur mitt on each arm, with a gap to allow a bare or thinly gloved hand through for those moments when you need to use fingers. The crew had received their *malitsas* the previous day and everyone thought I'd been mad to sit on the sledge all day in my modern clothing. I'd done it to see the difference for myself, and they were right to consider me mad – the difference in heat retention was amazing.

That evening the wind picked up. The whole *choom* creaked. Wayne followed me out into the snow to film me going for a piss and the conditions were rough, −30°C before the wind chill. But my new garb was wonderfully warm, even if I wasn't going to hang out with the other guys chatting outside the tents.

The morning brought another day of rest and retrenchment. The women headed off to collect wood while the men went over to the Second Brigade to find more stray reindeer. Wayne was still having trouble with his cameras, but I decided to try to do my best to help out anyway, to keep warm if nothing else. So I chopped wood, badly. Tried to saw it: worse. Unlike the Nenets, who expose their fingers to the cold for ages, mine nearly stuck to the steel of the axe or turned to painful blocks of ice in no time. I saw one guy working with bare metal for over an hour. Watching them, I knew I would quite simply get frostbite if I tried to do what they did. Whether this greater ability to deal with the cold was a racially genetic difference or simply toughness or long-term acclimatization I didn't know.

After the wood chopping, I went with Raya, the wife of Sergei's son Jova, and one of the other women to collect water. We commandeered a sledge, harnessed up some reindeer and set off down the hill to a nearby frozen lake. It took us a few minutes to find the previously cut hole, which had an inch or two of ice already frozen on since this morning. I broke through the thin layer with a heavy pike then began to fill two urns, ladling the icy water in with saucepans.

In the evening I joined the other side of the *choom* for the first time and had a great chat with Raya about love and marriage and bridal gifts and cultural ceremonies. As the men came back, the talk turned to reindeer and the migration: how the brigade is structured; how salaries are worked out; the price they can get for the animals, which depends on where they're sold and to whom. Then I quizzed Jova about his four years in agricultural college in Yarsale, which had led to him becoming the brigade vet.

We were up early the next morning to find a full moon shining above the horizon. It was as orange as the sun, and almost, it seemed, as bright. We were all dressed in no time, because this was another transit day. I made the mistake of wearing everything I had in anticipation of sitting on the sledge for hours of inactivity, my thermal gear from home as well as the *malitsa*. The result was that my temperature and sweat rate went up and down a lot in the first few hours of the day, which was potentially very dangerous. This time I was of more use with the dismantling of the *choom* and packing-up ritual. I was doing nothing of intricacy or skill, just carrying stuff or scraping snow or holding the odd rope and so on. But I was able to keep busy the whole time and felt better for it.

We had the usual pre-journey picnic of tea, salt fish and meat, then, as the moon set, we were off. It was −20°C. The snow was deep too, which meant the deer really struggled in places and the going was slower. At one treacherous point, the deer on the right of our team fell through a snow bridge and into a stretch of open, unfrozen river. The other deer were on the bank, so their strength and momentum enabled the animal to pull itself out, but our sledge was immediately behind and we nearly went right in ourselves. Luckily Sergei had pulled the other deer sharply to the left and I was, for a change, holding on tight to the sledge-ties, so was able to stop myself from toppling into the dangerously cold water.

Soon after that potentially disastrous incident, Sergei struck camp. He stopped his lead sledge and planted his pole in the snow. Up went the *choom*. Everyone was in good spirits now, and that evening we had another great group chat, this time about change and the environment and the future of the Nenets. Listening to Alexander and Sergei and Tatiana and the others made me want more than ever to challenge any audience preconceptions about these people's lives being romantic, remote or removed somehow from contemporary reality. These people were well educated and politically aware; they knew the pros and cons of the modern world, and had made the decision to live as they did.

We weren't moving in the morning so I had a bit of a lie-in. For the first few days I'd been unnaturally tired, often drifting off, despite the cold, while waiting for the tea to be brewed. Likewise on the sledge journeys. But I was definitely in the zone now. I was sleeping well and I could feel my energy levels returning. I felt great.

One physiological worry was that, because of my staple diet of meat and not much else, I hadn't had a dump since we'd been in Yarsale, over a week before. When and if I finally felt ready for it, it was going to be an excessively cold experience. Even taking a pee was a precarious activity. Fingers and dick would become painfully cold when exposed even for just a few seconds and you would generally be joined by three or four nearby reindeer, who love the salt content of urine and whose sharp antlers would come precariously close on a dark night.

After breakfast I went with Alexander to help bring in some fishing nets which had been set the previous day. To fix the nets in place a long pole had been used to feed the net through a hole in the thick ice before a second hole was smashed through at the point where the pole ended. The net was then held there in the freezing water, the pole pulled out of the original hole, taken to the new hole, and pushed back through with the net attached; and once again pushed to its end, where another hole was smashed. In this way, with a series of holes, the net could be extended under the ice for a hundred metres or so. We turned up this morning to watch a family pulling one of these nets back up through the original hole in the ice and bringing out a good number of fish in a variety of sizes – some very decent. I joined in for a little, but then realized that to do it properly I was going to have to go barehanded. No sooner were my hands wet and exposed to the bitter wind than they became like blocks of ice with no sensation or dexterity at all. I knew my body reactions well enough to realize that I had just minutes of exposure like this before I was seriously at risk from frostbite. The wind was quite strong and very cold and twice I heard Roza's translation – 'Hurry up, Bruce' – when I was getting tangled with the net and struggling to squeeze the fish out. In these temperatures it's dangerous to keep people hanging around, or to experiment with new skills. There simply wasn't time for that. For the crew, too, everything was so much harder. I had no idea how Wayne was able to hold the camera for so long. Any time I messed up a piece to camera I felt awful as everyone had to stand around freezing and waiting for my second attempt.

The next day it was surprisingly warm – a mere −1°C when we woke in the morning. This brought its own problems, as it started to rain. The snow was now thick and wet, which was very bad news, as once you got wet out here there was no easy way to get yourself or your clothing dry – even when the *chooms* were up – and serious moisture ruins the *malitsas*.

This was another migration day, but before we left, Alexander gave me a lassoing lesson, showing me how to loop up the long thin lasso – or *tenziang* – which is made from reindeer skin twisted into a circular plait. The skin is taken from a stag killed as he's preparing to rut, when testosterone levels are at their highest (after sex the skin becomes weaker, apparently).

This lesson was typical of the ever-pragmatic Alexander. He took me through the process once and then walked off. It was a migration day and he clearly had more important stuff to do. Left on my own, the tricky bit was finding the natural twist in the thread of the lasso and coiling it appropriately. This took a couple of goes to suss at all. After that I got the general knack, but my actual accuracy of throwing was still some way off.

Today I was travelling with interpreter and anthropologist Roza. We were on a sledge towards the back of our *choom* group, so for the first time I was able to see all the other sledges and reindeer stretching out in front of me – truly an amazing sight, like the most romantic Christmas card come to life. Appropriately, Roza and I spent some time discussing the influential St Nicholas and various bits of folklore of the Siberian reindeer-herder people. It's widely accepted that the myth of flying reindeer derives from Siberian legend, influenced as well by the shamans' custom of drinking the urine of reindeer which had fed upon the hallucinogenic fly agaric toadstool (known as *Amanita muscaria*, it's poisonous to humans until metabolized by the deer). The Father Christmas story may also have gained from the fact that shamans also went in for inducing spirits down the central pole of the *choom*, next to the chimney.

Our conversation came to an end when the wind picked up and the temperature dropped rapidly, and soon our wet-snow patches began to freeze. My previously damp fleece, which we were sitting on, became a solid ball of ice, the whole thing frozen into a clenched mass. I tried to do some filming with my Bruce-cam, but the lens was full of frozen mist and I couldn't clear it.

More frozen mist and spindrift came in with the rising wind, and soon we were in a whiteout. Conditions were so poor that

Sergei decided to halt the migration early. In the failing visibility, he couldn't guarantee that we'd get to his predetermined destination in daylight, or even to a place where there was good lichen pasture for the reindeer. His pole, stuck in the snow as usual to mark the camp site, was soon blown over. We all piled off and pitched in to get the *chooms* up before the wind made them impossible to erect.

The next morning the sky was clear again. Two snowmobiles arrived across the snowy wastes to take Sergei on ahead into Yarsale for a meeting with the slaughterhouse company. He needed to agree on meat prices, migration routes and the like. The petrol-powered machine that came to collect him may have been faster than a reindeer sledge, but useless too far away from town and sources of fuel.

Sergei was taking reindeer meat with him as a gift for his relatives in Yarsale, so a beast was slaughtered by ceremonial strangulation and quickly butchered. I'd eaten raw meat every day so far, but this was my first taste of unfrozen fresh meat, liver and warm blood. These reindeer only eat slow-growing lichen, which is intolerant of manufactured pollutants and a very pure food indeed; the animals are therefore very healthy and toxin free. And their meat was without doubt the subtlest and most delicious I'd ever eaten. One reason for the migration in the first place is for the herd to constantly search out fresh lichen pastures as it follows the seasons north and south each year – over 1,500 kilometres in total. None of these herders would ever dream of eating the artificially fed reindeer sold in town.

With the boss away, his son, the vet, Jova, had taken charge. That afternoon we headed off together to the main reindeer herd. There were so many animals dark against the snow and sky that it felt like being on an Arctic version of a blanched Serengeti plain with a mass of wildebeest.

Some animals from the transport herd had sneaked into the

main one and needed to be returned. I'd already lassoed the odd beast but never on camera and so I was desperate to get a good shot after so many filmed near misses. It was so frustrating. The noose was always really close, regularly touching the animal, but always just off target. More often than not the lasso would land on the bastard's back as it nonchalantly stepped forward.

I really wanted to lasso a running deer as it looked so cool and exhilarating to achieve, and is in fact easier as the animal will run into the hanging noose. But even though dozens kept running past me, I couldn't tell which particular animal the guys were targeting and so it was impossible to join in. Sensing my frustration, my friends pointed out the odd stag for me to have a go at. But I'd only get one in fifteen and never, it seemed, on camera.

The next morning we were on the move again, with Jova in charge. Our journey was now across a totally flat plain, not an undulation in sight. The snow was deep and the poor animals were having a hard time of it, sinking up to their bellies on occasion. In the end Jova made the bold decision to stop early. Although I understood why, I couldn't help but feel frustration with his plan. Having spent so many hours dismantling and packing up, it seemed crazy to stop and start unpacking again, when we could have gone so much further. This was a point of view not shared by our hosts. To them the packing and unpacking procedure was so routine that it was like getting up in the morning and catching a train to work. We, by contrast, wanted to be efficient and make the most of our efforts of the morning, translating that into distance covered towards our destination. Jova was taking a longer-term view, realizing that to exhaust his animals now might cause problems later. He was, of course, completely right.

Most evenings, it seemed, there was a special Russian day to toast – the latest had been Police Officers' Day! Tonight being

11 November I decided to tell them about our own Remembrance Day and elaborated on poppies and so on. Had the Cold War turned hot, I added, it might even have been possible that we could have ended up as each other's enemies, rather than sharing a *choom* as we were now – especially as the Royal Marines' NATO role was defending the northern flank of Norway. As the vodka went down our chat moved on to the futility of war, the merits and demerits of the UN, and corporate control of world politics. Alexander was still at heart very much a communist and thought that the reason for Russia's currently poor economy was what he called 'rogue-capitalism'. I fell into bed eventually with the issues spinning around my head.

After three days on the trot, the last speeding along on a crust of ice over the snow, Jova called a halt and we had a rest day. It was bliss to lie in for a change, rather than rising at five to pack up and dismantle everything. Breakfast included a huge jar of frozen fish roe, which was close to caviar and delicious on toast.

A few days earlier I had managed to finally break my constipated state and enjoy a proper call to nature out in the snow. It hadn't gone well. Quite apart from being freezing, I'd been joined by several curious reindeer and, to cap it all, slightly lost my balance while in the act. Today, though, I had a dream dump at last. The snow crust was solid. I found a small *sastruga*, pounded a little hole behind it and placed some old cut-off thermal underwear bottoms as a seat on the snow. So it was just a case of getting my *malitsa* out of the way and admiring the view, with the occasional dip of the head inside the cape to check my hand.

Later that morning, after the usual corralling and lassoing session I was given a sledge-driving lesson by Alexander – my first. On this instruction he took his time and went over things more than once. The left hand holds the pole, the right the rein – the 'steering and gas', as he put it. It was exhausting work and both my arms were in anaerobic hell in no time. The hardest factor of all, which I only realized halfway through my lesson, was that the reason the beasts were so unruly was that all they really wanted to do was rejoin the herd. Trying to make them turn away from their pals was next to impossible. Finally I managed to get them away from camp and the herd to a place where I was able at last to get a little more control out of them. But with a very wilful lead animal I was knackered by the time I finally managed to steer the beast back to my instructor.

After lunch Sergei returned from his trip to Yarsale. Little Danil was overjoyed and sat cradled happily in his grandfather's embrace. That evening Wayne and I had dinner on Sergei's side of the *choom* and after the usual toasts everything got a bit senti-mental and misty-eyed. Sergei talked about his childhood without a father; living with Alexander in harsh conditions and looking after his mother; his army days; his desire for the reindeer-herding tradition to continue; his love of the freedom and simplicity of the migrating way of life; how to him it is in no way a tough or an extreme life.

The whole continuation of this migration, of course, depends upon the land being empty and free to roam over, which is now threatened by the discovery and exploitation of the huge gas fields in these remote regions. The Bovanenkovo field alone holds the equivalent of three-quarters of all the North American fields put together. Both Sergei and Alexander were heavily involved in the fight against the development of the Yamal Peninsula, but knew that in the end they would have to coop-erate with the might of the Russian government and the Gazprom gas company rather than try, futilely, to fight them. Alexander even envisaged a time when his son, who was study-ing ecology at university in Tyumen, would work for Gazprom liaising with the Nenet people in the region. I was impressed by his intelligent and rational pragmatism.

Compensation to reindeer herders had been agreed by the

state. Discussions were underway about how to make gas pipelines reindeer-friendly, by raising them up from the ground as in some parts of North America. But many believed that in the end not much would actually be done to help keep the migrations continuing. Sergei had already been flown to a gas field in the north of the peninsula where a tarmac road interfered with a herding migration route. In the end, after protests, it had been agreed that a sand crossing would be put in for the reindeer. But that hadn't been in the original plan, so of course turned out to be far more expensive.

The bottom line was that the Nenets needed the outside world to know that they were not some remote people living in the Stone Age, who were inevitably going to have to modernize to survive. They had chosen the migration way of life because they valued it. In its relationship with nature and its ecological efficiency, indeed, despite the traditional methods used, it was a supremely modern way of living.

The next day everyone stayed put. It was time for Sergei's brief with the rest of his brigade about the coming months: the dates for corralling and slaughtering, as well as when some members would be given time off. Florian explained that each member of the brigade is granted a month's leave every year, which they take in a block every three to four years. This 'holiday' away from the main herd often takes place in the same general location, which is how the holidaying family are able to take their herd away with them. So the upcoming corralling of the herd was an excellent time for them to identify and separate their reindeer before heading off.

The meeting took place in our *choom*. It was odd having so many extra faces sitting around. Both sides of the room were tidied up and Sergei and Jova sat together at the central table with school exercise books of graph paper, a page for each person, lined up with meaningful-looking numbers, crosses and squiggles. The visitors were all men and none of them removed their *malitsas*; half never even lowered their hoods. The mood was jovial, as dates were discussed and made firm, and decisions made about who should go with Sergei the following week on a helicopter recce for usable winter pastures free from the treacherous ice-crust that we were increasingly seeing around us.

We were close to Yarsale now and all thoughts were focused on the upcoming corral, when reindeer destined for slaughter or holiday were to be split from the main herd. Tensions were high because if the herders failed to entice the herd into the corral's gates first time the deer would not go near it again. Just a bit of litter blowing in the wind at the wrong time could spook them, apparently, and that would be it for the year. No cash or holiday for anyone.

This was the last time all the *chooms* in the brigade would camp together for a while. Departing from our campsite today, the various groups would take up separate positions around the corral, so that once the animals were apart they could be taken to their respective positions without fear of mingling with the other deer again. The main herd would continue south to cross the frozen River Ob and on to the brigade's winter pastures. Our *choom* would take selected older animals into town for slaughter before joining the main brigade later; and the two holidaying families would go their separate ways and join the main brigade in a few months' time.

Normally we had been the first to depart in the long line of caravans, so it was strange but sublimely beautiful to watch the other reindeer sledges heading off without us. Once we'd got going, our first stop after about an hour didn't bode well. While we'd had that rain shower further north, there had been a torrential downpour at this latitude. As a result, there was more of the dreaded ice-crust that we'd been seeing, which the deer couldn't break through with their hooves to feed on the lichen beneath. If they went two days without eating they could easily die, Jova told me, so everyone was now tense. The herders were paid by carcass weight and all the animals were fit and healthy now. It had been a great year. For the animals to lose their fat or die at this eleventh hour would be a disaster. We had to hope that there were decent feeding grounds up ahead.

Despite this potential crisis, Alexander chose this moment to invite me to take the reins of the sledge. And what a difference to my earlier attempts! Whether due to the ice, a good lead animal or the movement of the whole herd, my steerage animal was thoroughly responsive today. The slightest pull or tap had the reindeer going in the desired direction. I could easily move out of my slipstream position and into a new lane made by myself and come alongside or even overtake the other sledges. It was magical, racing along over the icy snow towards the huge sun, setting in an orange explosion on the white horizon. The deer raced ahead, with impressive frosty antlers, and I found myself having one of those wonderful moments when I felt completely at peace and happy with myself in the world.

We struck camp that evening twelve kilometres short of the corral village of Portsy Yak. Luckily we'd found a sizeable patch of usable pasture within the main body of the continuing ice-crust and the deer could once again feed. So we stayed put for two days, preparing for the corral round-up.

Mid-morning the next day, Alexander, Florian, the crew and I headed over to the corral, which lay beyond the village to the north, on a steep slope like a small knoll. It was buzzing with people, while sledges littered the slope and frozen river below. The pens inside the corral were teeming with deer who had been brought in by the herders during the night (we'd not gone with them for fear of spooking the animals). The mixed herd was being pushed through some holding pens, before small groups were let in to a central sorting pen. Here the animals were set upon by a mass of herders, all doing different jobs. Some were vaccinating those deer which were not going to be slaughtered – they received an identifying cut to the rear haunch. Other less fortunate animals were marked in ways that meant they were destined for the cull.

I tried to get stuck in and help, but there wasn't much for me to do. The men in the middle were all highly proficient and there was no time to initiate a newcomer. The sorting process was going to take them all day and night for two days anyway, without me slowing things down. The earmarking by age, sex and destiny was too complex. I tried shovelling shit from the doorway every now and then, but it was all a bit marginal.

Going back to the *choom*, I took the second sledge and once again had a magnificent ride. My animals were wonderfully responsive and hardly ever in need of a pole up the arse. Admittedly I was following the first sledge, but I felt that I now really had control. Things were made even better because I decided I'd do something I hardly ever did while living with a family, but I couldn't resist it: I listened to my iPod under my fur hood without anyone seeing. I had a random shuffle mix on and felt as if I were in some magical Christmas dream, as 'Here With Me' from Dido was replaced by 'Pure Shores' from All Saints, then some psychedelic trance and finally the ethereal chants of 'Misereri Allegri's'. The music made the experience all the more surreal.

Two days later the animals were all sorted and we moved on to Yarsale. We rose very early, so as to get the herd into the slaughterhouse corral before it was light. As we approached the little town there was no moon and the lights burned bright in the distance. Neither these nor the smoky chimneys of the buildings around the abattoirs put off the deer at all, and they followed us easily to their final destination.

A few transport animals had got mixed up with the slaughter herd by accident and now had to be lassoed and removed. If only they had known why they were being collected they would have been less reluctant! I got more involved than at

any time earlier and missed a deer kick in the balls by a millimetre. I was grabbing them by their antlers, rugby-tackling
them, and generally getting down and dirty. Great fun.

Wayne was allowed into the slaughterhouse to film and it was
all very modern and automated – one minute from living animal
to skinned carcass. This gave rise to some interesting conversations
among the crew about the pros and cons of meat-eating.

It was strange, later, seeing the brigade members in town, away
from their sledges and animals. But they didn't seem in any
way out of place. Alexander and Sergei both owned town houses
and had done for years; in relative terms they were both well
off.

Once the slaughter was over we joined them for a farewell
dinner. Their homes were full of all the facilities and gadgets
you'd expect in a modern house, the TV was on in the background, and they looked like any family in a Siberian town. We
had a great evening, and toasted all our futures many times.

Theirs was such an interesting case. Here was a group of
indigenous people who knew all about the modern world, had
embraced those elements of it they wanted to, but managed to
maintain their traditional life too. And not in some quaint or
false fashion, but in a way that made them comfortably off as
well as fulfilled in deeper, unmaterial ways. They didn't want
to be patronized by the outside world and told they should
move on because life was better elsewhere. They knew the
score, and were acting on it.

'During my life,' Alexander concluded, 'I've lived in many
places. It's very comfortable in town. But I can't live within
these four walls, I find it very hard. We have everything here:
a bathtub, a washing machine, even a television, but I don't
need any of them. I have peace of mind out on the tundra. To
live here would be a prison sentence.'

I wondered how things would shake down with Gazprom
and the development of these Arctic gas fields. I respected

Alexander, Sergei and their families enormously, not to mention their ideas and ideals, but I knew that, like so many indigenous peoples around the globe, their chosen way of life was in the balance in order to make way for the massive consumption of the modern world.

14. Blood and Honey

The Akie of the Masai Steppe, Tanzania

I was back in Africa, trekking through the Tanzanian bush to reach a little-known tribal group who live on the edge of an area known as the Masai Steppe. But these people are not Masai, that proud, cattle-herding race – tall, dark and high-cheekboned. They are a group who don't keep cattle and, until recently, never cultivated crops. They subsist, I'd been told, as hunter-gatherers. They are called the Akie, or at least that's how they describe themselves – *A-kie-ey*, 'the people of the land'. The Masai call them 'Ndorobo' which literally means 'without cattle' or, because cattle are a sign of wealth, 'poor'. Even to the discerning eye, the two groups look almost identical. But there is a telling story about how you can tell a Masai from an Akie. You ask the individual you've met whether the Masai and the Akie are equal. If they say yes, they are Akie; if they say 'no way' they are Masai.

For me, these local pecking orders weren't important. I was on foot in the bush with a couple of guys whose company I was loving. Lemalale and Alois were a right pair, always ready with a laugh. Lemalale was short, bald and full of character, marching along in his crimson *shuka*, the traditional Masai shawl which the Akie have adopted; he was my guide and knew well the Akie village where I was hoping to stay. Alois was my interpreter, a young Masai with a lively face; he was taller than Lemalale, and his body was strung around with multicoloured beaded leather belts and necklaces. We had all been a little concerned that having a Masai interpreter was a risk and that Alois might act aloofly towards the Akie, but he and Lemalale seemed to be getting on just fine. In fact he was using words to describe his new, older friend which meant respect and friendship. It was a good sign.

It was so great to be trekking again. Partly because it's the best way to assimilate yourself to a culture's climate and terrain before arriving, and partly because I needed the exercise. I'd become rather fat and bloated since living off raw reindeer meat for a month in Siberia and I still felt uncomfortably bloated and distended.

We paced on. There was a path of sorts, but every twenty metres or so the bushes either side had grown together; they were covered with sharp thorns, so a careful manoeuvre was required to get through without being badly scratched. On the plus side, there was plenty of evidence of game: tracks of eland, kudu, giraffe, elephant, leopard and more. Every few minutes, it seemed, we surprised some sand grouse or a guinea fowl, flapping away noisily through the undergrowth. Then if we saw a gathering of birds, Lemalale was off on tiptoe with his bow and arrow, trying to stalk them before they saw him. He never got there, except with one group of sand grouse that I spotted and pointed out to him. He already had two arrows in hand, ready to fire, and I was initially thrilled to be so close to an expert in action. He took a few steps, then quietly strung his arrow and pulled back the bowstring. But I was a little surprised to hear the twang and see the arrow fall horizontally at his feet. Unperturbed, he picked it up and stalked closer, this time to within a few metres. Brilliant. This was surely a kill. But the bow was flexed and the arrow once again bounced off his rubberized car-tyre sandals. By the time he'd picked up his arrow to fire again, the birds were long gone. I began to harbour a few doubts about just how good a hunter my new friend was.

A little further on Lemalale led us off the path through some really dense bushy thorn to find a beautiful (and huge) baobab tree. These 'upside-down' trees have wonderfully bulbous trunks and short branches and look like something out of a Salvador Dalí painting. I knew Lemalale was looking for honey, as these trees are where they find this major part of their diet and income. I just hoped he wasn't expecting me to help gather it, as I have a healthy fear of bees – I've had a severe allergic reaction to venomous stings before; not just local swelling but full-blown and potentially lethal anaphylactic shock. In preparation for this shoot I'd undergone some tests and been diagnosed allergic to wasp and hornet venom, though thankfully non-allergic to bees. The crew had received some medical training for the treatment of severe allergic reactions (anaphylaxis) in case I had a bad day, so I'd been feeling relatively cool about the whole thing. Then, only the day before, I'd read that such allergy tests were inconclusive and there was a good chance that I could react equally to both types of venom. Not great for my confidence. I knew that at some point during this shoot I was going to have to face up to my fear and try and join in. The crew consensus was that we shouldn't risk it until the end in case I needed to be evacuated.

So I stood a few metres away and watched Lemalale and Alois climb the tree. The grey-brown surface of the massive trunk was pockmarked with hundreds of holes where climbing pegs had been hammered in over the years. The guys now used these as finger- and toeholds. There were three obvious crevasses in the bark where the hives could be. Lemalale stuck his head in one and I heard a loud whimper. I could barely stop laughing as I watched them both clambering down again as fast as they could. Alois was on the ground first, then Lemalale followed, his head swarming with bees. He ran off and thrust it in a bush – jerking it around trying to get rid of his assailants – with his arse sticking out. When he emerged from the undergrowth he still had four or five buzzing round him as he ran back to the tree to collect his bow and quiver. It wasn't the most promising start to honey-collecting, and for the second time that day I wondered just how great a hunter he was.

After a lunchtime nap under a tree we trekked on. The GPS I had with me told me we'd now covered twenty-five kilometres, which meant ten left to go. If we were going to film my arrival at Olmuti, the village where we were hoping to stay, in daylight, we needed to get a move on. Mid-afternoon, dark grey rain clouds appeared out of nowhere and drenched us in a downpour of tropical rain. We went from burning hot to freezing cold in about thirty seconds flat. None of us saw it coming and Matt Norman, our affable and talented cameraman, did amazingly well to save his precious equipment.

It was lucky it was only a few more kilometres on to Olmuti. Here we caught up with the other Matt (Brandon), the director/producer on this shoot, who had driven on ahead. Though it was our first time working together, he was a veteran of many similar types of presenter-led documentary; he had a wonderful gentle way of directing, which I was just beginning to get tuned in to. With him were my old friend Willow Murton and our fixer, Peter Jones, an intelligent and very knowledgeable safari guide. Though an Oxford-educated British-passport-holder, Peter had been born in Germany to American and Danish parents, had gone to school in Afghanistan, and had now settled in Tanzania for thirty years. Originally a flint-knapper and archaeologist, he was a world expert on the Akie and had been instrumental in setting up the location and recommending the personalities for the film – including the irrepressible Lemalale.

With them was Lonyokie, the headman of the village, a tall guy with a fabulous laugh and easy smile.

Peter's very professional team had already put up a tented camp for the crew, so as we arrived we were able to have a hot cup of tea, a bun and a bag of sweets, huddled in one of the tents with Lemalale, Alois, Lonyokie and other assorted locals. Matt had decided not to film my arrival until the next day as we were now looking like drowned rats, completely different from the footage we'd shot earlier on. Not having filmed the storm, this made sense.

The only problem being that I was now meeting everyone from the village off camera. There was no alternative. Olmuti was only 500 metres away and the Akie had all come over to see us, calling out '*Akiyanti*' or '*Waree*', both of which mean 'How are you?'; the first said by older people, the second by younger. They were all wonderfully charismatic. The women crouched on one knee as they greeted me, which I did in return, trying to get respectfully lower.

Later that night we settled in for a sumptuous crew supper of soup and steak with all the trimmings. This was by far the best crew camp service I'd ever seen – African five-star safari. The tents had mozzie nets, mattresses, pillows, lamps, mozzie repellent, you name it. Peter was looking after the crew royally and though I was looking forward to moving in with the Akie, it was going to be a tough one living in a mud hut when I knew just how luxurious the crew area was.

Another tropical downpour at lunchtime the next day solved our continuity problems. Cameraman Matt filmed me wandering round the damp undergrowth a little to establish our wet surroundings, then it was time for me to finally visit the village.

A few straggly fields of maize separated us from the settlement proper. I was surprised to see a thick encircling thorn fence, just like those of the Omo pastoralists, or a Masai *boma*.

One lady spotted me first, just at the fence entry point. Her reaction was immediately positive. Others came to join us and there were lots of smiles and warm handshakes. I started in on my usual explanations and got some good replies from Lonyokie, who acted as spokesman.

More and more faces appeared from the various huts. I produced some grain tea and tobacco we'd picked up as an arrival gift; then packets of sugar for each of the households, which went down very well. So well, in fact, that a song and dance session took place as soon as it had been received. This was great fun and I got stuck in, much to everyone's amusement, though not of course understanding what they were singing until the translations were made much later:

> Tell my beloved child not to leave his god
> Don't leave your god
>
> Tell my beloved child not to leave his god
> Don't let your mother trick you into leaving your god
>
> Tell the Akie not to leave their god
> Don't let the Masai trick you into leaving your god
>
> Tell this man who loves me . . . not to leave his god . . .

And so on. Then they brought out some sweet honey in a small transparent plastic water bottle, which was deliciously smooth and very smoky in flavour. We sat down and I explained that I wanted to stay with them and learn from them. That would be fine, they said, but I'd need insect repellent because the huts were full of bugs in the night. I told them I wanted to try without. They laughed. The shocked looks on their faces suggested they had a serious problem.

I decided to tell them about my fear of bees, at which they laughed some more. Lonyokie told me I could always just watch when they were gathering honey. When I explained that I might like to have a go anyway they said my arm would look like an elephant's trunk after the stings of a first attempt. After so many raids, these people were all desensitized to the venom; I, on the other hand, could only imagine the worst.

Otherwise, it was all going extremely well. We even talked a bit about their relationship with the Masai, after which one lady, who seemed a bit tipsy, kept repeating that they were Akie, not Ndorobo. It no longer seemed to matter that my official introduction to the village had been a day late.

I made the most of my last night in crew luxury and didn't join Peter and director Matt Brandon in the morning when they went over to the village to finalize details of payments and gifts. Peter's idea was that we would leave credits in the local school and medical centre, in addition to the usual cash payments for individual work done. When we discussed it over lunch it seemed there was some worry from the community about the school being Masai dominated. Once again we had to step back and get our heads round the reality of the complex local politics. As an alternative, the Akie had suggested a maize-grinding mill, which they said they really wanted. We agreed, provided we could find someone to show them how to maintain and fix it.

I didn't make it over to the village myself till around four. The storm clouds were threatening and there was rain all around, but none right above us. Lonyokie met me at the gate through the thorn fence and we had a quick exchange, before heading off to his hut and talking for a good hour or so about all sorts of stuff: what life was like for them when they were young; how his father had once owned cattle and farmed; how the Akie maintained their hunting skills, which they were taught as children; how the training was that they were given one arrow, then had to sit at night until an animal came, then shoot at it with their one arrow, and if they missed the target they were beaten.

Lonyokie's hut was spacious, with three rooms inside. We sat talking in the entrance room, which took up half of the main building. It was completely free of decoration, apart from one tattered old calendar, a red bucket, and three beautiful carved round stools, like old milking stools, the largest of which was offered to me. A hen and her brood of chicks clucked around in the centre of the floor, narrowly avoiding cameraman Matt's booted feet. Lonyokie's wife Ana joined us, crouched in the doorway to the two rooms beyond. She was a delightful woman, always smiling, and surprisingly tactile.

One of the rooms beyond was clearly the master bedroom, with a sizeable bed, raised up to hip height, and comfortable looking. A big cowhide lay on top of a base of woven twigs and straw. They had put my bags up on it – because, Lonyokie said, the rats would attack it if it were left on the floor overnight. Near its base was a tiny fire. A small pot stood on three raised stones, bubbling away with cornmeal. Next door I wasn't shown into, but it looked like a private room for Ana and her children.

After our long chat, Lonyokie gave me a bow and a quiver. We went outside to have a better look at it. The bow was old and had been strengthened because of slight cracks, but still looked strong. The shaft and the string, made from giraffe tendon, had each taken a day to prepare, Lonyokie explained. In the quiver were five metal-tipped arrows, each one a work of art, with arrowheads made from old car springs, all covered in a thick black poison paste. As is common with such weaponry, the arrowheads are designed to detach from the wooden shaft when they hit an animal. The poison is extracted from the roots of a tree called the desert rose (*Adenium obesum*). There is no known antidote, so every strike is fatal. Beside the arrows was a hollow wooden tube with a metal end (from a car stereo antenna) to blow smoke into beehives; two rubbing sticks for making fire; and finally a knife blade. All these were packed inside a roughly stitched leather quiver with a lid.

As the light faded, the crew disappeared back to camp. I was left with Lemalale and Alois to settle down for the night. It felt weird, as I hadn't had the full *Tribe* experience of being alone with the locals in this way for some time. On my last shoot in Siberia I'd been with the crew day and night.

Of course, despite some early trepidation, I loved it: the genuine hospitality, the curiosity and acceptance you get on your first day. Already the guys were running around and ignoring me, getting on with their lives as I caught up with my diary. The light was fading. Outside the hut, a chicken was being killed noisily.

'Please,' I said, gesturing, 'no special treatment for me.'

But they were, they said, going to kill it anyway. Idiot. As usual, in my oversensitive way I felt awful for arrogantly presuming that this was some kind of welcome treat for me. Ana then plucked the bird, cooked it over the fire in the room with the raised bed and we ate it with cornmeal. Afterwards we sat on a log watching the sunset. Half the village, it seemed, crowded round, talking about me in their native tongue, while I sat smiling and nodding. Hot sweet tea was a welcome nightcap and I tried some honey mead too, which was incredibly sweet.

Inside the hut I tried some of the snuff we'd brought as a present. I've done snuff on a number of occasions, but this variety was strong and I did way too much in a big old hedonistic snort. Everyone pissed themselves laughing then exclaimed how dangerous it was to do what I'd just done.

'That was a bit different to what I was expecting,' I gasped. 'That really is like . . . doing pepper.' They were all evacuating their throats and nasal passages on to the floor after their snuff inhalations, but I took myself outside to do the same – it was my first day after all, and even if they were doing it, I thought gobbing and snotting on your hosts' floor on your first day wasn't very English.

Four of us bedded down that night on the high bed: Lonyokie,

Lemalale, Alois and me. I took one end, but ended up with no cowhide at all. Luckily I was able to pull one of my *shuka* blankets over my head to keep off most of the insects. As was usual with all my stays in mud huts and treehouses, it was a fitful sleep.

Matt Norman was already in the village filming as I was getting up. Outside the hut, the villagers dressed me up royally in no fewer than three *shukas*. The first two were placed over alternate shoulders by knotting together their respective shortest ends so that they draped down to below the knee on both sides of my body. The outer of these was then tied at the bottom corners too, so as to form a kind of pouch. The third was then worn as a shawl.

We set out without breakfast into the bush. I was given a bow and a quiver, but I was already aware that in Akie hunts only one person ever shoots. Before long, we came across numerous tracks, all very fresh and obvious after the night's rain. Most prevalent was warthog, though Alois calling it a 'warth-og' confused me at first. Soon we came across a watering hole, and near it two hides. One of them had been recently used by one of the big-game-hunting companies whose visitors pay top dollar to hunt in these parts. The bait of, say, kudu would be hung, Lemalale explained, fifty metres from the watering hole, so the leopard would be sure of finding it. The hunter would then sit in the hide just ten metres away and have a clear shot from that range. The hide was right next to the road, so the quarry could be easily slung in the vehicle while the hunter headed back to the camp or hotel. Not much prowess required, really.

The Akie have very mixed feelings about commercial hunting. On the one hand they are often employed by the hunters as trackers, bringing in much-needed income. On the other hand they perceive these companies as competition, depleting the available game stocks. The truth is complex, and as one would expect, some hunting companies are good, some not so good. Regardless of ethics or taste, it is a sad indictment of modern Africa, but generally considered true, that without the hunting companies' rigorous anti-poaching patrols (against bush meat and animal parts' trade poachers – not traditional hunters) most of the game would have disappeared long ago. Legally, the hunting concessions have to pay a decent percentage of the hunting revenue back into the local community and this is monitored. But whether the Akie are ever the recipients of such payments is difficult to know, especially with the Masai running most things locally.

Until recently the Akie were even banned from hunting with bows and arrows, facing prison if they were caught; while visiting tourist hunters with enough cash could take home trophies to hang on their walls. Luckily, these laws have changed recently and the Akie, who have lived in these parts much longer than many well-established nation states, have been allowed to hunt traditionally again.

Walking on from the commercial hides, we were following more traditional methods. An hour further on we found some Akie hides. There was no kudu bait for us here; indeed we'd have been thrilled to catch the kind of game the hunting companies use as a lure. To maximize our chances, we decided to split the group: the two Matts and Lemalale into one of the hides; me, Lonyokie and Alois into the other. Our hide needed a bit of work, but five minutes of adding fresh green foliage and it was ready for action. The three of us crowded in, stripped down to the bare essential of clothing, and settled in for a long morning.

Outside, the long bleached grass waved silently in the sun. The warm breeze shifted the green tops of the thorn trees. We were all alert, waiting for the snap of a twig, or the rustle through the undergrowth that would announce the arrival of a warthog or kudu. But there was nothing. Just the buzz of flies and the odd cry of a bird overhead.

I'm not a big fan of hides. One irony of my life is that despite seeing so many wonderful ways of living and gaining an understanding about the important aspects of existence from tribal cultures, I'm unable to put much of it into practice. My life is so full of amazing and different sensory overloads of every kind that I've become almost addicted to constant stimulation. I get very fidgety if I stop for even a minute. I simply go mad if I'm not active in some way, even if I realize the stupidity of it all. No matter how important the kill we were waiting for, or the adrenaline release that would come from hitting a target, to me it wasn't worth staring at nothing all day.

But for these guys this wasn't an endurance activity, it was a necessity. If they didn't catch anything, their village would be without meat. I tried to sit patiently, remaining alert and looking out, but also fiddling silently with anything to hand: in this case Alois and Lonyokie's arrows and knives and Alois's colourfully beaded belt. And of course, the camera, Bruce-cam, cradled on my lap, ready to spring into action should anything actually happen. I was longing to rewind it and take a look at some of the footage of the previous night, not because there was anything I particularly needed to see, but just to keep me busy. Anyway, it was gloomy in the hide and just right for reviewing. But I knew the mechanism would make too much noise. In the end I couldn't help but nod off. I hadn't had a great night and in the drowsy heat I found it nigh on impossible not to doze. I woke after some time to hear Lonyokie's snores. Alois was sleeping too. Brilliant. I didn't feel so bad then. Who knows what had walked past us in the previous hour or so.

They woke and we waited some more. Nothing. After another hour I realized even Lonyokie was beyond bored. We agreed to walk up to the second hide and see what was happening with the others. They had seen a warthog and wanted to give it another hour, even though their hide was infested with biting ants. So we returned and waited some more.

Suddenly we heard something. Lonyokie had an arrow out in a flash and was drawing his bow for a shot. It was a warthog and her piglets, right in front of us, five metres away. I was trying to focus the camera, but it was all happening too fast. Lonyokie let fire, missed, and the hog family scattered. Lonyokie left the hide and stalked after them, Alois in hot pursuit. Lonyokie fired again and missed. Luckily I caught this on film.

They returned after a bit. Lonyokie reckoned he had fired twice and hit once. They were going to wait an hour before tracking the hog's blood trail and hopefully finding the dead quarry. But if he thought he'd hit with the second arrow I had to put him right. I reviewed the tape on the camera and played it over to him in slow motion. He'd missed. We went out and searched for the arrow and, sure enough, found it on the mud with the head still intact. The others had had no luck either. We returned to the village for a meatless lunch of cornmeal and beans.

The next day we had another go at catching some game. This seemed to be the Akie routine. Up very early, take a slow walk or head out to a hide, then sit and wait for game. So while cameraman Matt Norman went off in a vehicle with one load of guys, Lemalale, Lonyokie and I, accompanied by director Matt Brandon, trekked out thirteen kilometres to a rocky outcrop where a couple of new hides lay waiting for us. There were some good tracks on our way: leopard, giraffe and hyena spoor, and we saw a couple of dik-dik and a lesser kudu. It was a hopeful sign.

The four of us trekkers took our places in the hide. This one had a low front wall and inside the dirt floor was on a slope. So the only place to sit was right at the front, or else you'd be completely in view of any passing game. But once again the heat and stillness got the better of us, and we were all asleep after about four hours of tedium. Nothing big enough to wake us passed by, so it was another fruitless morning. We decided to up sticks and walk to the rocky outcrop where we knew that Matt the cameraman and the others were waiting. The view from up there was spectacular, a sea of green scrub below, with the occasional small mountain jutting up like a rocky island from the bushy plain. We filmed us walking against that for a bit, then, at Lonyokie's suggestion, decided to go and look for honey.

The honey tree was back along the long sandy road we'd walked out on in the morning. So we all drove back down the track to a clearing where the guys had spotted some old weaver birds' nests, up in the trees. We cut a few stout lengths of stick to throw at them and a couple of good shots brought three nests crashing down. All were empty, one was a bit new and too green to burn, but the other two were perfect for the purpose the guys had in mind: to make thick smoke to sedate the bees.

A kilometre or so further on we scrambled a few hundred metres through thick thorny scrub away from the vehicle and found the beehives we were looking for in another big baobab tree. The Akie were brilliant to watch as they got to work. The birds' nests were broken open and placed on long strands of moist green grass – lots of dry nest over a small amount of green. Then the green was folded together, enclosing the dry innards, and the whole thing was bound tightly with moist strands of thin vine to make a flattened cone. Then the guys got going with the fire, rubbing sticks. One was held upright and spun round and round at high speed in a friction hole in the other until the heat produced smouldering embers and ash from the lower stick. This had already been laid on an axe head on to which the tiny smoking particles were now pushed down a dedicated groove. The axe was lifted carefully and the embers dropped into the middle of the straw cone and blown on. In seconds the dry tinder of the nest was alight and the whole cone was billowing with smoke. It was all incredibly skilled and very quick.

The hive was at shoulder height, so no climbing was required today. The smoky grass was shoved into the entrance and the metal-tipped blowing straws used to oxygenate the fire and direct the smoke into the hive. The effect was amazing. The bees seemed unable to mount a counter-offensive. Drugged by the smoke, they either stumbled round the hive edges or flew in sleepy circles. Lonyokie now bravely shoved his bare arm deep into the hole, immediately pulling out big chunks of waxy comb, dripping with honey. One was passed round for us all to try and it was truly delicious. The comb was a strange, almost synthetic texture, which crushed in the mouth to a chewy mass, while the sweet honey exploded on the palate. The smoke made it taste even better. One or two combs were golden and pure, but most dripped with darker honey, and one or two were black and almost dry. Lonyokie let out the occasional yelp as he was stung on his forearm, hand and fingers, but this didn't stop him delving inside the hive for more, pausing now and then to reintroduce the smoking cone to calm the buzzing bees down. Occasionally he would shout out and slap his hand against the trunk to kill and smother a bee that had stung him. This surprised me a little as I had been told not to kill a bee at any cost as this would trigger their attack. The honey, meanwhile, just kept on coming.

Lemalale and Lonyokie were having a right old good-natured bicker at each other while I stood by, holding the leather bag that they use for collecting the honey. It was fairly clear that Lonyokie knew what he was doing and, once again, Lemalale was more the enthusiastic amateur. For me the whole thing was certainly a test of nerve as the combs were brought out and put in the bag, the bees flying and crawling all over me. But amazingly I was OK. When we stepped back from the tree with my collection bag full of honeycomb, I'd not had a single sting. Matt Norman had been close by me, getting lots of good shots. He had a specialist net over his face and beekeeper gloves on his hands, but still managed to get stung on the ankle.

★

For the next few days we fell into the Akie's routine of going out hunting early, and if there was no luck with game, returning home mid-morning via a honey tree, invariably a large baobab. Honey seemed to be the one thing the Akie were relatively confident of getting. Indeed on most days, it seemed, if they'd not caught anything by about 10 a.m., they'd shift their attention to getting honey before the sun got too hot for any animals to still be up and about.

One day there was no morning hunt and we just stuck around in the village. I decided to see what the women got up to while we were out. I went along with Ana on her twice-daily water-collecting round. This involved a walk to a rocky pool about a kilometre away. We both took big twenty-litre plastic drums. Once there, Ana told me to step in and immerse the whole drum, which stirred up all the mud and shit from the bottom; it didn't look very appetizing, but Ana explained that this was the only surface water for miles around. Not a spring but just a stagnant rock pool full of pathogens. The Masai used the pool for washing: both their cattle and themselves. I'd seen the cattle piss in it several times. But for the Akie this was the only water source so they had to make do.

'The Masai come and wash in it,' she told me. 'Then we drink it, sweat and all. It gives you stomach problems. It brings cholera. It really affects us. But if we don't drink here, where can we drink? The Masai keep on washing here and we keep on drinking here. They think they're superior to us, just because we're Ndorobo.' (I was always impressed that Alois never wavered while translating these negative sentiments towards the Masai. In private later he said he considered that much of it was indeed true.)

I needed a shave, and Ana asked if she could do it for me. I was cool with this, as long as Lonyokie was happy too, as Ana was prone to being quite flirtatious with me and I didn't want to cause any problems. As it turned out it had been his idea and he was going to get one afterwards. I carried a number of razors as gifts, so I gave her one and she got going. It hurt so much I was thinking I'd better ask her to stop. It felt like pulling teeth – thousands of them individually. In the end I offered her another razor brand. Thank God that was much smoother, though I found out later I was covered in small cuts. Still, it's always a nice sensation being shaved – rather self-indulgent and luxurious.

'Well,' I said, 'do I look a little bit younger? A little bit?'

'Yes,' she replied. 'You look younger. You look like a little boy.' She laughed.

After that we had a bit of a party. Ana had spent the last few days preparing mead, a kind of honey beer, made from honey and water into which the pith of an aloe root is intro-duced. This ferments and becomes alcoholic very quickly – within a day.

Now we were to taste it. It was brought out of the hut in a huge yellow tub and everyone gathered around. The long crescent of pith was removed from the tub, and the remaining, rather bitty broth was filtered through a fresh section of tree aloe pith into another tub, then scooped up in a bowl and poured into a variety of mugs. I was the first to drink it. It smelt very sweet but was delicious to taste. I gulped it down in one and got handshakes and laughter all round. Probably the best reception I'd had for any one activity in all fourteen episodes of *Tribe* so far. Then everyone followed suit and instantly the mood changed. The mead was quite alcoholic, and I'd felt the buzz instantly, but the others were laughing like pissheads as soon as they'd had a drink. Verbal blessings followed, then some spit-sprayings from the mouth. Lonyokie was calling on the spirits of his ancestors to help us in our hunting:

> Bless us with meat,
> Come to us now, spirits, and drink!
> All my grandfathers,
> Come and drink now,

Prepare the path for our hunt,
Let the chameleon guide us,
Let the baobab give us strength.
Send the lions away,
Don't let them disturb us in the bush,
My grandfather!

That done, the dancing began. There were lots of different styles and songs and everyone was in the best of spirits. Then the women did a little pantomime with bows and arrows, pretending to fire at their menfolk. In my experience, boozy sessions like this can go one of two ways, and any underlying tensions are quick to come to the fore. But with this wonderful community it was obvious that everyone was on the best of terms with each other right then. We laughed and danced for hours.

We were up again well before dawn and out into the bush under a bright moon, hoping for some help from the spirits and luck at last. Lonyokie and I were out front, with the whole entourage behind. It was great watching Lonyokie identifying animals at every turn from their tracks. I had a guess each time, and was pleased to get quite a few right. But despite the numerous tracks, we saw no animals in the flesh, all day long. Back in camp we had a long chat to review our options. It was clear that trying to hunt with a full crew accompanying, noisy and smelling of suntan lotion and mozzie repellent as they were, just wasn't working. Maybe I should go along with them alone, I said, taking Bruce-cam.

The Akie's suggestion was that we all go to a dedicated hunting camp of theirs for a few days and hunt intensively. The camp was an hour's walk further on from the rocky hill and outcrop we'd visited before. So the next day we trekked out there and spent our time hunting in different groups. Mostly we sat in hides but sometimes we headed out in small groups on foot. But our luck didn't improve. We saw some baboons

380 sledges spread back
to up to ten kilometres

A simple structure
that stood up to all
conditions

As soon as you stopped moving, you really felt the cold

Jova's wife, Raya

I loved our evening chats

Bird-watching

Great banter
every evening

In an open clearing, we would be able to see any lions approaching

Everywhere I go, they have a different butchering technique

The Akie of the Masai Steppe, Tanzania

Smoking out the bees

Having fun in the waterfall

Emang with dinner

Instant rucksack

Thick secondary forest
made the unwieldy
blowpipe hard to use

and had some near misses but nothing was caught. We began to worry that the Akie might start to feel pressure about us catching something, which was the very last thing we wanted, as the aim of the programme was, of course, just to follow their normal lives. The whole thing became a bit artificial, because we couldn't work out whether they were doing all this hunting for themselves or for our benefit. Their answers to our questions varied widely depending on who we spoke to and when. It was a frustrating time.

One time while stalking a kudu on our knees I caught up with Lonyokie and realized he'd lost a poisoned arrow tip somewhere during the crawl. I'd been following his exact route, and when we finally found it in the sand I saw my own knee print had missed it by a millimetre. If I'd knelt on it, it would almost certainly have proved fatal. It made me wonder what I would have done and said to the camera in my last hour. There would have been no point in getting upset or angry. I like to think that I would have played it cool. It was a sobering moment, if a bit morbid. After that I was more careful.

After days of fruitless hunting Lonyokie started to feel unwell, then Lemalale too: they had a fever and painful mouth ulcers respectively. We gave them both some medication and Lonyokie made a rapid recovery. Lemalale didn't. He was in a bad way, his usual Jack-the-lad smile only lasting a moment before his face contorted with pain.

Almost a week went by before we decided to move to a new camp. We drove out through a huge, open, typically African grassy plain. There were signs of life everywhere, which was great. Lonyokie's fever had returned, so while the crew and driver started setting up camp, I went with him and Lemalale and a couple of others to a nearby Akie village to look for treatment. We had offered to drive him to the clinic in Kitwai, the nearest proper settlement, which had Western medicines, but he was insistent that he wanted local treatment. He knew of a woman who could cure him, he said.

Her village was much like Olmuti, except that the houses comprised A-frame roofs with a porch of sorts and mud for walls. The old lady was a traditional healer and very happy to help. She laid Lonyokie down on a cowhide in her hut and rubbed oil into his stomach, a pale, almost milky liquid which she kept in an old plastic half-litre drinking water bottle. Lonyokie was in obvious pain even with the massage, which didn't bode well. Then she brought him outside, laid him down again on the cowhide mat, and got going on him with a razor blade. She took big pinches of flesh and made perpendicular cuts into the rolls of fat in line with the length of his body. There were maybe twenty cuts in a row above his navel, then another two rows the same beneath. Droplets of blood slowly oozed from each cut, then she spat huge gobs of spit all over the wounds and rubbed in a powder made from crushed burnt leaves. Lonyokie's stomach was a mess and his face showed the pain. You would have thought that would be enough to put anyone off the local healer for life. But at this moment, Alois suddenly exclaimed that he wasn't feeling 100 per cent either, so he promptly lay down for the same treatment. Sitting next to him in the car on the way back, he said his stomach didn't ache any more, but it wasn't half painful. I can't say I was surprised.

By the time we got back to camp everything was set up. We had a bit of lunch and retreated to two new hides which Papake, one of the village hunting experts, and Matt Norman had built, right in the middle of a nearby field. Both hides had a brilliant 360-degree view for hundreds of metres in every direction, which would make staying alert so much easier. Nonetheless, hours went by with zilch happening as usual. We saw the others emerge from their hide to retrieve an arrow they'd shot at a kudu we'd not spotted. But that was it. Nothing actually caught.

The old lady's razor-treatment had not improved Lonyokie's condition much. The next morning he agreed to go with Willow to the clinic in Kitwai and try Western medicine. Lemalale decided to go too while I stayed in the hunting camp.

I was woken mid-afternoon by a shake from Matt. One of the master hunters, Leyanne, had apparently gone off on his own, tracked and successfully shot a warthog. Now he'd come back to find us so we could join him as he tracked it. Brilliant! At last! This was what we needed: a track to follow. We set out with the camera and high hopes, which were only slightly discouraged by the treacherous undergrowth, the worst yet, thorns everywhere and no path at all. My bare feet in sandals were taking a battering from every conceivable direction: acacia seed pods between sandal and foot; grassy seeds spiking my bare feet; thorns under the toenails.

Eventually Leyanne got us to the point where he'd shot the warthog. It was here, after an hour of walking, that our tracking really started. What an expert he was! I've tracked in many places before and definitely know the basics, but to watch this guy in action was a real treat. The tracks were obvious at first, the telltale signs of a sprint, accompanied by the obvious blood drops, but as long grass and more thorns came into the route it all became increasingly difficult. After all the recent rain the place was greener than it had been for ages. Leyanne would often be on his hands and knees searching each individual spoor. There were other criss-crossing tracks and more than once we followed the wrong lead, only to find it was, say, a small kudu, so we had to go back and start again. We'd been looking for the warthog for hours and had only gone a few hundred metres. Now the rain clouds were looming again and dusk was just around the corner. We were all getting desperate. It was becoming clearer and clearer that we were not going to find our quarry after all. Although it was disappointing to all of us, in a way we were telling the truth as it was: game is scarce out here, and what with the changing environment and wildlife availability, the Akie are having a tough time of it these days. For me, that was a story in itself.

It rained and rained in the night, so there was no point in trying to find the warthog in the morning as the tracks would have been totally obliterated. Later on we packed up camp totally and returned in the afternoon to Olmuti. Peter Jones was waiting for us. He was as disappointed about our lack of success as we were. We drank margaritas round the fire to drown our sorrows.

The next afternoon the rain swept in again. Matt and I were in the mess tent when two bedraggled hunters suddenly appeared, grinning broadly. It was Papake and his mentor, Leyanne, our two master hunters, shivering with the wet and cold, but with fantastic news. They had stalked and killed a greater kudu. It was late and they hadn't brought it back with them because it was so big. And they wanted us to film it before it was butchered. Awesome! But could we get to it before dusk fell?

We decided to go for it, even though cameraman Matt was over in the village. We threw everyone into pick-ups and raced off, following an old hunting track that hadn't been used for a while. This turned out to be too overgrown to drive down, so we took to our feet and then got completely lost; both while trying to find the dead animal, then, when we'd finally abandoned that idea, while trying to get back to the vehicle, in pitch dark across ground littered with the sharp shrub they call Spanish bayonet, fearful of any big game that might have been about. We made it eventually, when I gave up on Lemalale's decidedly unhelpful tracking advice and turned to the stars and the GPS, its battery now dangerously low.

At first light we trekked out easily to the clearing where Papake and Leyanne had set up their hide. And yes, amazingly, thirty metres away in the scrub the kudu was lying, stiff as a board. We dragged it out of the thick bush into a large clearing to butcher it. This was so that we might be able to see any approaching lions, drawn by the smell of the offal. Everything was hung around on trees and branches in the area as the guys took their reward: first raw liver, then bone marrow, which was sucked out of the bones with great relish. They offered me some and it was delicious: a very delicate taste, melting in the mouth and quite creamy.

'It's Akie food,' said Leyanne with a happy chuckle.

Back in the village the meat was shared all around. Every household brought a pot to get their bit. Soon the atmosphere became very jovial. We sat around as huge chunks were passed on to groups, who then sliced it up into manageable morsels. Every last piece was boiled or roasted and eaten that day. Nothing was smoked to be kept for later.

We had one more day out looking for honey and now, at the very end of the shoot, when it didn't matter so much if I had a severe allergic reaction and had to be flown home, I risked putting my arm into one of the holes in the side of a baobab tree. There were two hives in the tree and close up the humming of the bees inside made an eerie sound. The first was tackled by Leyanne, but though visibly well stocked with bees, it contained no honey. Now at last it was my turn. Hanging from a branch several feet from the ground, I went through the full procedure with the smoking grass, terrified about what might happen if I didn't sedate the bees properly. Finally my moment had come. I plunged my hand deep into the hole, all set for the pain of the first sting. But, as it turned out, it was a worse dud than the other one. Not only was there no honey, there weren't even any bees.

The guys assured me that the empty hive was as much a surprise to them as it was to me, but it was still a bit disappointing. It had been a tough call for me to pluck up the courage to do it, and now I felt somewhat cheated that there was no reward after all. Simultaneously, though, it was obviously a massive relief to me not to have an arm swelling up like an elephant's trunk; or worse still, a full-on allergic reaction. But that was it. We were leaving in the morning and they didn't know of any other live hives in their territory. They'd been saving these two for our last day, having spotted them a week previously. Damn.

We had spent almost two weeks of non-stop hunting with the Akie, and caught one kudu. Lonyokie summed it up beautifully as I was leaving. Change was now essential for them. They had to learn about planting corn and other crops because their old ways simply couldn't sustain them any more.

We left them with the present of a corn-grinding machine: a huge thing, and an expensive item by the standards of the area. Yes, of course, it would be another facet of change for this culture. And we were responsible for it. People were going to use it for miles around, and it would be based in this community of Olmuti. But that was it. It had been their choice, based on hard facts and the evidence of their changing lives. They were ecstatic with it and although it felt strange giving a traditional hunter-gatherer community such a gift, I was happy for them.

15. Fear and Loathing in Borneo

The Penan People of Sarawak, Malaysia

It was my last ever trip for *Tribe*, and we were going undercover deep into the forests of Sarawak in Malaysian Borneo. In this remote location a desperate battle is being fought out between the Penan people, who are still attempting to lead a nomadic life in the virgin forest, and the mighty logging companies, whose profits depend on having unfettered access to these swathes of empty jungle.

The Sarawak government is on the side of the loggers, and very cagey about anyone reporting the issues, let alone filming them. Permits are invariably blocked. The only way we were going to get to meet the Penan and experience and film their lives was by doing what we'd done with the Kombai in Papua New Guinea – going in under the wire. Researcher Matt Fletcher had already gone ahead and done a substantial recce of the area where the Penan mainly live. Now director Gavin Searle (who'd made the Bhutan film), Matt and I returned, posing as birdwatchers.

Trouble started even before we got out to our location. A couple of days after we'd flown into Miri, a coastal town and capital of the province, where we were staying at the Marriott Hotel while prepping our expedition, we were told that word was out as to our plans. A local government spy had got wind of who we were. There was a whole posse of police, apparently, patrolling the area we hoped to visit. Then our fixer John (not his real name) got an anonymous call threatening him and saying that the authorities knew exactly what we were up to.

It didn't look good. Gavin and I stayed put in the Marriott while the rest of the team returned to base. Besides Matt and John, this consisted of a young Malaysian woman I'll call Seda, who was acting as our liaison with the Penan, and an interpreter I'll call Toby. Our biggest concern was not to incriminate these guys, who were putting themselves at risk to help us make our film. Logging is big business and we'd heard plenty of stories of aggressive tactics, including rumours of people going missing and the like. Most famously, in May 2000, the well-known Swiss activist Bruno Manser, who had been actively involved over many years in promoting the Penan's cause, had disappeared and never been found. I didn't think any of us would be personally harmed, but our associates might well have some trouble after we'd gone. We entered a couple of days of careful replanning, with various conspiracy theories flying around. Eventually we discovered that the police patrol in the area was involved in other business, which reduced our worries a little. Having discussed sending one vehicle off as a decoy in another direction, we eventually decided to head directly through the Mulu National Park, then on through the checkpoint into the Penan plantation. If we were picked up, we were picked up. At least we hadn't done anything incriminating yet.

As it turned out, there was no trouble at all at the checkpoint. As for the endless plantation beyond, it demonstrated all too clearly what serious logging could do to the landscape. The roads were dead straight lines, cutting through mile upon mile of featureless terrain. What once had been primary forest was now row upon row of oil palm trees. Demand for palm oil has risen dramatically in recent years, not just because of its use in soap, shampoo, cosmetics, detergents and cooking oil, but ironically because of global warming: it is a 'green' biofuel, widely considered to be a sound ecological substitute for oil. More than 85 per cent of the world's palm oil comes from Malaysia and Indonesia.

In the morning we arrived at the little Penan settlement where John had arranged for us to stay. It was barely a hundred metres from the road. As befitted a nomadic people, it was a temporary settlement, a series of shelters they call *sulaps*. These quickly assembled structures are set on small platforms raised about two metres off the ground; then covered with dirty blue and orange plastic tarpaulin roofs to keep the rain off. They are built from cut saplings, approximately wrist-thick, bound together with rattan twine. Leaf roofs are now very rare, but sometimes leaves are added to plug holes in the plastic. Inside, up on the platforms, fires burned in their soil hearths.

I was hoping for a warm welcome, but hardly expecting the one we got. They knew we were from the BBC, and that – being a British institution – seemed to mean a great deal to them; historically the Penan had been served surprisingly well by the colonial British. In 1841, the Sultan of Brunei awarded a British adventurer called James Brooke the feudal title of Rajah of Sarawak, and the Brooke family continued to run the country for a hundred years, before finally ceding control to the British government in 1946. During this time the Penan were allowed to roam free in the forests, protected by a series of laws (which halted as well their exploitation by the more settled tribal groups by, for example, guaranteeing the price of their forest products in organized markets). After 1963, when Sarawak gained independence and joined Malaysia, the interests of development increasingly became more important than those of the nomadic hunter-gatherers. The state now only recognizes land rights of those who cultivate land; and since the Penan are dispersed forest-dwellers, this doesn't include them.

So now I was hearing questions like 'Why did you leave us?' and 'Have you forgotten about us?' as if I and the team were representatives of the fondly remembered British come to rescue them. They all looked at me earnestly and shook my hand, softly, without closing theirs or squeezing in any way. I was struck by their deep sense of calm and tranquillity, but also this definite feeling of expectation as they watched me. 'Seeing you,' said a man called Jeffrey, apparently the chief of this small group, 'there is hope that the forest will remain.'

We sat down for a meeting. Alongside Jeff was a man called Arau, who had a fair resemblance to Bruce Lee, with a pudding-bowl haircut and a thin moustache. He was bright-eyed and very enthusiastic, and if not the chief, then at least the chief talker. I told them I wanted to understand what it was like to live in the jungle with them; not just learn about what they did, how they hunted and so on, but how they thought. Arau told me how they could feel the difference between an untouched forest and one that had been logged; the noise, the smell, the light, even the temperature is different. To them a secondary forest is dead. This certainly reflected the statistics of modern environmentalists, who calculate that on land that has been logged even once, biodiversity is reduced by 66 per cent.

They welcomed me to stay with them as long as I liked, and follow them as they moved. There were thirteen families gathered in this little settlement, and they would congregate like this, they said, every month or so, before drifting off in different directions to hunt or collect sago (which, as with the Kombai, is a staple of their diet). Then they'd meet up again at a designated rendezvous. I was struck by how my questions wouldn't immediately be answered by Jeff or even Arau – as with some chiefs in other areas – but discussed among them all for a good few minutes, before an answer was offered, with many of them chipping in.

John had previously brought some baby sago plants with him, which he intended the Penan should plant nearby. The cuttings sat there in black plastic plant-bags beside us, but none of them seemed to have any idea what to do with them, as planting is not something they are familiar with. It would take about seven years for each tiny sapling to grow to maturity, before it could be felled and mashed in the traditional way, strained and dried into flour. Though the loggers don't specifically target sago, the act of selective logging and road building destroys the mature plants and things were apparently getting desperate out here.

The next morning was a Sunday, a day of rest for the Penan, who are newly Christianized; the first Penan in the 1950s, and this group, apparently, as recently as 2003. Jet-lagged and still on London time, I was glad of the lie-in as I'd been unable to get off to sleep, even in my favourite comfy hammock. Gavin and Matt slept nearby under a tarp, along with Seda and Toby. As in Bhutan, Gavin was totally happy to muck in, eating and sleeping with the locals, not away to one side in some luxury tented camp. This meant that we were already so much more at one with the Penan and it was an infinitely preferable way to make the film.

That evening I was due to move in with Selapan, one of the older guys in the group. Gavin had chosen him because he was a good talker and had a large family, with children and grandchildren. They had a pet rhinoceros hornbill, which was always hanging noisily around camp. It was only a few months old and had yet to develop its full beak colour and famous horn; it had been brought into the fold after its nest tree had been felled earlier in the year. Pets are very much part of Penan culture. There was a baby boar and a little grey macaque monkey in camp too. Once an animal has been brought back to camp, it becomes a pet and therefore taboo to kill it, even if it came from a traditional prey species.

I'd done nothing much all morning, except chat with John and learn more about the Penan, their struggles with the government and their uncertain future. Suddenly, in the early afternoon, the call came for us to make ourselves scarce. We quickly camouflaged up our stuff in the crew area then headed upstream into the jungle. It was a false alarm, as it turned out; just some Malaysian TV crew trying to do a news piece about the Penan for a Malaysian charitable cause. But it certainly set our hearts going for a moment. The crew didn't stay long and we were soon back in camp again, albeit at the far end, away from the road and beyond a screen of trees.

'Many Malaysian people come to take pictures of us,' came Toby's translation of Arau's damning words. 'But after they leave, nothing improves. The logging companies still come and disturb our way of life.' He continued in this vein for quite a while. Though generally tranquil, once they got started on the subject of their dispossession, it was clearly hard to stop.

In the morning, our hosts were keen for us to move on; to make a new camp, deeper in the forest, well away from the road.

'I feel worried about our visitors,' said Selapan about us. 'I don't feel nice if people see them staying with us. We should find a new place to take them. If they're seen here, we might be in trouble. More and more people are coming to the settlement because they know these people are here.'

Before we left we filmed the would-be sago nursery and I tried to find out from the Penan how it felt to be planting after generations of being in a culture of collecting and gathering as needs arose. They did a good job of expressing how alien it was to them. But there was no anger; it was more puzzlement at their changed circumstances. The forest had changed; what should they do now? For them it wasn't just about learning a new skill – it was a completely new concept. Instant return societies live in the moment; farmers plan for the future. This was a huge change for them.

Our move up to the new campsite was very easy going. We followed the larger of the two streams by the sago nursery upriver. This meant a fair amount of wading through the water, with an occasional steep climb over the odd spur before rejoining the stream. We stopped at one very pretty waterfall for a bathe in a rock pool. The whole trek took little more than an hour.

Our new site, right above a crystal-clear river, was overgrown, but it didn't take long for the four families with us to clear it, cut neat sapling poles, then tie them up in criss-cross formation to make their little wooden shelters, which this time were closer to the ground (for fear of us and our heavy gear breaking them, I guessed). Everyone worked in groups, with no obvious gender divide. There was a fair bit of friendly banter between the male and female couples about hut levels, stability and sturdiness, which was fun to watch. These relationships, like marriages, seemed to be based on necessity and respect and it looked to be a pretty even workload. The only thing women didn't do, apparently, was hunt. 'They don't know how to hunt,' Arau said.

It was calm around the new campsite that evening. At six o'clock, the background hum of chirruping cicadas was broken by one that was as loud as a car alarm (so regular you could set your watch to it – it reminded me instantly of my many visits to Borneo in the past). Fires were lit, and well away from the road and outsiders everything seemed tranquil, except for the rumbling of thunder in the distance.

I took the opportunity to chat to Arau and his wife Tapi, asking them my usual questions about how they'd met and joined together and so on. Arau was very forthcoming, his eyes twinkling away as he explained how they'd met when he was visiting their family, how they'd started to work together whenever they could, and eventually got together without ceremony. Tapi was much more diffident. Even when I asked her a direct question she kept her head at right angles, facing away from me, her fingers working busily away at the rattan she was weaving. Arau explained that she was just very shy.

In the morning Jeff and Arau took me, Gavin, Toby and Seda up into the forest to look for sago. Two other guys, Emang and Lucas, were going out hunting too, but they didn't want us along with them as they needed meat for the camp and success was important. That was perfectly understandable. So we crossed the river and climbed the steep slope on the far side. Quite soon we came across a logging road, maybe fifteen years old, a huge scar on the landscape, but at least it gave us a good view of the entire area. Jeff and Arau could make out only two sago groves on all the surrounding slopes. Before the loggers came in, the place would have been abundant with them.

The slope beyond the road was steep, and here, the guys told us, we were in untouched forest. I found this hard to believe. We were close to the road and there were no obvious big trees. But Jeff and Arau said they could just tell; here everything was alive, while back in the logged forest they had felt anxious. As we climbed Arau pointed things out to us: certain bird calls, partic- ular fruits, a wild boar's burrow-nest with distinctive scrapings of foliage around the entrance. We found a lone sago palm, cut it down and removed its heart from the point where the branches spread out from the main trunk. It tasted just like the ones we'd had with the Kombai, and was clearly regarded as a delicacy here as there: a deliciously soft, moist vegetable texture, with a taste somewhere between asparagus and artichoke heart. Then we climbed further to a sizeable grove of sago trees. Here the guys set to work chopping down four of the stems, which became a bit of an epic task – they didn't fall to the ground at first but got caught in adjacent trees. I tried to help but was told it would be dangerous, with their extremely thorny trunks falling in all directions. So I sat with Gavin and Seda and watched. It started to rain, increasingly heavily. We waited patiently for them to collect the hearts, getting colder and colder in the downpour.

Once on the move again we warmed up nicely. It was a slippery trek back down the hill. The river in the valley was quite high now, and dirty brown with silt. Arau explained that this was another side-effect of the logging. The binding roots of trees are removed and the soil is exposed. Once, he said, these rivers had been crystal clear at all times and never used to flood so badly.

Emang and Lucas returned later that afternoon with a mother and piglet wild boar. The baby was particularly plump, which the hunters expressed by marking the depth of fat with the thumb against the pointing finger of the same hand. Arau and Jeff quizzed them about what they'd found, and how they'd caught it. The mother had been cut in two to be carried home. Now the meat was cut up further to be divided among the families. Some Penan from the settlement we'd left down by the road had anticipated the kill and so had made their way up to us to collect their share. Bowls were put out for the families present (the Penan and us) and further bowls for the families over the spur downriver. The division was meticulous and each type of meat was cut down to the smallest morsel so that everyone got a share of each cut: fatty back, lean back, ribs, liver and so on.

Our meat was cooked that evening: cooked liver and spare ribs, with the main bowl of meat diced into a curry. I decided to avoid the curry and slept like a baby, for the last time in my comfy hammock before moving in with Arau. My original host, Selapan, hadn't moved upstream with us, so I would stay with Arau and Tapi.

I moved my backpack over to their shelter the next morning, then watched Arau collect wood and rattan from the forest to make supports for the raised platform that Gavin would be filming from. Nearby another guy was outside his shelter making darts and stoppers for his traditional blowpipe, which like those of the Matis, are wonderful objects, a couple of metres long. I had lunch with my new hosts: boiled and burnt boar, accompanied by gelatinous sago, neither as bad as they looked. We had planned to spend the afternoon applying poison to some blowpipe darts, but news came of a sick person in the other camp, so Arau and Seda had to leave us. With Tapi next door in their sleeping shelter, I spent my first evening in my new home watching the rain pour down with only a very frustrated tied-up pet monkey for company. Luckily the Penan use mozzie nets, so I felt able to erect mine, a godsend in this insect-infested place. In the middle of the night Arau and Seda returned and cooked up a meal; then very early in the morning my host was up again to light the fire. Quite a busy body was our Arau.

So all in all I felt pretty tired as we headed off to harvest the felled sago. Jeff was off visiting relatives, so Arau and I trekked back up the spur and over the logging road, with Gavin, Matt and Toby along with us. We weren't a strong enough team, Arau said, to work with the logs we'd felled previously, so we found some new sago palms and felled those. Once on the ground the trees were chopped into three two-metre lengths, stripped with a sharp *parang* of their spiny covering of thorns, then carried, de-spined, down the hill to a place where Tapi had found an old processing area. The logs were split lengthwise with an axe, then their insides pulverized by a swinging wooden pole into a pithy mash. Tapi, meanwhile, had made a square wooden platform with slightly raised sides over a collecting area. A woven mat was placed in it, then the sago pith added on top. She then stood upon the platform and mashed the sago with her feet, adding water from a bowl, working round the four corners of the platform as if treading grapes. Gradually the mashed starchy paste filtered through on to the collecting cloth below.

This went on all day. I had a couple of goes at pounding the sago, but clearly didn't have Tapi's fine technique. Arau had sliced his foot quite badly, so when he took his turn it left a spreading red stain over the creamy starchy white. At one point there was a sudden downpour, but Arau and Tapi had a shelter erected in two minutes, so we were spared the worst.

At the end of our long session we had a precipitated stodgy residue of sago, which was wrapped up in a cloth and placed in a tube-like wicker backpack. I carried this home, the only thing I was allowed to do all day. Back in camp our very late lunch was, of course, more wallpaper-paste sago, with thankfully some lovely lean bits of pork to give it variety. I was eager to chat with my family, but Gavin had monopolized both translators in another shelter, talking about astronomy. So I decided to get my iPod video out and show Arau and Tapi how the Kombai process sago with just stone and wooden tools. We were soon joined in our shelter by most of the camp and everyone was spellbound. They couldn't believe that there were people in the world with fewer tools than them. They listened with awe as I described a life without pots, pans, knives and *parangs*.

I was starting to settle in and enjoy myself. My only disappointment was my relationship with Tapi, which continued to be, for some reason, very strained. She refused to meet my eye or interact with me at all. When we ate, she faced away. And she looked positively upset when I offered her, say, a piece of fruit. Such a contrast to her husband, the ever-active, gregarious Arau.

My sleep was fitful due to the uneven floor and the family's pet monkey going mad above my head. Eventually Arau got up and took it away to another shelter, as it was keeping the whole camp awake. In the morning he had to leave us after breakfast to go back down to the other camp, because a local pastor was turning up there. All those who'd been staying before had apparently left, and Arau thought it might look suspicious if there was no one there to greet him. It wouldn't be wise for me to go with him, he said, as he wasn't sure how trustworthy the pastor was (which made me smirk).

So Gavin and I went out with Emang and Lucas to have a look at a jackfruit tree, another of their traditional sources of food. It was a sunny day and a nice walk. Not that you'd notice until you were on the logging road, which we followed for ten minutes or so. The guys were pointing out interesting stuff everywhere, from bent saplings – indicating the way a monkey had gone – to different kinds of trees and the medicines they produce. But when we got to the tree they'd had in mind it was stripped of fruit. Monkeys and birds had got there first. Emang went off to find sago palm hearts, and we hung out with Lucas, who was turning out to be great fun and suddenly quite verbose on camera. We talked about logging, virgin forests, resistance, sago and the concerns of the Penan in general.

When Emang returned, we decided to go off and find a tajem tree, their traditional source of poison. The trunk was cut with deep grooves, up to five metres from the ground. They had obviously been taking poison from it for years, and to my mind showed a continued use of this area far better than any amount of new sago plantations. We had no bamboo in which to collect the poisonous sap, so we agreed to leave it for another time.

Back at camp all was quiet. I had the shits quite badly, but Emang told me it was fine to go and sort myself out downriver, which made things much easier and more soothing.

Sunday again, the day of rest. I'd been having such good conversations with everyone that I longed to discuss Christianity with them. I wanted to know what they'd been told (or maybe felt) which had made them all believe so suddenly, and what the consequences might have been if they had rejected their new religion. Instead I did lots of pieces to camera about the political side of the Penan's situation: logging rights, land rights, the law as it stands and so on. It was fun working with Gavin to get these right. He's a born activist, a very knowledgeable anthropology graduate, and most definitely on the side of the Penan against the loggers and the Sarawak government. As he said, I owed it to these people to tell their story. I was uneasy with suddenly becoming an eco-enviro-human rights activist on camera, because I knew this was a hugely complex story, and one that we could only touch on in the film. In any case, much of what I'd have liked to say was bigger than this small and local example. But then again, as Gavin pointed out, I did think what the logging companies were doing was wrong, so why shouldn't I say that? It was a tough one, and once we'd started recording there was no going back. I found myself energized by it all. I had now come further off the fence than at any time since the start of *Tribe*.

The day of rest over, we went back to the poison tree with Arau, this time with bamboo containers to collect the sap. One tiny drop entering the bloodstream can be fatal, so we had to be excessively careful. To get up to an area where there were fresh cuts Arau climbed an adjacent tree and I decided to join him. It wasn't the most elegant ascent, but soon we were both astride a branch eight or so metres from the ground, opposite to where the tree was relatively untouched. Now Arau pulled our tree closer to the larger poison tree and with his axe cut a slot facing vertically down, into which he pinned the top of the bamboo collecting tube. Then above that he cut a myriad of small grooves at oblique angles in an arrowhead formation, so all the sap trickled downwards to flow into the bamboo. With the first grooves there were plenty of chippings flying around but little evidence of sap, but soon I could see droplets of lethal poison flowing in all directions. At this point I realized how many open wounds, bloody blisters and cuts riddled my hands, arms and legs; also why Arau was wearing a T-shirt for the first time since I'd met him.

We got back to camp to good news. Lucas and Emang had been out hunting and had some success: three baby boar and a huge sow. The usual hour-long dividing of the meat ensued, and after that a scene of happy activity in the camp, with large fires and pots overflowing with pork.

I was sitting writing my diary in Arau's shelter the following evening when I looked up to see three strangers coming towards me. They were all a fair bit older than our group – old in Penan terms – a couple and another man. Both men had black loincloths and one wore a shirt over that. On wrists and calves they wore bracelets. One had large copper rings which pulled his earlobes down a good inch or two.

'We heard that you are here, so we came to see you,' said the man called Koling, who had a mullet haircut with a high fringe. After a little more introductory chit-chat, during which I introduced myself and told them why I was there, Koling launched into a diatribe. Even though I couldn't immediately understand his words I knew he was talking about logging and Penan issues. He had that same way of talking they all had when they got on to this emotional subject.

And once it had been translated I was deeply struck. He said that the three of them had walked all day, crossed a big river by barge, then spent several hours walking down an open logging road in the baking sun in order to be here and meet us. They had come to ask a question. Could I give them some indication of how to save their forest? They had seen, they said, their friends die, their trees disappear and their whole world changed. 'To us Penan,' Koling said, 'there is no life in the forest if the animals and the sago are gone.' Could I tell them what to do to stop it?

Again, these were powerful words to be presented with and demanded huge expectations of me. I had no idea what to say. As the rain poured down, rattling on the tarpaulin, and darkness fell, I tried to tell them what we were doing. I explained that I couldn't promise anything, but we would try to do what we could for them. At the very least our film might give them a voice. So they decided to stay the night. Gavin and I now asked them questions about the past, their memories of the Brooke era and so on, and they were very forthcoming.

'When I was a young girl,' said the old woman, 'I used to be so happy walking in the forest. I used to sing while I was looking for sago. I loved to see the green leaves of the trees. When I went walking I could hear the sound of the wild peacocks, the hornbills and the gibbons, and when I looked at the forest it was lovely.'

In the morning they talked some more about their plight. Then, at Gavin's instigation, we asked them to show us some of the signs the Penan traditionally use to pass messages along a trail. This was brilliant stuff. Just a single arrangement of message sticks and leaves could carry so much information: distance, time, welfare, items carried or wanted. There were signs for such distinct messages as:

'I'm going back to the shelters and I am hungry. You must hurry.'

'I'm going to catch and eat wild boar.'

'I'm going to go to that sago tree on the mountain, process the sago, and stay there overnight.'

After that they showed us the sign that they put out for the logging companies, a stone in a cleft stick. The stone represented a curse, that the hearts of the loggers would turn to stone and they would die.

After they'd gone Jeff got on with making the poison from the sap we'd collected. He'd made a funnel out of waxy leaves, with moss at the bottom to act as a filter. He now poured the milk-chocolate-coloured sap through this and into an oblong waterproof container, also made of leaves. This was then placed on a rack to slowly heat over the fire, and the liquid reduced to a thick residue. The whole process of boiling down the poison took so long that everyone gradually slipped off. In the end I did too, knackered from my night up talking with the old folks and wanting an early night, as we would be up before dawn to go hunting.

I was going out with Arau and one other guy, Leyong, which was great. No crew to slow us down; just Bruce-cam to film. My bumbag was only small so I ditched all my usual safety gear to make room for it. A bit of a risk, perhaps, but to me the most important task was to keep up and allow them to hunt as if I weren't there.

We wandered downstream for a bit, then turned up a steep slope into the forest. Their skills were soon apparent: knowing immediately what all the different bird calls were, brilliant at spotting spoor. Soon some birds flitted into the trees above and they started firing. I was surprised they bothered. The birds were no larger than a blue tit, and they were wasting precious poison darts on them. In the background we could hear the calls of bigger game, but they kept on stalking and firing at the little birds.

After a while we came across a new boar track, and then a place where it had obviously made quite a mess feeding. We stalked it silently for a while, until the tracks vanished into very dense foliage. Even if they were able to follow it in there, Arau said, there was a chance that if it ran away wounded they would never be able to find it. So they left the trail and returned to the birds.

An hour or two of thorns, slips and slides, and stream-walking later, we came to an open bit of forest, the nearest thing to virgin forest we'd yet seen. Here we saw a squirrel which Arau downed with a single shot. I have to hand it to them: they were incredibly accurate with their darts. It was a shame they only had such tiny birds and rodents to aim at. We returned from the hunt with the squirrel and one tiny green bird – barely a mouthful.

Back in camp more people had pitched up. I played back the tape of the hunt to a gathering of fifteen or so fascinated Penan. Frustratingly when we were halfway through this yet more people arrived: a girl with cerebral palsy and her knee locked half closed, carried by a tiny man of my age, who had her in a piggy back, with a bark sling holding her to his shoulders. Next came an old boy in a loincloth, carrying a rattan basket with a full-sized macaque monkey clinging to his arm. Along with the rest of the group was a string of similar pets, including three blind puppies, five dogs and a tiny baby monkey.

After we'd eaten that evening there was lots to talk about with these new arrivals. There were fires blazing everywhere you looked. All thirteen families of the original settlement were up here now. Between the little shelters the rain bucketed down, one of the heaviest downpours I could remember.

One couple were Penan from a different valley, visiting relatives. They explained that the previous week, the logging company had turned up, told them they didn't have a legal claim to their land, then said they were about to start logging, extracting the biggest trees in a 'first pass'. This guy didn't know where to go for help and so was appealing to me. Once again, it was an indication of how desperate they were that they had come to a total stranger like this. And the sad truth was that even if our programme managed to bring this issue to the attention of a wider world, it was probably too late for this group. Their ancestors had lived in the area for many generations, but because they could not fulfil the legal requirements of proving their ownership, the loggers had the right to extract the wood under concession. In truth, however, there are many ways in which the Penan could prove their land ownership through detailed local knowledge, poison tree harvesting and historical accounts; it's just that such evidence is inadmissible in Sarawak law. It is almost as if the laws were made to exclude the Penan who, as nomadic hunter-gatherers, are obviously unable to provide the necessary evidence of cultivation before 1958, which is the only way they can secure any tenure.

The plight of the Penan has reached international attention

before. In 1987, assisted by Bruno Manser, the Swiss environmentalist who was later to mysteriously disappear, Penan from
the Eastern group erected a series of blockades against the
logging companies that were encroaching on their land. Images
of this protest reached the media in Japan, Australia, Europe and
North America and aroused much sympathy. In 1990 and 1992
Manser even took representatives of the Penan to the USA,
where he held a press conference with Senator Al Gore. In the
UK, the issue was addressed in a speech by Prince Charles, who
described the treatment of the Penan as 'collective genocide'.

Both the BBC and National Geographic made documentaries on the Penan. The story was written up everywhere from
the *New Yorker* to *Rolling Stone*. The Australian film *Blowpipes
and Bulldozers* and the Swedish film *Tong Tana* reached large
audiences. Universal Studios apparently even developed a script
in which the forest wisdom of the Penan saves the world from
catastrophe. The issue was discussed at the Rio Earth Summit
and raised at the UN General Assembly.

The Malaysian government's response was sophisticated.
Prime Minister Dr Mahathir Mohamad described the campaign
as 'eco-imperialism'. In reply to a much-publicized letter from
a ten-year-old boy lamenting the fact that there would be no
jungle animals left for him to study when he grew up, and
calling what was happening in the Sarawak forests 'disgraceful',
Dr Mohamad replied in kind:

> It is disgraceful that you should be used by adults for the
> purpose of trying to shame us because of the extraction of
> timber from our forests . . . the industry helps hundreds of
> thousands of poor people in Malaysia. Are they to remain
> poor because you want to study tropical animals? . . . If
> you don't want us to cut down our forests, tell your father
> to tell the rich countries like Britain to pay more for the
> timber they buy from us.

*

It was a powerful argument, and one that remains telling to this day. But in response to the strong counter-offensive by Malaysia, many of the NGOs went back home to dutifully 'sort out their own backyards' first. The talks then went to international levels and the attention shifted towards 'sustainable' logging and certifications for authenticity, which proved so difficult that many of the original environmentalists opted out of the schemes. Sadly, the voices that originally started the whole campaign, those of the Penan themselves, became lost in red tape and high-level discussions, with the result that no one was watching the continued disappearance of their lands.

Gavin had gone down with flu and was confined to his sleeping bag, but I continued to follow the daily activities of our hosts, which the next day meant collecting rattan, another of the Penan's dwindling raw materials. Ten of us left camp and trekked back to the waterfall, along a logging road, then into a part of the forest that contained thousands of huge rattan plants with central stems the width of a finger going up to the treetops. While the men kept guard, the women got to work ripping the rattan out of the trees, then using *parangs* to strip it of its thorny exterior, leaving the lovely cane centre we call wicker. This was then cut into lengths, split into four, and the square core discarded.

Back in camp the next day, Sunday, the women got to work with their raw material making baskets: some of the backpack type, open lattice, stiff backs with open sides. Tapi, meanwhile, worked on a closed-weave basket the size of an office waste-paper bin. Starting after breakfast, she'd pretty much finished by last light. Another girl soaked her rattan slivers in brown mud to stain them black.

Meanwhile, Emang sat in front of his little shelter, method-ically applying poison to his thirty-centimetre-long darts. He wasn't using the sap we'd recently collected, but an old batch that Jeff had stored, a tested mix; once reduced, the new poison has to be tried out in the hunt. If an animal hit by a dart froths at the mouth while dying, then the mixture isn't strong enough. If an animal stays rigid while dying – which is potentially disastrous, as it could stay stuck high in a tree – then chilli has to be added to the poison to ensure a writhing death. Such are the Penan's tricks of the trade, built up over generations.

By Monday Gavin had recovered, was up and about, and was now concerned about a new issue: were the Penan really telling us what they believed, or what they wanted us to hear? I walked in on him having a serious session about this with Seda, Matt and John. It seemed that the Penan had been so heavily politicized over the years that some messages had filtered down to all levels and become stock answers. Which was not to say that the Penan's feelings weren't strong about hating the loggers and fearing a loss of their way of life, but that they weren't necessarily being completely honest about what they wanted. They talked about wanting to stay roaming the forest, and not settling or even having the tiniest slice of the pie of developed society. Apart from the Kombai who were relatively ignorant of the outside world, this was the first time I'd ever heard this and I wasn't sure that this didn't have an element of political stance about it. They have been heralded for so long by romantic environmentalists as guardians of the forest that they now believe that whenever they talk to white people they should reiterate how they just want to stay in the forest, a mantra that always makes the white man happy. But really, when the forest Penan see the settled Penan or Kalabit, with their shiny new toys, health and education, what they see is their own world in decline. Their forest is disappearing. Their cash crops, such as the rare resinous *gaharu* wood, have massively dwindled. They see the difference between themselves and their neighbours becoming an increasing gulf, so they run back and hide where they feel safe. But what no one had told them is that they could have both: the freedom of the jungle and the advantages of the modern world.

With all this in mind, Gavin was now confronting our hosts with the idea that perhaps they had a different answer for outsiders to what they tell themselves in private. Initially, they denied this categorically, saying there must be a problem with the translations. But then, when pushed, they said they were never against development per se. Yes, of course, they want decent health care and education if they can get it, but their priority is that they don't want to lose the forest. Because that is all they know, and the only way they know how to live. They have no skills or trade to offer the wider world, so how would they live if they left the forest? They had heard so many horror stories of other Penan groups being persuaded to leave the forest and become settled while their forest was destroyed as soon as they'd left. Our new friends were so scared of this scenario that they'd decided to not risk ever leaving the forest in case it happened to them.

It had been a shaky twenty-four hours but we felt, after this, that our film was safe. The 'guardians of the forest' voice that they all had was authentic, just not the whole story. As Selapan had said when I'd first met him, 'We'd be happy to settle if somebody showed us how.'

I felt we were at last breaking through with these diffident, hard-to-read people and getting to a deeper level of under-standing. Another conversation with Arau and Jeff produced a fascinating insight: the Penan really seem to have a very different sense of time to ours. They don't follow months or seasons or years. For all their amazing understanding of nature they can't predict, for example, when a tree might fruit. They see signs and hear from others, but they don't count years or seasons. Menstruation is probably their only real cycle as they seem to pay scant attention to the moon. They have little oral history about the past and no real concept of the future. Theirs appears to be simply a dynamic present. This is why, perhaps, the larger world outside seems so bizarre to them. We were talking about what might happen in a hypothetical future; they were only concerned with now.

Furthermore, their political system is as close to an anarchy as I've ever come across. In some areas you could see where this form of living has its problems. In relationships, for example, you can marry who you like, and if that doesn't work out, you don't feel your husband is providing well enough for you, or you fancy someone else, you just move on. Kids can be sorted out somehow between you – your own selfish desires take precedence. There are no rules as such and no governing body to arbitrate, so some social issues are never sorted and as a result just fester. But on the other hand they are free of all the class and society issues that might otherwise hinder the freedom of their lives. There are no preachers or politicians to manipulate them, give advice or demand anything of them; no rituals to adhere to. They seem to have a natural moral code, which generally works very well. In a funny way I felt a great affinity with their way of life. Clutter free, mobile, dynamic and resourceful.

There was an old logging camp not far away that they wanted to show us. So the next day, Jeff, Arau, Gavin and I trekked up there. Some kids with blowpipes joined us on the first steep climb out of the camp; then we were on our own along a small path and on to a logging road, which was wide and well cleared and led into an even wider road, from where we had amazing views of the surrounding forest. The road was hot in the scorching sun and the guys visibly hated it. Eventually we came down a slope to the camp.

It was a huge clearing at the bottom of a small valley, which had contained about 500 workers and their families during the second logging of the area. The place was now thoroughly overgrown and the wooden buildings derelict. I asked about the loggers themselves, hoping to hear that they were decent enough people (as there is no need to demonize the loggers because they are just trying to feed their families). But Jeff and Arau told me that twice they had brought sick people down to the camp in the hope of receiving help, or even a lift to a clinic, and the loggers had met them with machetes, looking for a fight.

Originally, when the first logging road was put in, they said, they had been told that it would give them a route to clinics, education and development, and that the houses here would be theirs to keep after the loggers went. But the road was now so full of landslides that it would have been quicker to walk. The loggers' dwellings had been stripped bare before they left, the ground littered with nails. The bridge over the river gave a good idea of the sort of waste and devastation that had taken place: it was made of maybe forty criss-crossed logs of enormous proportions, bigger than anything I'd seen to date. It was now half collapsed, with these huge logs strewn everywhere. The men were angry, and I was on their side.

We were coming to the end of our time with the Penan, but before we left they wanted to take me to see a stretch of untouched primary forest, such as had existed before this logging nightmare descended upon them. The trek was not actually that long from the camp, but involved crossing the river, which was still running very high. Normally they would ford it, but today it was so high we had to cut down a big tree to cross it. Surprisingly, quite a few of them seemed scared of the crossing, and we had to erect two rattan handrails before everyone would go over. Perhaps this was because such flooding was a relatively new phenomenon.

The untouched jungle was on a steep slope – probably only left like this because it was too steep for the machinery to get up – and it contained visibly bigger trees in among the rest. The ground was bare and brown and you could see for some distance. There were lots of saplings, but they didn't branch or leaf till well above eye level, giving a clear view through, something I hadn't seen in the forest we'd been in before. With such large trees there was little light and it was very cool in temperature. There were no puddles or marshy areas, but well-bound soil with good drainage. Looking up, I had the sensation that it was all going on above my head. Although I'd spent a fair amount of time in forest like this in Indonesia and Papua or Malaysian National Parks, rarely had I noticed the distinction so markedly. This forest was alive in a different kind of way and I could feel it.

Others had been out hunting and before we finally left our Penan friends we had a bit of a feast of wild boar in camp. Seda and Matt had already gone, taking our rushes a back way to Brunei for safe keeping: we didn't want to be stopped on the way back and deprived of all our hard work. Then Tapi left, off to some religious gathering, apparently. As well as the cash she and Arau were getting for being our hosts, I gave her a new black vest, a metal pot with a tight-fitting lid and a silk-lined sleeping bag that I'd brought along but not used. She was next to tears as she said goodbye. Our relationship had been almost the weirdest I'd had with any adult during all the *Tribe* shoots. At first I'd thought she just didn't like me; then later I realized she was merely incredibly shy and retiring. Towards the end she'd even joined Arau and me for meals. She never answered any question I asked directly. Even when Arau wasn't there she'd shout through to Emang in the next-door shelter to answer for her. But her few glances in my direction had eventually been warm. She had been very kind to me in her way and I would miss her.

The rain came down heavily as usual in the evening and for a while it looked as if the feast was off. When the downpour finally stopped I'd already eaten with Arau and was about to go to bed, but the others said they wanted to have this special meal. They had chopped down half the forest, it seemed, to make a set of benches, which looked like church pews once they'd been set out. They had used a tremendous amount of wood – ironic given the theme of our film, and it made me think all the way back to my difficulty with the Babongo when they chopped that first tree down and I struggled to know what to say.

Everyone had cooked rice and there was a huge pot of boar made into a curried stew, washed down with lots of orange squash and coffee, which we had provided. Every member of all thirteen families came out from their shelters and joined in. It was a lovely occasion and I decided, impromptu, to say a few words, so I told them all about the film and wished them well.

I'd loved living with the Penan. They had surprised me in so many ways and I was so interested in their society and world-view. Sharing is key to their existence, every house is completely open and every family activity is there for all others to see.

Arau had been a particularly fantastic host. As his farewell gift to me, he gave me a traditional blowpipe and spent the last couple of days making poison darts for it. In return, we gave away nearly all our possessions as not only was it the end of the shoot, but the end of *Tribe* for ever. I had been on the road for nearly four years, living with so many wonderful communities across the world. I had a number of new tribal names, umpteen brothers and sisters, mothers, fathers, uncles and aunts, and had been initiated or become a man in more than a few cultures. I had learnt so much from so many people and wanted to put some of it into practice in my own life back in Europe, if that was going to be at all possible.

As I waved goodbye to my Penan friends I knew that their plight was a tough one. Their future wasn't so much in the hands of the loggers or the politicians but in our own, we in the 'developed' world who continue to buy hardwoods or palm oil products with little consideration about where they come from and what effects our choices have. It was a sobering thought, and I wondered, if the Penan had known the whole story, whether they ever would have welcomed me at all.

I'm Often Asked . . .

Some deeper thoughts on my experiences

The three series of *Tribe* have been over four years in the making and for everyone involved a most profound and enlightening experience. The general public reaction to the programmes has been largely warm and positive (even amongst some of those who were initially against the idea). The programmes have been – and continue to be – shown in over thirty countries worldwide and appear to have chimed with the growing understanding of so many of the global social and environmental crises that face us all.

One of the many aims of the series was to challenge overly romantic views of tribal communities. The misconceptions of historical explorers have influenced us all and too often been continued by the modern media, who actively reinforce existing stereotypes. To counter this, we wanted to go against the tide and highlight the similarities between human beings rather than accentuate their exotic differences. To those who've travelled at all widely, such an approach might seem obvious; but one of the more common reactions I had to the screening of the first series was surprise that fundamentally 'we are all the same'.

To me, all humans experience the same emotions and are subject to the same motivating forces: forging out ways to physically sustain ourselves; propagating our genes; trying – occasionally – to escape the normality of life; maybe even aspiring to become something bigger than the sum of our physical parts. Within each society there are of course massive individual differences, in everything from physique to character. Humanity comes in all shapes, colours and sizes; there are extroverts and introverts; more or less altruistic; and so on – but beneath that, there's not much to distinguish us.

Having said that, with each new culture that I visit the thing I notice again and again is how much people are products of their society's unique interaction of environment, genetics and culture. Once you grasp this huge diversity of mankind it quickly becomes too simple to label any particular group in either a negative or a positive way. We're all products of our own culture; indeed, I would argue that many of us hold beliefs based on little more than what we've been taught as kids, to which we mix in cognitive and emotional reactions based on our experiences in later life.

In my own case, I've long been battling my 'given' beliefs against my 'found' ones. For many this isn't such a struggle, as they have had the chance to reason such issues out early in life, but for those of us who had a strong religious upbringing or strict social constraints, such a battle can be all-consuming. Indeed, my interest in spending time with tribal peoples in the first place – long before I joined the BBC – had a lot to do with my own personal journey seeking answers to the bigger questions of life.

Actually living with tribal people, as I did on each of the fifteen *Tribe* shoots, has given me a whole new set of ideas for assessing the world, which, in turn, I've tried to use to investigate the driving forces of my own society and where we may be going right or wrong. I've also hoped to better understand previously inexplicable aspects of my own life and see how I too am not much more than the product of my culture.

Realizing the importance of challenging my own preconceptions was an extremely useful starting point for getting the most out of living with tribal groups. In order to best discover their most cherished principles, I wanted to enter their world without prejudice or strong opinion. This resolve was tested repeatedly. All too often people from the 'developed' world put tribal cultures on a pedestal, seeing them through rose-tinted spectacles as pristine and gentle with perfect environmental credentials and a great sense of community. This may contain some truth in comparison to our own culture, but to sweepingly brand such societies as idyllic is deeply patronizing. Time and time again my views were fundamentally challenged while trying to understand such difficult cultural practices as cannibalism with the Kombai, female circumcision with the Dassanech, the warfare between the Suri and the Nyangatom, the endless inebriation of the Sanema, or the whipping of the Hamar women.

The learning curve I went through with each of these issues has, I hope, been described in the book already. But to really explain the central lesson I've been taught, which is about tolerance through understanding, I'm going to risk criticism by highlighting perhaps the most contentious issue of all – female circumcision. There are not many people in Europe or North America who would suggest that female genital mutilation (FGM) is anything more than a barbaric act with horrific consequences. Deep down I agree. But I nonetheless still hold true to the conclusion I reached after my time with the Dassanech, that it's not for me to judge existing cultural practices. This is why:

When looking at any cultural trait or belief or practice of a society, I try to figure out how or why it might have come about. To achieve this I start by going back to its historical roots to see what geographical, political or societal issues might have been most at work in that culture. In the case of female circumcision many would argue that such a cruel and demeaning practice could only have its roots in misogyny or exercise of power. Whatever its origins, the reasons are complex, span back several centuries, and are bound up with all sorts of influences, including warfare and slavery, honour and shame, membership of a particular ethnic group, and the inheritance of property through the male line. There may even have been other explanations for it in harsh nomadic desert conditions, such as to avoid unwanted pregnancies. Who knows?

My point is not that I want to justify the act – far from it. But simply this: after living with people who practise FGM (like the extraordinary Abanesh), I still find it hard to judge or blame them, no matter how abhorrent their beliefs and actions might seem to me.

Should we impose our views and way of life on such people without knowing the full cultural significance of how they live? Can we be so sure of our own beliefs when the repercussions of following the assumptions of the so-called 'developed' world can have even bigger environmental, social or other negative ramifications? In any case, any dominant culture which tries to oppress such strong overriding cultural or religious feelings is often doomed to failure, sometimes with the result that such practices become even more entrenched. Examples are easy to find throughout history.

By the end of the second series I'd decided that it was OK to agree to disagree with the people I was visiting without prejudice or hatred. Even in the extreme cases like FGM or the apparently cannibalistic practices of the Kombai, I didn't feel it was ever my place to pass judgement.

I know from my own life just how hard it is to distance oneself from a powerful belief system, as there is undoubted comfort in accepting what one has been taught when young. I was brought up as a committed Christian, and it took me many difficult years to realize that, much as I respected those who wanted to follow this faith, it wasn't for me. And that was with all the benefits of travel, reading, time to think and question. So I understand all too well that so long as people like Abanesh live within their close-knit community, where all their peers think and feel the same as each other, it's almost impossible for her to escape her cultural beliefs and practices – and, actually, it's not a priority in an already tough life. Clean water and a more stable livelihood would be more important to people like her. After which the issue of circumcision could be addressed, once it's dragged out from the shadow of grinding poverty.

Of course it is possible for someone to escape the worst aspects of their culture and upbringing if they want it enough or receive some form of enlightenment, but I feel strongly that people will generally only change their views if new conviction comes from within. You need a brave character like Keri, the Hamar woman who had rejected the whipping culture she was born to, to start to make the difference. Again, it's patronizing to think that we outsiders have a responsibility to change these 'barbaric' cultures, whether it's about the rights of women, animal welfare, or any number of contentious issues that the programmes have covered. Inform them, persuade them and help them, yes; but to try to order them and enforce alien rules is not the best way, I am sure.

In order to improve all societies, ours as well as others', surely cultural exchange is a key. Mixing people up. Separating us all from our one-sided views. Just as a tribal community may wish to learn new methods of gender equality or animal welfare from us, maybe we, by looking at or spending time with tribal people, can assess our own society too.

Right now we are heading towards a homogenized world. Not one of cultural exchange but rather of cultural takeover. If this continues, there may be no litmus test to see where we've gone wrong or right, no way to tell whether our so-called 'development' is really meeting our physical, emotional and social needs. Without people like our indigenous communities there will be no 'control' element of the human experiment from which to learn or remember the different ways of community living in the natural world.

We're entering an era of ever-increasing individualism where no one seems to be dependent on anyone else any more. Just as my Adi friend Taman Tamak was discovering with his new corrugated-iron roof, we no longer need our neighbour's help to survive, so it's easy to ignore him. We no longer have respected elders to help us through the important rites of passage from childhood to adulthood. There is no longer a culture of shamans passing on sacred knowledge about how to deal safely with dangerous substances. Hardly surprising that so many of our young people get it wrong for lack of society's guidance.

In this atomized world of ours, few of us know or care where our consumed products originate from or what is happening in some distant corner of the globe when we buy our hardwood furniture, cheap burgers, biodiesel, shark-fin soup and the like.

Our global systems are in dire need of reassessment. Politicians, craving re-election, act only in the short term. Their sponsoring corporations transcend nation states, and pander primarily to the interests of their collectively greedy shareholders, while operating within an economic system which accentuates disparity of wealth and where natural products are only worth anything at all when they've been plundered and destroyed.

Many of us in the 'developed' world see some sort of global disaster coming. But as modern societies, presently at least, we seem to be continuing in the same vein, feathering our expensive nests, raiding our natural resources, while simultaneously looking romantically over our shoulders at 'how it used to be'. Many of us cherish the idea that there are these 'pristine' cultures still living in harmony with the planet. It provides us with a strange form of comfort to know that such people still exist. Yet too few of us are doing anything at all to stop our collective progression towards something potentially catastrophic.

The sad irony is that even as we destroy these tribal cultures, now is the time when we need them more than ever. Rather than wrecking the planet, we could be listening and learning from their long-standing knowledge about how to lead a more sustainable life and how to protect the environment. Yes, they're still only human. Yes, they still get it wrong sometimes and they're certainly not pristine or perfect. But they still have lots to teach us. If only we would listen.

Acknowledgements

This book is about my experience and the lessons I learnt while making the BBC television series *Tribe*. Quite a few of the people that I need to thank are therefore those who helped me make the series itself, especially those who have influenced me personally.

The programme was commissioned by Richard Klein, who recommended me for the job and who I can never really ever thank enough for such an amazing opportunity. Steve Robinson became the Series Producer for *Tribe*. Without question the series bears his stamp above all other people; his leadership, ethics, poetry and friendship are beyond words. Thank you, mate.

Thanks to Adrian Davies, who runs the Factual Department in BBC Wales.

All the researchers over the years have been fantastic and many of them have come out to work on the shoots. Through endless discussions Willow Murton, Rachel Webster, Matthew Fletcher, Matthew Dyas, Renée Godfrey, Bethan Evans and Jane Atkins have all helped me to understand the difficulties of the subject better. Along with Hannah Griffiths, the Assistant Producer, and Michelle Baars, the Production Team Assistant, we've all grown as a family.

Our Producer/Directors were central to the programmes and in many ways to the book too. Thank you for ever to James Smith and Matthew Brandon; and Jon Clay, Graham Johnston, Wayne Derrick and Gavin Searle, who were also cameramen. I love you guys. My praise and thanks can never be high enough.

Sam Gracey and Tim Butt were two of the cameramen who have brought the tribal peoples and their lives to life. The amazing editors, who have had to sit and listen to my endless waffle for weeks at a time to get the best out of me, and make a complicated story understandable, deserve special thanks here – John Parker and Gwynfor Llewellyn in particular. They are all magicians of their trade.

There are many others who helped make the films what they are: mixers, graders, musicians, press agents and the like. Too many to list here but all worked hard.

My understanding of the cultures I've visited would be next to nothing without the tireless fieldwork of many eminent anthropologists, local experts and fixers that I've learnt from, both in person and on the page. I'd especially like to thank Philippe Erikson, Zablon Beyen, Judy Knight, Richard Feinberg, Florian Stammler, Peter Jones and Marcus Colchester.

I am so glad to be with the vibrant Penguin team: Nick Lowndes, Alison Rae, Helen Reynolds, Carly Cook and Georgina Atsiaris have all done so much. Likewise, Liz Smith, Jane Rose, Clare Pollock, Ana-Maria Rivera and Naomi Fidler have all beavered behind the scenes to help make it all happen.

The phenomenal look of the book is largely due to the creative eye of Andrew Smith. And my editor, Katy Follain, needs the highest praise as a marvel of tact and understating. You were always right to rein me in. Katy, thank you.

I must thank Sheila Ableman for her generous support from the outset and, indeed, acquiring me this book deal in the first place.

I must also thank my ghostwriter, Mark McCrum, for all his efforts. Ours has been the greatest collaboration of all in this book. My terrible affliction of being an insufferable control freak and wanting to rewrite or add to all his hard work must have been a very difficult issue to deal with. Luckily, he was able to gently reword my new scribblings into readable prose, and the result is better for his strong will and good sense. Thank you and sorry, Mark.

I am especially grateful to Sam Organ, our brilliant Executive Producer, whose wisdom and judgement so deftly shaped this series. Willow Murton shares such a similar vision to me on the subject that her advice and literary help on this book have always been welcome. Love ya, Wills.

Lindsay Davies, the Production Manager, is the single most important person in the *Tribe* team. Her organizational skills are mind-blowing, and she worked night and day to keep the schedule and budget on track. Without her, there would be no *Tribe* and my life would be a comparative hell. Lindsay, you make *Tribe* what it is. From all of us, thank you, thank you.

The other most influential woman in my world is Nikki Hemmings, my assistant, who helps in every aspect of my life so that I can have a little time to rest and play. Thanks, Nikks.

Much of the book is also based on lessons I've learnt in life from family and friends. Many thanks to all of them, but none more so than Madeline Dempsey, who started me first on my journey of discovery which helped influence my conclusion and which she looked over too.

Lastly, the most important thanks of all goes to all the wonderful indigenous people of the world, especially those who I've been lucky enough to meet and who this book is about and dedicated to.

Bruce Minanga Opang Lokorlam Parry
Ibiza
July 2007

BRUCE PARRY

AMAZON

Explorer Bruce Parry embarks on an epic journey down the Amazon – the world's greatest river, its largest forest, the most bio-diverse habitat on the planet and home to some of the last uncontacted tribes left on Earth.

This book, which will accompany a landmark TV series, will follow Bruce on a breathtaking journey from the Amazon's source on a slope of Nevado Mismi, a mountain that towers over 5000 metres in the Peruvian Andes, to its vast mouth on Brazil's Atlantic Coast.

He will travel over six thousand kilometres, by foot, light aircraft and boat to stay with the tribes that live beneath the rainforest canopy. He will explore high mountains, wide savannahs, deep jungle and the most powerful river in the world. And he will tell the stories of the people that inhabit the greatest forest on Earth.

The book will seek to show the Amazon as it is now, at the beginning of the twenty-first century: a complex, shifting environmental war; the lungs of our planet. It will combine adventure and exploration with Bruce Parry's unique immersive anthropology. He will live with the tribes and share their lives.

But it will also tell the changing story of Amazonia and the people who live and work there, the coca growers, the cattle farmers, the loggers and the illegal miners who strip the jungle for traces of gold.

To be published in autumn 2008

He just wanted a decent book to read ...

Not too much to ask, is it? It was in 1935 when Allen Lane, Managing Director of Bodley Head Publishers, stood on a platform at Exeter railway station looking for something good to read on his journey back to London. His choice was limited to popular magazines and poor-quality paperbacks – the same choice faced every day by the vast majority of readers, few of whom could afford hardbacks. Lane's disappointment and subsequent anger at the range of books generally available led him to found a company – and change the world.

'We believed in the existence in this country of a vast reading public for intelligent books at a low price, and staked everything on it'
Sir Allen Lane, 1902–1970, founder of Penguin Books

The quality paperback had arrived – and not just in bookshops. Lane was adamant that his Penguins should appear in chain stores and tobacconists, and should cost no more than a packet of cigarettes.

Reading habits (and cigarette prices) have changed since 1935, but Penguin still believes in publishing the best books for everybody to enjoy. We still believe that good design costs no more than bad design, and we still believe that quality books published passionately and responsibly make the world a better place.

So wherever you see the little bird – whether it's on a piece of prize-winning literary fiction or a celebrity autobiography, political tour de force or historical masterpiece, a serial-killer thriller, reference book, world classic or a piece of pure escapism – you can bet that it represents the very best that the genre has to offer.

Whatever you like to read – trust Penguin.